How God Acts

TITLES IN THE SERIES

How God Acts

Creation, Redemption, and Special Divine Action

Denis Edwards

FORTRESS PRESS

MINNEAPOLIS

HOW GOD ACTS
Creation, Redemption, and Special Divine Action
Theology and the Sciences series

Cover image: "Creation and the Universe I," Yvonne Ashby
Cover design: Ivy Palmer Skrade
Book design: PerfecType, Nashville, TN

Library of Congress Cataloging-in-Publication Data

Edwards, Denis, 1943-
  How God acts : creation, redemption, and special divine action / Denis Edwards.
    p. cm. — (Theology and the sciences)
  Includes bibliographical references and index.
  ISBN 978-0-8006-9700-6 (alk. paper)
  1. Providence and government of God—Christianity. I. Title.
  BT135.E39 2010
  231'.5—dc22
                            2009037224

The paper used in this publication meets the minimum requirements for American National Standard for Information Sciences—Permanence of Paper for Printed Library Materials, ANSI Z329.48–1984.

Manufactured in the U.S.A.

Contents

Foreword

Understanding God's action in the world—what divine action means, how God acts, and how God does not act—is central to all theological reflection. This fundamental issue has received increased attention over the past thirty years, as the dialogue between theology and the natural sciences has broadened and deepened, and as the persistent challenges to anthropomorphic images of God's interaction with us and with the world from our experiences of natural and moral evil have increased. Many have repeated the basic distinction between God's universal creative action in nature and God's special action in history. Whereas divine creation has been relatively easy to understand in light of the full range of our understanding, divine special acts—such as the incarnation, resurrection, miracles, God's answering prayer—have challenged theologians and philosophers of religion at a more profound level. How do they fit into the overall fabric of reality without entailing outside micromanagement, aggravating the problem of evil, or trivializing and disrespecting who God is for us?

We commonly follow Anselm by defining theology as "faith seeking understanding." Here Denis Edwards has done this in an extraordinary way, probing both old and new avenues to understanding special divine action in its central manifestations. He has critically appropriated and developed Rahner's insights on creation as divine self-bestowal, and integrated his treatment with the wisdom of Thomas Aquinas on creation and primary and secondary causality and with the vision of Athanasius on redemption as participatory transformation, while at the same time respecting the integrity of the particular divine acts themselves. Supplementing this with confirming insights and conclusions carefully distilled from physics, chemistry, biology, and from philosophical reflections on the laws of nature, and with strong suggestions of recent christological scholarship, Edwards presents us with an elaborate portrait of how special divine action can be understood as deeply relational and also as "noninterventionist." God is always working as Creator in and through the secondary causal structures of the world—but in a highly differentiated way—instead of intervening or micromanaging the regularities, processes, and relationships of nature. From the limited perspective of our scientific knowledge, and of our impoverished concepts of God, we may interpret God's special divine acts as "intervention." But that is relative to our very limited understanding of God, creation, and the laws of nature. From Edwards's broader ontological framework, based on Rahner and on the others I have mentioned, God's action—which is always the action of one who creates—is essential, immanent, and therefore operative within creation itself.

What results from this integrated exploration are the strong provisional beginnings (much more remains to be done, of course) of a consistent integrated model of divine action, which carefully and intimately links God's saving acts in history with God's universal creative action, takes the incarnation and its consequences with profound seriousness, emphasizes the ongoing mystery of who God is and God's overwhelming love, and at the same time finds in the well-supported conclusions of the natural sciences profound consonance with Edwards's, and the church's, theological understanding of the key aspects of Christian faith.

William R. Stoeger, S.J.

Preface

When a natural tragedy brings death and destruction, as with the South Asian tsunami of 2004, Hurricane Katrina, or the recent bushfires in south-eastern Australia, one of the responses is the question "Why is God doing this?" The question is asked both by churchgoers and by those who have abandoned church practice. Sometimes it appears in the secular press, along with answers from a range of religious authorities. The same question arises spontaneously in more personal situations of unbearable grief and loss, as when death takes a child or a young parent or a dear friend.

Among the answers offered to this question are these: "It's God's will"; "God sends these sufferings in order to try us"; "God does not send us more than we can bear"; "Suffering brings us closer to God"; "God sends sufferings as a punishment for our sins"; "This hurricane, or this death, is the result of immoral living and the rejection of God's law"; "God sends us suffering so that we can offer up our sufferings with Jesus on the cross"; "God sends us sufferings because God loves us especially"; "Suffering is sent by God to teach us to grow to maturity in our spiritual lives."

All of these answers seem at best inadequate, and some of them can be extremely damaging. They intensify the pain of the sufferers, either by making them feel they are responsible for the suffering or by making them feel that God is punishing them or has in some way targeted them. Such answers can distort the Christian gospel of God. There is little of the good news of the God proclaimed by Jesus. In particular, it is essential to ask whether it is appropriate to think of God, the God of Jesus, as deliberately sending disasters to some people while saving others from them. This, of course, raises a fundamental question about how we think of God acting in our world. It also invites a critical question about the pastoral practice of the Christian community: What view of divine action, and what view of God, is encouraged by the practice of the church?

Every generation has had to struggle with the ancient problem of evil. There is a new intensity to the problem of evil in our day, however, because of our twenty-first-century scientific worldview. We now know that the evolution of life, with all its abundance and beauty, has been accompanied by terrible costs, not only to human beings, but also to many other species, most of which are now extinct. The costs are built into the system, into the physical processes at work in the geology of our planet, such as the meetings of tectonic plates that give rise not only to mountain ranges and new habitats but also to deadly earthquakes and tsunamis. The costs are built into the very biological processes, such as random mutation and natural selection, that enable life to evolve on earth. What is beautiful and good arises by way of increasing complexity through emergent processes that involve tragic loss. The costs are evident in the 3.7-billion-year history of life with its patterns of predation, death, and extinction. We know, as no generation has known before us, that these costs are intrinsic to the processes that give rise to life on earth in all its wonderful diversity.

Our awareness, not only of extreme human suffering, but also of the costs built into evolutionary emergence, presents a fundamental challenge to contemporary theology. A theological response might be attempted in at least two different ways. One is through a philosophical or theological theodicy, which attempts to defend or explain the goodness of God in relation to suffering. But theodicies need to be treated with caution, because they run the risks of seeming to know what is unknown in God, on the one hand, and of trivializing suffering by putting it in an explanatory framework, on the other. A recent example of a partial theodicy that avoids these traps is Christopher Southgate's *The Groaning of Creation*.[1] An alternative strategy, the one I will adopt in this book, is to contribute to a renewed theology of divine action. This strategy is based on the analysis that a particular theology of divine action in Christianity, a theology that sees God in highly interventionist ways, has contributed to the problem we have in dealing with suffering. A renewed theology of divine action will not remove or explain the intractable theological problem of suffering, but it may remove something that exacerbates the problem.

In response to the costs built into evolution, a theology of divine action has to be able to offer a view of God working creatively and redemptively in and through the natural world to bring it to healing and wholeness. Such a theology of divine action must meet at least three requirements. First, it would need to be a noninterventionist theology that sees God as working in and through the natural world, rather than as arbitrarily intervening to send suffering to some and not to others. Second, God's action in creating an emergent universe would need to be understood in the light of the resurrection and the promise that all things will be transformed and redeemed in Christ (Rom 8:19-23; Col 1:20; Eph 1:10; Rev 21:5). Third, it would need to be a theology in which God is understood as lovingly accepting the limits of creatures and actively waiting upon finite creaturely processes, living with the constraints of these processes, accompanying each creature in love, rejoicing in every emergence, suffering with every suffering creature, and promising to bring all to healing and fullness of life.

While a Christian theological notion of divine action cannot offer a full explanation of suffering, it can remove common misunderstandings that spring from traditional Christian notions of divine action. It can offer an alternative to the popular view of an interventionist and arbitrary God, a view of God who acts in and through all the interactions of creatures, always respecting their integrity and their proper autonomy, enabling and empowering creaturely entities and processes to exist, to interact, and to evolve. It would also need to be a theology that can account for special divine acts, such as the Christ-event, and the experiences of grace and providence in everyday life. Such a theology would need to be in creative dialogue with sciences such as cosmology and biological evolution. It would need to offer an eschatological vision that sees suffering in the context of hope based on the resurrection. Such a theology would need to be eschatological from the ground up. It would need to offer hope not just for human beings but for the whole of creation.

I will begin this work with two chapters that attempt to set the scene, the first addressing some characteristics of the universe revealed by the natural sciences, and the second exploring what can be discovered about divine action from the Christ-event. What I see as two central chapters follow: the first on creation as the self-bestowal of God, and the second on special divine acts in the history of the universe, the life of grace, and the history of salvation. Then, in the fifth chapter, I take up the question of miracles in relation to the laws of nature and follow this with a chapter on the resurrection of Jesus. This leads to two chapters on the divine act of redemption in Christ, which I explore in terms of deifying transformation. The penultimate chapter is on eschatology, the final deification of the whole of creation. Discussions of divine action seem to lead to important questions about the meaning of prayer, so the book concludes with a chapter on prayers of intercession.

The title of this book could be a little misleading. It will become evident to readers that there is a sense in which I believe we *cannot* say how God acts. We cannot describe the inner nature of divine action any more than we can know or describe the divine nature. In this sense, the title promises more than can be delivered. But we can seek to articulate some characteristics of divine action that we perceive from the way God is revealed to us in the Christ-event, from creation itself, and from our own experience of the grace of the Spirit at work in our lives. This book is an attempt to describe these characteristics. In this sense, it is possible and proper to explore how God acts in our world.

The first and most important acknowledgment I need to make is to William R. Stoeger, S.J., who has collaborated with me on this whole project. Bill is an astrophysicist who works for the Vatican Observatory Research Group in the Steward Observatory of the University of Arizona. Before beginning this work, I enjoyed the hospitality of the Jesuit community of Tucson and spent many hours talking over the project with Bill. At several points in this book, I incorporate and build on his published works in the field of science and theology. He has read and offered critical comments on each chapter. I have learned a great deal from him over many years, and this book owes much to him. I was able to travel to Tucson to meet with him because of the generous bursary provided by the Manly Union's Ongoing Formation Fund. My sincere thanks to the president, Fr. Peter Christie, and the executive of this fund.

In September 2005, the Center for Theology and the Natural Sciences in Berkeley, California, and the Vatican Observatory cosponsored a conference on the problem of evil, held at Castel Gandolfo, Italy. The focus was on the suffering built into the natural world, in the light of recent developments in physics and cosmology. My work benefited greatly from this conference; from the original impetus to write a paper on this fundamental issue; from the stimulating engagement with scientists, philosophers, and theologians gathered from around the world; from their critical comments on my own work; and from their various contributions to the conference and to the book published as a result.[2]

I was able to do a substantial amount of work on this book in the second half of 2007, when I was made welcome at Durham University as the St. Cuthbert's Senior Visiting Research Fellow in Catholic Theology. I am very grateful to the faculty of the Department of Theology and Religion at Durham University. I owe particular thanks to the Durham University Catholic Chaplaincy and St. Cuthbert's Catholic Church, and to the community that made me feel so much at home. I owe a great deal to Dr. Paul D. Murray and Fr. Anthony Currer, above all for their friendship, but also for their generous interest in this research, their critical questions, and their constant encouragement.

As I was beginning this work, Bob Russell and Ted Peters of the Center for Theology and the Natural Sciences at Berkeley graciously took time to discuss the issues of this book with me. I have learned much from both of them in many such discussions. Alastair Blake, Visiting Research Fellow in Physics at the University of Adelaide, and my colleagues James McEvoy, Patricia Fox, R.S.M., and Rosemary Hocking, have read the manuscript carefully and generously offered very helpful comments. I have benefited greatly from their suggestions and encouragement along the way.

The first versions of chapters 2 and 3 were published as "Why Is God Doing This? Suffering, the Universe, and Christian Eschatology," in *Physics and Cosmology: Scientific Perspectives on the Problem of Natural Evil*, edited by Nancey Murphy, Robert John Russell, and William R. Stoeger (Vatican: Vatican Observatory; Berkeley: Center for Theology and the Natural Sciences, 2007), 247–66. Some of the material in chapters 7 and 9 first appeared as "The Redemption of Animals in an Incarnational Theology," in *Creaturely Theology: On God, Humans and Other Animals*, edited by Celia Deane-Drummond and David Clough (London: SCM, 2009), 81–99. A version of chapter 5 appeared as "Miracles and the Laws of Nature," in *Compass* 41, no. 2 (2007): 8–16. The basis for chapter 6 appeared as "Resurrection and the Costs of Evolution: A Dialogue with Rahner on the Costs of Evolution," in *Theological Studies* 67 (December 2006): 816–33. Part of chapter 9 appeared as "Every Sparrow That Falls to the Ground: The Cost of Evolution and the Christ-Event," in *Ecotheology* 11, no. 1 (March 2006): 103–23. A later development will appear as "Hope for Creation after Darwin: The Redemption of 'All Things,'" in *Theology after Darwin*, edited by Michael Northcott (London: Paternoster, 2009). I am grateful to the College Theology Society for inviting me to offer a plenary lecture at the society's annual convention in May 2009 at Notre Dame University, where I was able to test material found in chapters 3 and 4. This lecture is due for publication in *Horizons*. Scripture quotations are from the New Revised Standard Version.

1

Characteristics of the Universe
Revealed by the Sciences

What is the proper starting point for a Christian theology of divine action? A little reflection suggests that, if it is to be truly a Christian theology, then it will certainly be grounded in the Christian tradition and the central conviction of this tradition, that God has acted to bring salvation to our world in the life, death, and resurrection of Jesus and in the outpouring of the Spirit. This will be taken up as the theme of the next chapter. But, I believe, a theology of divine action depends as well on the worldview that the theologian brings to his or her work. And if this worldview is to be as faithful as possible to the world we actually encounter, it will be shaped by the best insights of the sciences.

When twenty-first-century cosmology describes the emergence and expansion of our universe, and when contemporary biology describes the evolution of life on Earth, the theologian takes these scientific findings seriously, because she interprets the history of the universe that cosmology describes, and the story of life that biology articulates, as the fruit of the divine act of creation. When the sciences come to a broadly held consensus that, for example, the observable universe has been expanding for 13.7 billion years from a tiny, compressed state, or that natural selection has played a fundamental role in the evolution of life on Earth, the theologian will see such a consensus as the best description we have to date of the concrete and specific ways in which God's action takes effect in a universe of creatures. Of course, such a theology will need to be revised if and when the scientific picture changes or develops. But this is the nature of theology, to be done again anew in new contexts.

In this chapter, then, I attempt to articulate key insights from the sciences that contribute to a worldview that will form a dialogue partner for the theology of divine action that follows. I will ask this question: What are the key characteristics of the world revealed by the natural sciences that are significant for a theology of the action of God? William Stoeger offers some guidance here. He has provided a response to this question from the perspective of a cosmologist and philosopher of science.[1] He speaks of a universe that is evolving at all levels, that is relational, that has its own integrity, and that possesses some directionality. A further theme, which will be fundamental for this book, is that evolution is costly for many creatures. Stoeger's assessment seems in general agreement with that of others involved in the contemporary discussion among science, philosophy, and theology, including Ian Barbour, Arthur Peacocke, John Polkinghorne, Robert John Russell, Nancey Murphy, George Ellis, John Haught, Philip Clayton, and Christopher Southgate.[2] I will follow Stoeger's line of thought, outlining an understanding of characteristics of the worldview revealed by the natural sciences that will be basic to the theology of divine action developed in the rest of this book.

A Universe That Evolves at All Levels

We owe the discovery of the evolution of life by means of natural selection to the work of Charles Darwin and Alfred Russel Wallace in the nineteenth century. The discovery that the universe itself is expanding and evolving is the achievement of twentieth-century science, as it built on Albert Einstein's theory of general relativity and Edwin Hubble's astronomical observations. With some confidence, cosmologists can now trace the history of the observable universe back to the first second of its existence, about 13.7 billion years ago, when it was unimaginably small, dense, and hot. They think a great deal happened in the first second, including the emergence of the four fundamental forces—gravitation, electromagnetism, and the strong and weak nuclear forces—and the fundamental particles, such as neutrons, protons, electrons, and neutrinos.

According to many influential theories in cosmology, early in the first second, the young universe went through a period of very rapid inflation. In the first few minutes, as the universe expanded more gently and continued to cool, protons and neutrons were able to combine to form the nuclei of hydrogen, the simplest element, and the first helium. By the end of the first three minutes, the observable universe existed as an expanding and cooling fireball of hydrogen and helium nuclei. When it was about 400,000 years old, it entered a new stage of its evolution. It was cool enough for nuclei to bond with electrons to form atoms of hydrogen and helium. In this process, matter was decoupled from radiation. The universe became transparent to the radiation that fills it—the cosmic microwave radiation. This radiation, predicted by the theory of big bang cosmology, was discovered in 1967 and is now mapped by astronomers, who find it gives them a kind of snapshot of the early universe.

As the universe continued to expand, slight unevenness in density meant there were locations where large clouds of hydrogen and helium accumulated, the beginning of galaxies. Under the influence of gravity, these pockets of gas eventually stopped expanding and began to collapse, heat up, and fragment. Massive enough fragments increased in temperature to the point where nuclear fusion processes were triggered, converting hydrogen into more helium. The first stars were born, lighting up the universe. Further nuclear reactions would convert helium into heavier elements, including the carbon, nitrogen, and oxygen from which we are made. Very large stars ended in supernova explosions that produced still heavier elements, seeding their galaxies with elements for the formation of further stars and their planets.

Our Milky Way is one of about 200 billion galaxies in the observable universe. The Milky Way contains more than 100 billion stars. Because of the material produced by stars and supernova explosions, and the subsequent chemical processing in cooler astronomical environments, interstellar clouds, comets, asteroids, planets, and moons contain complex organic molecules and amino acids. These are fundamental to the emergence of life on Earth. Our own solar system formed from a great molecular cloud of gas about 4.6 billion years ago. The raw materials for life were assembled as Earth took shape from the matter circling the newly emerged Sun and through the bombardment of the young Earth by meteorites.

Within about a billion years, life appeared on Earth in the form of bacterial cells without a nucleus (called prokaryotes). The next big step was the emergence of creatures that possess a developed cell nucleus (the eukaryotes). Early microbial forms of life began to change the atmosphere to one that was oxygen rich through photosynthesis. Developed multicellular animals appear in the fossil record from about 570 million years ago and took new and diverse forms in the seas of the Cambrian period (545 million to 495 million years ago). Dinosaurs, flying reptiles, and mammals appeared in the Triassic (248 million to 206 million years ago) and Jurassic (206 million to 144 million years ago) periods. Birds and flowering plants emerged at the beginning of the Cretaceous period (144 million to 65 million years ago). Various hominid species evolved between 4 million and 2 million years ago. *Homo erectus* emerged about 2 million years ago with a large brain and an athletic body and soon spread from Africa to other parts of the world. Modern humans seem to have evolved about 200,000 years ago, lighter than *Homo erectus* and possessing a much larger brain.

The universe and everything in it evolves in time. According to quantum cosmologists, time as we know it could not have been a characteristic of our universe in the tiniest fraction of the first second of its history (the Planck era), but emerged as the universe expanded from its primordial state. But ever since the first part of the first second, long periods of time have been essential to the emergence of the universe—above all of its galaxies and stars, with their capacity to produce elements like carbon, which then set the scene for the emergence of life and consciousness on a planet like Earth. The emergence of this kind of complexity requires something like the 13.7 billion years that have passed since the first second of our universe.

In a theological vision, this great story of an evolving universe is not only our story, but also God's story, the story of God's creation. The first particles, the emergence of stars, the production of heavier elements necessary for life, the development of complex molecules, the evolution of life on Earth—all of this is God's work, brought about by God working in and through the laws of nature over immense lengths of time and with great patience. Reflecting on this leads one to think that God must be a Creator who not only enables but respects and waits upon the processes by which things evolve in more and more complex ways. It seems that it is characteristic of God to create in an emergent and evolutionary way.

A Universe Constituted by Patterns of Relationship

When the various sciences look at an atom, a galaxy, or the most complex thing we know, the human brain, they find patterns of relationships. Quarks are the building blocks for protons and neutrons, and these combine in various ways to form the ninety-two kinds of atoms. Atoms form the basis of molecules, which combine to form macromolecules. Combinations of these make life possible in single-celled bacteria, in multicellular organisms, in neurologically developed animals with their social structure, and in human beings with their developed brains and their participation in and dependence upon society and culture.

At each level, entities are constituted from other entities structured in differentiated and cooperative interrelationships. Arthur Peacocke, among others, has described the picture of the world that the natural sciences give us as a complex "hierarchy." This word points to the way patterns of relationship nest upon one another: there is a series of levels of organization of matter, in which each member in the series is a new whole yet is constituted of parts that precede it in the series.[3]

Stoeger describes the patterns discovered by the natural sciences as "constitutive relationships." Constitutive relationships are "those interactions among components and with the larger context which jointly effect the composition of a given system and establish its functional characteristic within the larger whole of which it is a part, and thereby enable it to manifest the particular properties and behavior it does."[4] These relationships make an entity what it is, endowing it with unity of structure and consistency of action. Entities emerge and exist in such patterns of interrelationship. These include not only the interrelationship between the constituents that make up an entity, but also the interrelationship between the entity and its environment.

Each entity is constituted by more fundamental entities; each entity is interrelated with others to form a larger system. Thus, a carbon atom is constituted from subatomic particles (protons, neutrons, and electrons). But a carbon atom in my body is constituted as part of a molecule, which forms part of a cell, which belongs to an organ of my body. I am part of a family, a human society, and a community of interrelated living creatures on Earth. The Earth community depends upon and is interrelated with the Sun, the Milky Way Galaxy, and the whole universe.

At all levels from fundamental particles to atoms, molecules, cells, and the universe, one level of reality is articulated upon another in new patterns of relationship. Stoeger finds that this kind of articulated structuring is a universal feature of the world revealed by the natural and social sciences. At every level, this nested organization is realized through the interrelationships among the components, together with the whole–part relationships that determine the distribution and collective function of components.[5] Constitutive relationships involve all those interactions that incorporate components into a more complex whole, and relate that complex whole into another level of unity. They may be physical, biological, or social in character.

We human beings depend upon many different systems both inside and outside ourselves. Atoms that make up the neurons of our brains were formed in long-dead stars. We are dependent upon and interrelated with the universe. Closer to home, we become who we are in relationship to families, communities, and the land to which we belong, with its animals, birds, trees, flowers, insects, and bacteria.

When we move beyond science to theology, we can add that the most important constitutive relationship of all, one that operates on a radically different level from all the others and is not accessible to empirical research, is the relationship of ongoing creation. This is the relationship by which the indwelling Creator Spirit is present to each creature, enabling it to be and to become in a world of interconnected relationships. This relationship with the Creator endows all things with existence in an interrelational and ordered world. While science suggests a world of constitutive relationships, a Christian theology locates this in relation to a Trinitarian God of mutual relations. It sees God's being as Communion. While it insists that there is an infinite difference between all the interrelationships of creatures and the divine Communion, a Trinitarian theology of creation sees every creature, whether it be an insect, a tree, a star, or a human being, as participating in the life of divine Communion. It sees their differentiated relationships with each other as already a limited, creaturely reflection of this divine life, and as in some way a sacrament of Communion.

A Universe Where Natural Processes Have Their Own Integrity

While science sees everything in our universe as interrelated, it also sees each entity and process as possessing a level of integrity. And as new systems and new organisms emerge in the course of evolutionary history, the sciences see them as emerging and being maintained by natural processes with their own integrity. Some scientists are convinced that within nature itself, there are self-ordering and self-organizing principles and processes that can adequately account, at the level of science, for the emergence of complexity and novelty.[6] While some of these principles and processes are already well known, others remain a matter of speculation. The gaps in scientific knowledge have not all been filled, but more are being filled every day.

Appealing to outside intervention is not an accepted option for science. Science is rightly committed to methodological naturalism, seeking natural explanations for empirical reality. There is no need to appeal to the "god of the gaps." At the level of empirical reality, the level at which all the sciences work, the natural world is understood as possessing a kind of autonomy, in the sense that it evolves and functions on its own, according to its own laws. Science has learned to be confident that natural processes are to be explained by the laws of nature. Even when, at a particular stage of research, something cannot be explained, there is still a well-based assumption that a natural explanation is to be sought and found. There is an expectation that science, working with its understanding of the laws and processes of the natural world, will be able to explain the origin and existence of atoms, stars, cells, the world of plants and animals and human beings.

There are, of course, important questions to ask that take us beyond the empirical sciences. These sciences cannot tell us why there is anything at all. They cannot tell us why there is a universe or why there is order in it. They cannot tell us the meaning of our own lives and deaths. They cannot tell us the significance of this immense cosmos in which we find ourselves or our own place in it. They cannot deal with the endless searching of the human mind and heart. They cannot tell us whether the ultimate meaning of the whole universe is personal love or bleak emptiness. They cannot tell us whether we are ultimately forgiven and loved. These are all urgent human questions, but they are philosophical and theological questions rather than scientific ones.

Christian theology sees God as the Creator who is profoundly and intimately present to every aspect of the universe, enabling it to be and to become at every point. It proclaims that the ultimate meaning of the universe, and that which guides and empowers it, is the love revealed in Jesus and poured out in the Spirit. But with Stoeger, I believe that this kind of theological position is entirely coherent with a profound respect for the autonomy of the sciences, and for their assumption that it is the task of science to explain the emergence of the universe, the evolution of life, and the whole of empirical reality according to scientific methods, which involve methodological naturalism and do not invoke the "god of the gaps."

A theology that takes science seriously will respect the integrity of the natural sciences and the integrity of nature itself and will see both as God given. After all, Thomas Aquinas long ago proclaimed that God works creatively and providentially through the whole network of created causes, which he called secondary causes. This is something I will need to address more fully later in this book. For now, it is enough to note that Aquinas does not see this as a diminishment of divine power, but as the way divine power works. God acts in and through creaturely causes because of the divine goodness that wants to give creatures "the dignity of causing." Aquinas sees God as creating in such a way as to give creatures their own integrity and relative independence as causal agents.

A Directional Universe

Does the universe give evidence of purpose? Does science support a teleological view of evolution? At the beginning of the twenty-first century, it seems clear that the sciences do not offer clear evidence of a goal-directed universe. Some biologists, including Stephen Jay Gould, have challenged the general idea of "progress" in evolutionary history.[7] Gould also famously introduced the metaphor of "replaying life's tape," insisting that were the tape to be played again, the randomness and contingency of the process would mean that life would not evolve in anything like the same way.[8] While others fully accept the role of contingency in evolution, they come to a different conclusion. Simon Conway Morris presents many examples of parallel and convergent evolution, where very different lineages have evolved similar adaptations in similar contexts.[9] Evolution is not entirely random but is constrained along certain lines, as selection pressures organisms toward possible functional spaces. This means that if features of organisms are of great adaptive value and genetically possible, these features will eventually arise. Such features include intelligence, and Conway Morris thinks that something like the human was bound to emerge.[10]

The eye is a common example of convergent evolution. It has emerged independently at least three times: in vertebrates, in the cephalopods (squids and octopus), and in some marine worms. A case can be made for the independent but convergent evolution of intelligence, not just among primates (monkeys, apes, and humans) and the cetaceans (whales and dolphins), but also among crows and parrots.[11] The emergence of intelligence in birds is all the more remarkable, in that birds and mammals evolved from distinct reptilian ancestors and have very different brains. Their last common ancestor lived over 280 million years ago. It seems clear that recent work on convergent evolution supports the idea of some overall direction in the patterns of evolutionary emergence.

From the perspective of a cosmologist, William Stoeger believes that a strong case can be made that the sciences reveal some overall directionality in the evolution of the universe at large, and of systems within it. This overall directionality is indicated first of all by the fact that the universe is expanding and cooling and that its structure is dominated by gravity. This means that the universe in fact evolves in the direction of greater complexity, from quarks, to stars, to bacteria, to the human brain. Chance plays an essential role in this pattern, particularly at the level of random genetic mutations, which can have disastrous consequences for organisms but also give rise, in some cases, to new evolutionary developments. Chance is involved at the planetary level when a comet collides with Earth, bringing death and extinction of species. Such deadly chance events occur within a framework of lawfulness, and they can provide opportunities for the emergence of new systems or new species of organisms. In this sense, chance is not opposed to overall directionality but, when combined with the lawfulness of the universe, is part of the pattern by which it occurs.

Stoeger points out that science does not offer grounds for the idea that there is a preplanned outcome to evolution or for the idea that the evolutionary process is consciously directed. There is no evidence for the existence of a blueprint of the final outcome. Science does not indicate purpose or design, but neither does it rule them out. The kind of directionality that science indicates is that of a chain of realized possibilities that build upon one another: "The realization of any given possibility presupposes the prior realization of other possibilities, which are the stepping stones to those involving greater complexity or organization."[12] At any given point in the evolution of the universe and of life, there is a limited range of developments that either will occur or may occur. At any one point, there is a developing, nested set of directionalities. Some of these can emerge in specific ways in particular locales. So where a stable star system contains a planet that is rich in minerals and water, and is the right distance from the star to have a moderate temperature, there is the rich possibility of future evolutionary development.

The cosmological "anthropic principle" seems to support the idea that directionality is built into the evolution of the universe. This principle points to the insight that the universe has to be finely tuned in precisely the right ways if life, particularly human life, is to emerge within it. A very small change in any one of the many constants, such as the gravitational constant, that characterize the forces and particles of the universe would leave it completely lifeless.[13] These constants need to be precisely tuned, very close to what we find in the universe as it is, if galaxies are to form in the early universe, stars are to ignite to produce elements like carbon, and life is to evolve on a planet like Earth. It takes billions of years of star burning to produce the elements that make life on Earth possible. There is, then, a close relationship between the age and size of the universe and the emergence of life on our planet.

I am not suggesting that the anthropic principle proves the existence of the Creator, nor am I arguing that it proves the universe is designed. Advances in science, such as inflationary theory, may well offer ever better explanations for what we observe as the fine-tuning of the universe. All I am suggesting here is that the anthropic principle, as we now understand it, does fit naturally with a theological view of a God who is acting purposefully in creation. While there is this congruence with the anthropic principle, it is worth noting that there is no such natural fit between Christian hope for a future transformation of creation and cosmology's prediction of a universe endlessly expanding and dissipating into a bleak and lifeless future or, as seems less likely, collapsing back on itself. This issue has begun to be addressed by the science–theology dialogue, in the work of scholars including Robert John Russell and John Polkinghorne, and it will require much more work from theologians.[14]

Stoeger's generalization from the scientific evidence is a modest one. What the sciences show is that the universe does evolve with time, in the direction of increasing complexity that includes the emergence of stars, the appearance of the first self-replicating bacteria, and the evolution of human beings. The sciences do *not* reveal a divine design or blueprint. But the scientific evidence is open to a Christian interpretation. This modest claim, that the sciences support an overall directionality in the evolution of the universe and life, fits well with the idea of a God who is achieving purposes in creation, redemption, and final fulfillment. It is congruent with a view of God who acts creatively and providentially in and through the laws of nature, in all the randomness and lawfulness that allows and enables a life-bearing universe to evolve.

The Costs of Evolution

Following Stoeger, I have been proposing that specific characteristics of the universe that are relevant for a Christian theology of divine action can be distilled from the natural sciences: the sciences reveal a universe that is evolving at all levels, that is constituted by relationships, that has its own integrity, and that has an overall directionality. The evolutionary character of the universe is something that Christian theologians are able to embrace positively and to understand as the way God creates.[15] But evolution is costly, and this constitutes another characteristic of the universe revealed by the natural sciences. They reveal that the costs of evolution are intrinsic to the process.

It has become clear from the evolutionary biology of the past two centuries that competition for resources, predation, death, pain, and extinction are built into the evolution of life. They are not simply unfortunate circumstances that sometimes accompany the emergence of a world of beauty and diversity. They were already part of the pattern of life long before the emergence of human beings and cannot be caused by human sin, as many Christians of the past have thought. The costs of evolution are intrinsic to the process by which life has come to flourish on Earth.

In the world as we know it from the biological sciences, eagles, dolphins, and humans could not be what they are without death. The evolution of each species occurs only through the long processes of evolutionary history, the repeated cycles of birth, reproduction, and death. The evolution of organs like the eye depends upon the pattern of life and death repeated over countless generations, by which random genetic changes give an advantage in adapting to an environment and reproducing. Natural selection is unthinkable without the cycle of generations. It depends upon lives that end in death. Ursula Goodenough points out that part of the evolutionary strategy of organisms like our own is that their somatic cells are programmed for death. Death is the price paid for living in a complex world with developed forms of life, including sentient life. Death is the price we pay for a world in which there are wings, eyes, and brains.[16]

Both cooperation and competition for resources have shaped life on our planet, and the evolution of many species depends upon the predator–prey relationship. As Holmes Rolston puts it, "The cougar's fang has carved the limbs of the fleet-footed deer, and vice-versa."[17] Christopher Southgate takes up this theme: "No-one who has seen at close quarters the surge of a full grown orca through the water, the prowl of a leopard through long grass, or that quicksilver stalling turn by which a peregrine returns to the stoop—all products of the refinements of predation over millions of years—can doubt the value that arises from the process."[18] This value is, in some cases, closely related to behavior that inflicts pain on other animals: an orca batters a gray whale until it has no more strength, a leopard may take minutes to kill an antelope, a peregrine may maim its prey, leaving it to die a lingering death. Suffering among the weak, the young, and the less adapted is intrinsic to the evolution of the wonderful attributes of living creatures.[19]

Pain seems to accompany sentience. An increase in the brain's capacity to receive and store information brings with it an increase of an organism's sensitivity to its environment. Consciousness involves awareness not only of what is life enhancing but also of what is damaging. In the context of natural selection, pain has survival value. It acts as a warning and a spur to action. Pain is "an energizing force," which because of its high survival value, will tend to be selected for in evolution. Excessive pain would be counterproductive in terms of survival and would tend to not be selected for overall.[20] In the forms of life we know, increased consciousness involves the capacity to experience pain, and with the emergence of reflective consciousness, there is an increase in the capacity to experience suffering, in that what is painful can be remembered, dwelled upon, and feared.

Extinction is part of the evolutionary pattern of life on Earth. Species disappear, and new ones emerge. Only about 2 to 4 percent of the species that have existed on Earth survive today. In this sense, extinction is part of the natural cycle of life. But there have also been a number of catastrophic extinctions in the 3.7-billion-year history of life on Earth. In the worst of these, 250 million years ago, most of life was annihilated. In a short time, something like 96 percent of species was lost. In the extinction of 65 million years ago, the dinosaurs disappeared, along with perhaps 70 percent of the species on Earth. Today, many species are being driven to extinction or are under threat of extinction because of human activity. Something of value is lost with every extinction. Theologically, every species is an expression of God in our world, a word of God spoken on our planet. But it is also true that with the mass extinctions on our planet, life has emerged in creative new ways. With the extinction of the dinosaurs, for example, it seems that mammals had more opportunity to diversify and flourish.

Christopher Southgate analyzes the issues that might be thought to constitute the problem of evolutionary theodicy, including death, the pain involved in parasitism, predation and disease, the waste involved in the abundance of organisms, and the extinction of species. He sees death as a thermodynamic necessity, which does not need to be considered a problem if it follows a fulfilled life. He proposes that the two issues that need to be dealt with are the suffering of sentient creatures and the extinction of species, which he sees as always a loss of value to the biosphere as a whole.[21] I find logic to this position and the distinction it allows between pain that assists survival and death that follows a full life, on the one hand, and the suffering of sentient animals, on the other. This may well be helpful for the kind of theodicy Southgate is arguing.

For the purposes of this book, however, it is helpful to consider the costs of evolution as a whole. These costs are involved in the way complexity arises in one location by drawing energy from another, in the way life evolves through genetic mutations that are mainly damaging to organisms, in the way living creatures prey on others, in the way decay and death seem intrinsic to the evolution of the biosphere, and in the way that extinction seems to be part of the pattern of life on Earth. The costs of evolution are the pain, suffering, and loss that occur in all of these. It is all of these costs that I want to bring into the dialogue of this book.

In this chapter, I have outlined some of the key characteristics of the universe that emerge from the natural sciences: the universe is emergent and evolving, is constituted by relationships, possesses its own integrity, has a level of directionality, and has costs that are intrinsic to the process. I have proposed that each of these is relevant to a theology of divine action. With this kind of scientific worldview in mind, I will turn to the Christian tradition itself, asking what it brings to a conversation about divine action.

2

Divine Action in the Christ-Event

One of the themes of this book will be that creation is to be understood in the light of Christ. For a Christian theology, the God of creation is the God who gives God's self to us in Jesus of Nazareth. A Christian theology of divine action, then, is grounded not simply by reference to a general theology of creation, but in what Christians see as the decisive act of God in our human history, the Christ-event. I will use the expression *Christ-event* to refer to the life, death, and resurrection of Jesus and the outpouring of the Holy Spirit. In this chapter, I will attempt to build a basis for a Christian theology of divine action by asking two interrelated questions. First, what does Jesus reveal, in his words and deeds, about the nature of divine action? Second, what further insights come from pondering God's action, not only in Jesus' life, but also in his death, his resurrection, and the sending of the Holy Spirit? The first question asks what we can know about Jesus' own theology of divine action, while the second asks what we can learn from the whole Christ-event.

Jesus' Vision of Divine Action: The Reign of God

What did Jesus think and teach about divine action? This question seems rarely asked in theologies of divine action, but once it is raised, an obvious answer presents itself. Jesus' life and ministry revolves around a particular concept of God's action, which he calls the kingdom, or reign, of God. He sees his mission as proclaiming the good news of this coming reign of

God and as calling for radical conversion in the light of it: "The time is fulfilled, and the kingdom of God has come near; repent, and believe in the good news" (Mark 1:15). Not only his words but also his deeds proclaim this coming act of God: "But if it is by the finger of God that I cast out the demons, then the kingdom of God has come to you" (Luke 11:20).

The centrality of the reign of God for Jesus is widely attested to in the Gospel tradition. It appears in five distinct blocks: in the Gospel of Mark, in material that is common to Matthew and Luke, in material that is found only in Matthew, in material that is special to Luke, and in John.[1] When the Greek phrase *basileia tou theou* is translated into English as "kingdom of God," it can seem static. This is very unhelpful, since its meaning for Jesus is radically dynamic. It stands for the living God and for this God's saving action. The precise phrase "kingdom of God" does not occur in the Hebrew Scriptures (it appears in Wis 10:10), but these Scriptures are the essential background for Jesus' usage, with their concept of God as the one who creates, rules, and saves and their frequent use of kingly terms for God.

In the way Jesus uses it, the kingdom of God is a rich symbolic expression. It is a "tensive" symbol, which means it cannot be limited to any one reference but continually opens up to further meanings.[2] It is a symbol that evokes a story, the biblical story that embraces God's action in creation and salvation. N. T. Wright makes the point that the kingdom of God was Jesus' unique way of retelling the common Jewish story, the story of the God who is coming to restore Israel.[3] He sees Jesus as convinced that this story would be brought to its God-given climax in and through his own ministry. The reign of God is a rich and multivalent symbol, one that evokes the story of God's action in multiple ways. The best way of grasping its meaning for Jesus is by attending to the way he expresses it in both his words and deeds. In search of this meaning, I will discuss briefly some key aspects of this ministry, his parables of the kingdom, his healing ministry, his open table, and his formation of a new community.

Parables of Divine Action

Jesus not only acts like a prophet (Mark 6:4) of Israel in proclaiming the coming reign of God, but also stands in the ancient wisdom tradition of Israel (Mark 6:2; Luke 7:35). Like other wisdom teachers, he speaks of

God in language taken from the natural world and the everyday life of human beings. God is the God of continuous creation, who causes the sun to rise and rain to fall on all alike (Matt 5:45), whose provident care embraces the wildflowers and birds of Galilee (Matt 6:25-34), and who does not forget even one little sparrow (Luke 12:6). Jesus makes use of traditional wisdom forms of figurative speech (*mashal*) that include short sayings (aphorisms) and parables.

Typical short sayings of Jesus include these: "But many that are first will be last and the last first" (Mark 10:31); "It is easier for a camel to go through the eye of a needle than for a rich man to enter the kingdom of God" (Mark 10:25); "Love your enemies and pray for those who persecute you" (Matt 5:44). These sayings are filled with the urgency of God's coming reign. Some make use of hyperbole. It seems that they were deliberately provocative. They appear designed to challenge and destabilize settled worldviews and to invite hearers into a bigger world, the world of the kingdom of God. To hold together in one's heart and mind "love" and the person or group one has learned to hate as the enemy is to already begin to experience the breaking in of this kingdom.

The parables function in a similar way. They are the creations of an artist in words, someone who communicates in vivid stories with unusual skill. Biblical scholars have come to see the parables in their original form not so much as moral examples but as a communication of the coming reign of God. To listen with open ears to these stories is to experience something of the kingdom. It has been said that the parables of Jesus are not simply examples but revelation. They function like metaphor, where "we have an image with a certain shock to the imagination which directly conveys vision of what is signified."[4] The parables are "the preaching itself" and do not simply serve as examples.[5] They bring the kingdom of God into language and allow language to mediate the kingdom. As poetic metaphors mediate the experience of the poet, so the parables of Jesus give expression to his own experience of God and mediate this experience.[6] When our ears are open to receive the parable, it becomes a moment of grace for us, a kingdom event. The hearer of the parable not only learns about the reign of God but also participates in it.

The parable of the Good Samaritan (Luke 10:30-37) tells a story, all too familiar to Jesus' hearers, of someone being attacked, robbed, and left for dead. But there is a shock to the imagination when the traveler who comes to the victim's aid with extraordinary generosity turns out to be not one of those from whom aid might be expected, but precisely one who is regarded as a dangerous and alien infidel. To glimpse the possibility of such a person as a true neighbor, as a wonderfully generous and life-saving neighbor, is to enter the radically different world of God's reign. The parable of the Workers in the Vineyard (Matt 20:1-16) tells what is, at first, an ordinary story of workers being employed at different times in a day, from early in the morning until late in the afternoon. The shock comes at the close of day, when all are paid the same amount. This affronts all sense of what is right. Precisely because of this, the parable can open a hearer to the idea that the God of the kingdom may be radically other than all of our human notions about who deserves what. It can lead to a glimpse of God as boundless in generosity, a God not constrained by human notions of proper compensation, a God of the latecomer, a God of the poor, the outsider, and the sinner.

The presence and action of this God of the kingdom in our world is not always easy to discern. Jesus invites us to think of divine action as sometimes like the tiny mustard seed, which may be almost invisible but will grow into a plant whose leaves shelter the birds of the sky, or like the yeast a woman mixes with flour to make bread (Matt 13:31-33). This is a God who freely gives God's self to us, and this gift of God's self is the treasure of a lifetime that one discovers, the pearl of immense worth that one finds. For this, one needs to be prepared to sell everything and to risk everything (Matt 13:34-35).

Healing

Jesus not only proclaims God's coming action in parables but announces it in his deeds. The Gospels portray Jesus as a healer and an exorcist. He brings good news of God's reign by the healing of bodies and the liberating of minds and spirits. The Gospels contain not only summary statements of Jesus healing many people but also developed and vivid narratives, such as those of the leper (Mark 1:40-45), the woman suffering from a hemorrhage (Mark 5:24b-34), the blind beggar Bartimaeus (Mark 10:46-52), and the woman with a crippled back (Luke 13:10-17). John Meier has considered

Jesus' miracles in great detail, and he is convinced that, historically, Jesus was seen in his own time as a healer and wonder-worker, and saw himself as bringing healing in the name of the God whose coming he proclaimed. Jesus was known as both a prophet and a wonder-worker, and this combination helps to account for the excitement he generated.[7]

Jesus is remembered as often healing by touch but as driving out demons by verbal command (Mark 1:25). It seems clear that those suffering from what we would now call mental illnesses like schizophrenia and physical conditions such as epilepsy were among those who at the time were described as possessed. Jesus is remembered as using the language of the kingdom of these liberating acts: "But if it is by the finger of God that I cast out the demons, then the kingdom of God has come to you" (Luke 11:20). Meier comments that Jesus is seeing a specific and concrete act of healing in the here and now as an anticipation of God's eschatological act: "Jesus consciously chose to indicate that the display of miraculous power in his own ministry constituted a partial and preliminary realization of God's kingly rule, which would soon be displayed in full force. It was to underline this organic link between his own ministry in the present and the full coming of God's eschatological rule in the near future that Jesus chose to employ 'the kingdom of God' for both."[8]

These stories of healing and exorcism function as gospel, revealing God's will to save enfleshed in Jesus' compassionate words and deeds. The miracles express the healing and the *shalom* associated with the coming of God's reign. The healings are both a sign that God's reign is already present in Jesus' ministry and a promise of its fullness. They liberate the afflicted, not only from a medical condition (disease), but also from a situation of alienation (illness). In these actions, salvation from God is revealed as far more than a religious matter in the narrow sense. It embraces the body, health, sanity, relationships, community, and wholeness.

Compared with the suffering of so many in the global community, Jesus' healings are actions on a small scale. But these limited actions point to and anticipate God's future action in which all will find healing and liberation. Edward Schillebeeckx has said of Jesus, "He saw a distant vision of final, perfect and universal salvation—the kingdom of God—in and through his own fragmentary actions, which were historical and thus limited and finite."[9] Jesus recognized these specific actions as practical anticipations of salvation to come. Reflection on this suggests that our own practices of healing and liberation, incomplete and limited as they are, may be seen as a participation in and an anticipation of God's coming reign. The limited healing ministry of Jesus "confirms the permanent validity of any practice of doing good which is incomplete because it is historically limited."[10] The kingdom practice of Jesus invites and challenges us to action that participates in the way of the kingdom, in what Schillebeeckx calls the "orthopraxis" of the kingdom.[11]

The Open Table

Early in Mark's Gospel, we find Jesus and his disciples at table, eating with many tax collectors and sinners. This provokes a challenge from some scribes of the Pharisees: "Why does he eat with tax collectors and sinners?" Jesus responds, "Those who are well have no need of a physician, but those who are sick; I have come to call not the righteous but sinners" (Mark 2:15-20). In Luke, Jesus eats with Zacchaeus, a chief tax collector and public sinner. Zacchaeus repents, and Jesus declares, "Today salvation has come to this house, because he too is a son of Abraham. For the son of man came to seek out and to save the lost" (Luke 19:1-10). Because of such meals with sinners and outcasts, Jesus is remembered as being called a "glutton and a drunkard, a friend of tax collectors and sinners" (Matt 11:18-19).

Many historical scholars agree that eating with public sinners was one of the striking characteristics of Jesus' regular activity. James Dunn points out how Jesus' practice differed from that of other Jewish groups including the Essenes and at least some of the Pharisees. To eat with another forged a bond with that person. To refuse table fellowship was to deny the acceptability of the other. Some Pharisees, as well as the Essenes, thought their meals should express Israel's holiness, its being set apart from others.[12] By contrast, Jesus stressed the importance of inviting to the table "the poor, the crippled, the lame and the blind" (Luke 14:13, 21). According to Dunn, "Jesus was remembered as deliberately posing his vision of open table-fellowship in direct antithesis to the ideal practiced at Qumran."[13] Jesus' meals thus became a "bone of contention" between Jesus and his chief critics.[14]

Wright points out that when Jesus' practice of an open table is linked to the claim that he was inaugurating the long-awaited kingdom, it becomes deeply symbolic.[15] The meals anticipated the great eschatological feast of the kingdom. Wright sees these inclusive meals as connected to another strong tradition about Jesus, that he did not fast (Mark 2:18-22). Jesus defends his practice of not fasting with the parables of the wedding guests, the unshrunk cloth, and the new wine (Mark 2:19). As Wright points out, in his refusal to fast and in his embrace of celebratory meals with sinners, Jesus is making a claim about eschatology: a claim that the reign of God is already present in his ministry.[16]

When Jesus sends his disciples out on mission, he instructs them to expect hospitality in the villages of Galilee (Mark 6:7-13). John Dominic Crossan sees these instructions for mission as connected to Jesus' meal ministry. Both are aimed at bringing about egalitarian community in an honor and shame culture.[17] In assessing this claim, it is worth remembering that in Jesus' parable of the great banquet, the servants are told to bring to the feast whoever they can find (Matt 22:9-10; Luke 14:21-43). Classes, sexes, and ranks will be all mixed up. Crossan rightly makes the point that Jesus *lived* his parable. If the reign of God is present in a non-discriminating table, this depicts in miniature an open and nondiscriminating society.

Jesus' meals with his disciples and outcasts and sinners are anticipatory celebrations of the coming kingdom of God. They call sinners to conversion and are a pledge of God's forgiveness. Sanders points out that, while all of Judaism would have rejoiced at the conversion of sinners, Jesus causes grave offense by welcoming them without the authorized process of temple and priesthood. He is speaking for God, claiming for sinners a place in the reign of God as forgiven and free.[18] He welcomes outsiders and untouchables as friends at table, not shrinking from their touch (Luke 7:28), but welcoming them into the community of God's reign.

The Community of Disciples

Jesus did not act as an isolated individual. On the contrary, he set out to form a movement that was concerned with the gathering and renewing of Israel in the light of God's coming reign. He calls followers into a lifelong relationship. Some are called to a literal following of Jesus, leaving families and livelihood and traveling with him, receiving his teaching at length, and sharing his ministry (Matt 19:21; Mark 1:16-20; John 1:43). Others are part of a wider circle who stayed at home, implementing Jesus' teaching in ordinary life and offering hospitality and support to Jesus and his itinerant disciples.[19] They include Simon (Mark 14:3-9), Joseph of Arimathea (Mark 15:42-47), Mary and Martha (Luke 10:38-42), and Zacchaeus (Luke 19:1-10).

In a symbolic act, Jesus appoints the Twelve and sends them on mission. These will sit "on thrones judging the twelve tribes of Israel" (Matt 19:28; Luke 22:30). They represent the twelve patriarchs at the beginning of Israel and symbolize Jesus' intention to gather and reconstitute Israel. Peter is given a leadership role (Matt 16:18; John 21:15-19). Women are significant in the group that travels with Jesus. Mark says of the women at the cross, "Among them were Mary Magdalene, and Mary the mother of James the younger and of Joses, and Salome. These used to follow him and provided for him when he was in Galilee; and there were many other women who came up with him to Jerusalem" (15:40-41). Women disciples, above all Mary Magdalene, remain with Jesus at the cross and are the first witnesses to resurrection.

The disciples of Jesus constitute a new family. When Jesus is told that his mother and brothers are outside, he says of those around him, "Here are my mother and brothers! Whoever does the will of God is my brother and sister and mother" (Mark 3:31-35). He claims that the disciples who have left everything will find it a hundredfold in the new community (Mark 10:29-30). In this new family, as Elisabeth Schüssler Fiorenza has said, tax collectors, sinners, women, children, fishers, slaves, and those who have been healed or set free from bondage to evil spirits all find their place, confident in their dignity and equality as God's beloved children.[20] Every form of dominating power is forbidden within the new community. Domination is to be replaced by authority exercised as if by a servant, modeled on Jesus, who gives his life as a ransom for many (Mark 10:42-45). There is to be no oppression, no coercion, no violence directed to anyone inside or outside the community of the reign of God.[21]

Jesus' parables of the kingdom, his healing ministry, his open table, and his formation of a new community all help give content to Jesus' vision of the kingdom of God. What becomes clear is that the symbol of the kingdom in the ministry of Jesus, his symbol of divine action, is many-faceted and cannot be limited to any one referent. In particular, for Jesus, the action of God is not exclusively present, nor is it exclusively coming in the future. I think the parables of Jesus, his healings, inclusive meals, and new family are all locations where what is coming—God's future act—is already made present in anticipation. These acts of Jesus are partial anticipations of God's coming action. With Meier, quoted in the discussion of Jesus' healing, I see in Jesus' ministry "a partial and preliminary realization of God's kingly rule." And with Schillebeeckx, quoted in the same section, I see Jesus' actions as "fragmentary," "historical," "limited," and "finite" anticipations of salvation to come.

Marcus Borg is among those scholars who reject a strong view of "imminent eschatology," the idea that God is going to bring about the kingdom in the near future. He sees Jesus' emphasis more on God's presence and action in the here and now. As I have made clear, I think Jesus proclaimed a kingdom that has both present and future dimensions. The kingdom is the promised action of God that will transform and heal our world. It is something that comes to us from the future but is already present in anticipation in Jesus and his actions and, I would argue, in the grace that invades our lives in the twenty-first century and calls us to discipleship and to commitment to peace, justice, and love. Because of this, I am very much with Marcus Borg when goes on to talk about "participatory eschatology."[22] He believes that the kingdom Jesus preached involved following his way, and that this involves us as participants in God's work of the kingdom. We are called to share God's passion for the world and to share the commitment of Jesus as he sought to open the eyes of the blind, to set free the captives, and to proclaim the jubilee of God. Borg writes:

Does participatory eschatology mean that Jesus thought the kingdom of God, God's dream, would come about through human political achievement? By no means. I do not imagine that he thought that. It is always *God's* kingdom, *God's* dream, *God's* will. And it involves a deep centering in the God whom Jesus knew. So did he think God would bring in the kingdom without our involvement? I do not imagine this either. Indeed, the choice between "God does it" or "we do it" is a misleading and inappropriate dichotomy. In St. Augustine's wonderful aphorism, "God without us will not; and we without God cannot."[23]

I believe, with Borg, that the choice between "God does it" and "we do it" is misleading. Jesus' kingdom theology is radically centered on God yet fully participatory. This same false choice reappears again and again in contemporary discussions of divine action. What is needed is a theology of divine action that understands God as the one who achieves the divine purposes in and through created causes, who delights in and respects human freedom and the integrity of the natural world. By God's choice, divine action has a radically participatory character.

Divine Action for Jesus

Jesus proclaims the God who acts, among other ways, in his parables, his healings, his open table, and his formation of a community of disciples. The preceding discussion of these practices of Jesus, brief as it is, suggests some conclusions about Jesus' view of God's action:

- God's kingdom, the great act of God, has the character of future promise but is already present, in anticipation, in Jesus and his ministry, including his words, his healing, his table fellowship with sinners and outsiders, and the shared life of his community. These are limited, anticipatory participations in God's reign that point to its fulfillment where all will be healed and reconciled.
- The focus of Jesus' ministry is always on God, and always on God who acts. The God of Jesus is not a remote God, but one who is actively and vigorously engaged with human history and with the whole creation.
- The character of God is revealed as radical love and boundless compassion. It is a love that is personal and interpersonal. It is a love that gives priority to the poor, the lost, and the hurt.
- Divine action involves God's creation of the universe, God's ongoing creation of all things, God's providential care for all creatures, God's saving actions in the history of Israel, God's action in the Christ-event, God's gracious engagement with each of us, and God's fulfillment of all things.
- The community of those who follow Jesus is invited to share in Jesus' intimate, personal, and trusting relationship with God.

- Divine action, while it is always God's free act, also has a participatory character. It involves those who follow the way of Jesus not only in the demands of Christian community, but also in a life of commitment to the poor of the earth and of love for the enemy. The proclamation of the reign of God calls for a radical conversion, which entails orthopraxis, action in accord with God's kingdom.
- The kingdom of God, the action of God, is encountered now in our own graced experiences, including our prayer, our love for others, our community life, and our participation in acts of healing, liberation, peacemaking, and care for the community of life on earth.

Divine Action in the Light of the Whole Christ-Event

Jesus proclaimed good news concerning a new and wonderful act of God. God would act graciously to restore and renew the whole of Israel, and through this act bring salvation to the whole world. This act would involve a privileged place for the poor, the afflicted, the sinners, and the outcasts. The aim of Jesus, as Ben Meyer puts it, was "to win over all Israel to eschatological restoration." This restoration would be the way to, and the beginning of, the salvation of all the nations.[24] The response Jesus sought was faith, a faith that involved participation in a new way of life.

His confronting words and deeds, including his provocative action in the temple, led some leaders of his people to fear him as a dangerous troublemaker. They handed him over to the Romans, who executed him by crucifixion as a political subversive. The New Testament recounts that the demoralized and defeated community of disciples encountered him after death, raised up by God, radically transformed and radiant with resurrection life. The Spirit of God was poured out upon them, constituting them as the community of Jesus for the world. They saw the risen Christ as the promise of general resurrection and of the final transformation of all things. In the power of the Spirit, they went out to proclaim that God has acted in Jesus' life, death, and resurrection to bring salvation to the world.

This, then, constitutes the central Christian insight into divine action. The God who acts in creation, the God who acts in the history of Israel, has now acted in Christ to bring healing and hope to the world in a new creation. What has already begun in Christ will reach its promised fulfillment when all things will be transformed and made new. While there is much more that could be said about this divine action, I will focus on only two aspects that will be important for the rest of this work: first, God is shown to be a God who actively and lovingly waits upon creation, and second, God is revealed as a God whose power is a power-in-love.

God Who Lovingly Waits upon Creation

The early Christian community could look back on the Christ-event and see the inner connection between Jesus' life and his death and resurrection. It was not only that his life lived in love for others found its final expression in his death for others. It was also that the saving action of God, the great divine act of healing, forgiveness, and liberation that Jesus proclaimed in his lifetime, was now seen to have occurred, even though it had yet to reach its fulfillment, in and through his death and resurrection.

Paul builds his theology around this conviction, which is a tradition he himself received: "For I handed on to you as of first importance what I myself received: that Christ died for our sins according to the Scriptures, and that he was buried, and that he was raised up on the third day in accordance with the scriptures" (1 Cor 15:3-4). At the center of Mark, there are the three passion predictions (Mark 8:31; 9:31; 10:33), where Jesus warns his disciples that "the Son of Man *must* undergo great suffering" (Mark 8:31; emphasis added). In Luke, the risen Christ asks the disciples on the road to Emmaus, "Was it not *necessary* that the Messiah should suffer these things and then enter into his glory?" (24:26; emphasis added).

The early church clearly did see salvation as coming through the death of Jesus, but was this true of Jesus during his lifetime? Did he see what he proclaimed as coming about in some way through his death? It seems clear that the details of the passion predictions, particularly in Mark 10:33-34, are influenced by the later events. But in his lifetime, Jesus had before him not only the fate of the prophets (Luke 11:47; Mark 12:1-12) but also that of John the Baptist. There is good reason to think he would have considered the possibility of death and pondered its meaning in terms of his mission.

Joel Green argues that Jesus saw his coming death as part of a new event of exodus and covenant renewal: "Taken together with his prophetic action in the Temple, the symbolic actions at the table of Jesus' last meal with his disciples suggest that he viewed himself as the focal point of God's great act of deliverance."[25] James Dunn proposes that Jesus may have thought of his death in the light of Jewish traditions of the suffering righteous ones and the suffering Son of Man, and in terms of the Baptist's metaphors of fire and water and the idea of covenant sacrifice.[26] Dunn sees Jesus as placing his hope in God's vindication after death, possibly in terms of his participation in general resurrection.[27]

If this is so, then we need to allow for a change in the way Jesus saw God's reign taking effect. His earlier proclamation of the coming reign of God and his call to conversion were clearly genuine. He hoped for a positive response. God's work of restoration and salvation would take shape in and through the gathering and renewal of Israel. But he met opposition and failure, which culminated in the events in Jerusalem. This meant he now had to find God and God's saving love at work in rejection, failure, darkness, and death. The later Christian community could build on this insight, seeing Christ's death and resurrection as the act of God's saving and transforming love. It could interpret his death in light of the Scriptures, particularly the suffering servant of Isaiah 53. In this sense, it could speak of the death of Jesus as "necessary."

When the death of Jesus on the cross is described as necessary, it can lead to serious misunderstandings. Such talk can give the impression that the violent act of crucifixion was planned and required by God. Of course, if salvation comes to us through an incarnation that involves God taking up and transforming not only life, but also death from within, then not only Jesus' life, but also his free embrace of death and the transformation of death in his resurrection, is fundamental to salvation. But the particular death of Jesus, nailed to a Roman cross, was utterly cruel and humiliating, like many others in human history. It was an act of extreme violence, an evil and objectively sinful act. It should not be thought of as directly willed by God.

We need to start from the premise that Jesus' call to conversion in the light of the reign of God authentically expressed God's positive will. This would mean that God's will, first of all, was that Israel and ultimately the world would respond to Jesus' proclamation with faith and commitment. When, instead, human beings resist and reject the divine initiative that finds expression in Jesus' ministry, and when they attack and kill the bearer of good news, in defiance of God's will, God continues to be a God of healing and life and transforms this murderous act in the Spirit so that it becomes the bearer of salvation for the world.

We need to be able to proclaim God's bringing salvation to the world through this event of the cross without suggesting that God plans and wants the evil act of the crucifixion. Edward Schillebeeckx points to Aquinas's refusal to locate evil in God and applies this refusal to the cross of Christ: "*Negativity* cannot have a cause or a motive in God. But in that case we cannot look for a divine *reason* for the death of Jesus either. Therefore, first of all, we have to say that we are not redeemed *thanks* to the death of Jesus but *despite* it." Despite the evil human act, God transforms what is evil into something that finally we Christians rightly see as blessed. Evil is transformed in the power of the Spirit: "Only *in* the overcoming of it can we say that the negative aspects of our history have an indirect role in God's plan of salvation: *God is the Lord of history.*"[28] On the one hand, God does not will the evil act of crucifixion. On the other hand, the God of Jesus brings new life, freedom, and healing through the cross, because the destructive act of crucifying Jesus is transformed by God into a vehicle of liberation and life.

Herbert McCabe says something similar. He asks, "Well, then, did the Father want Jesus to be crucified? And if so, why?" He replies to his own question: "The answer as I see it is again: No. The mission of Jesus from the Father is not the mission to be crucified; what the Father wanted is that Jesus should be human."[29] To be human is to live in love, in wholehearted love of God, risking love for others in the world. Jesus' mission was to form a community of mutual love and forgiveness instead of domination, and it proved to be a failure. Love is a dangerous, disturbing, and subversive force in a world of sin, fear, and domination. Jesus came up against the power of the establishment in religion and colonial power. As McCabe says, Jesus was so human he had to be killed.[30] Jesus accepts his failure and death and entrusts all to God to bring God's purposes to fulfillment through his death. He put up no barriers, loving those who hated him, and giving himself finally in love to God. This act encapsulates the prayer of his life lived in love. This most radical act of self-giving love is answered in the resurrection, and God's Spirit is poured out upon the world—the Spirit in which the world is to be transformed into a community of love, the kingdom of God.[31]

What does the death and resurrection reveal about the nature of divine action? I will focus simply on two interrelated lines of thought. *First, in the Christ-event, we find that God's self-giving and saving love actively waits upon creaturely response.* It does not overwhelm or coerce. In his lifetime, Jesus consistently refuses to perform spectacular or authenticating miracles. His proclamation of the coming reign of God calls for and depends on a free human response. When, instead, the response is complete rejection and condemnation of Jesus, God does not intervene. There is no miracle, no "twelve legions of angels" sent to protect Jesus (Matt 26:53). God does not step in to change any one of the countless contingencies, human and natural, involved in Jesus' death. When Jesus cries out in his agony, asking the one he calls *Abba* to take away the cup that is before him, the cup is not taken away (Mark 14:36). This does not mean that his prayer is not heard. As the Letter to the Hebrews tells us, his prayer was heard, and he gave himself in loving obedience and fidelity to his mission, becoming for all of us the source of eternal salvation (Heb 5:9).

Second, while God does not intervene to overturn natural law or to coerce human freedom, God acts powerfully to achieve the divine purposes. The violence inflicted on Jesus is met with defenseless love, a love that will finally disarm all violence. Sin is met with forgiveness. The death Jesus experiences becomes the beginning of victory over death for the whole creation. In the power of the Spirit, God transforms sin, violence, and death into new life in Christ. The promised reign of God is brought into existence through the death and resurrection of Jesus, as a promise of the final transfiguration of all things in Christ, which is enfleshed in the Spirit-formed community of disciples.

What is specific to Christian theology is that it sees in the Christ-event the revelation of God and of God's purposes for the world. I take this to mean that the way God acts here might offer some clues as to a Christian theology of divine action more generally. Reflection on the Christ-event suggests a theology of divine action in which God actively waits upon creation, upon the unfolding of natural processes and upon the freedom of human responses, yet acts powerfully, faithfully, and lovingly to fulfill the divine promises.

The Vulnerability of Divine Love

On the basis of the self-revelation of God in the life, death, and resurrection of Jesus, it can be said that God enters into and embraces the suffering of a suffering world. It is important to recognize, however, that the biblical idea of a God who feels compassion for creatures and suffers with creation stands in some tension in the Christian tradition with the long-held conviction that God is unchanging (impassible). In recent theology, there have been new attempts at a theology of a God who suffers with us, but also defenses of the tradition of God as unchanging.[32]

While I count myself among those who advocate a theology of divine compassionate suffering with creatures, this kind of theology needs to respect and incorporate key insights that have been long upheld in the tradition of an unchanging God: First, God is unchanging in being divinely constant in love and faithful to the divine promises. Second, God is not thought of as trapped in creaturely suffering, but remains all-powerful in the sense of being able to bring all things to their promised fulfillment. This divine form of power, I will suggest below, is not a power that acts over against creation, but a power-in-love. Finally, God remains the utterly transcendent Creator and not a creature, and this means that when God is said to have the capacity for compassionate suffering with others, this is attributed to God only in a strictly transcendent and divine way that recognizes the limits of analogical language. In the view proposed here, God's capacity to feel with suffering creation is seen not as a creaturely limitation, but as the expression of a love beyond all loves, the fullness of compassionate love that only God has.

A theology that can hold to these values can take seriously the biblical picture of a God of boundless compassion, who sees people's misery, hears their cries, knows their sufferings, and comes to deliver them (Exod 3: 7-8). It can think of God as one who could say, "As a mother comforts her child so do I comfort you" (Isa 66:13). Above all, it can build on the divine love revealed in the cross and see this as the revelation of true divinity and of divine power as power-in-love. Paul tells the Christian community at

Corinth that Christ *crucified* is the "the power of God and the wisdom of God" (1 Cor 1:24). In the crucified one, divine power looks like utter foolishness and weakness, but, Paul insists, "God's weakness is stronger than human strength" (1 Cor 1:25). The true nature of divine power is revealed in the vulnerability of the crucified—and in the resurrection of the crucified.

In Philippians, the Christian community is urged to take on the mind of Christ Jesus, who, though he was in the form of God, emptied himself to the point of death on a cross (Phil 2:3-11). While this text has usually been taken as implying Christ's preexistence, some scholars dispute this, but in either interpretation, Paul sees Jesus Christ as the revelation of God. And he clearly sees the self-emptying love of Christ as revealing the nature of divine love for us. This self-emptying love proves to be immensely powerful: Christ is raised up and exalted and given a name above every name. Here, as elsewhere, Paul sees God's purposes being powerfully achieved in Christ in a way that is contrary to all human views of power.

What is fundamental for a theology of divine action is that this self-emptying love of Christ reveals what is at the heart of God. Self-emptying love is found to be characteristic of divine action. Walter Kasper is a helpful guide at this point. He insists that the self-emptying love of Christ's cross is not to be seen as the abandonment of divinity, but as the revelation of true divinity. It is the manifestation of the truth of God: "On the cross God's self-renouncing love is embodied with ultimate radicalness."[33] The cross of Jesus is the utmost expression of God's self-surrendering love. It is the "unsurpassable self-definition of God."[34] The cross reveals a God who acts in history, a God faithful to the divine promises, a God of unfathomable and divine love. It is the revelation of the true nature of divine transcendence and divine omnipotence:

> For the Bible, then, the revelation of God's omnipotence and the revelation of God's love are not contraries. God need not strip himself of his omnipotence to reveal his love. On the contrary, it requires omnipotence to be able to surrender oneself and give oneself away; and it requires omnipotence to be able to take oneself back in the giving and to preserve the independence and freedom of the recipient. Only an almighty love can give itself wholly to the other and be a helpless love.[35]

The love revealed in the cross is extreme in its vulnerability, but it is also filled with the power of life. In and through the vulnerability of love "for others" to the end, resurrection power breaks in upon creation. Together, the cross and resurrection redefine divine power. In this light, divine omnipotence can be seen as the transcendent power of self-bestowing love, a love capable of bringing life to all things.

Kasper sees this divine vulnerability in love not as the expression of a lack, but as the expression of divine fullness. It expresses the capacity to love in a transcendent and divine way. God does not suffer from lack of being, but suffers out of love which is the overflow of the divine being. Suffering does not befall God but expresses the divine freedom to love. Kasper insists that "to predicate becoming, suffering and movement of God" does not mean that God is to be thought of as a developing God. It is not a passage from potential to act. Rather, "To predicate becoming, suffering and movement of God is to understand God as the fullness of being, as pure actuality, as overflow of life and love."[36]

In Kasper's view, it is precisely because God is the omnipotence of love that God can enter into vulnerability and death and bring life. If the cross is the self-revelation of a God who loves in freedom, then this points to a God who from all eternity is self-communicating love, to a Trinitarian life of mutual self-giving love. What we experience in Jesus and in the Spirit is the self-bestowal of God, and we rightly see this as a revelation of the dynamic and ecstatic self-bestowing love that is the divine life of the Trinity. Rowan Williams points to the way that God's self-giving in Christ leads us to see God's act in creation as one of kenosis, and how it also points to the dynamism of self-giving love in Trinitarian life:

> The divinity of Jesus is what we recognize in finding in him the creative newness of God: his life and death and resurrection *as a whole* effect the new creation. Thus that life and death and resurrection are in a highly distinctive sense the act and the speech of God. Because they create by renunciation, by giving away, we learn to see God's creative act as in itself a giving away, a letting go; and because the giving away of Jesus is itself a response to the giving God whom Jesus calls *Abba*, we learn that God's act includes both a giving and a receiving, that God's life is itself in movement and in relation with itself. The ground is prepared for a doctrine of God the Trinity.[37]

The cross and resurrection reveal the true nature of divine power, as the infinite capacity for self-bestowing love. This is a love that does not overpower but works in and through creaturely processes to bring life. God's power is revealed in Christ as a power-in-love, as a relational power. It is the very nature of God to be self-bestowing love. It is the very nature of divine power to enable the other to flourish in all the other's integrity and proper autonomy. If the cross is the self-definition of God and the true revelation of divine power, then what is found to be true of divine action in the cross and resurrection of Jesus can be thought of as governing the other forms of divine action explored in the rest of this book.

3

Creation as Divine Self-Bestowal

Science puts before us a universe that has been expanding and evolving over the past 13.7 billion years, and a history of life on our planet that goes back about 3.7 billion years. Christian theology learns what it can from sciences like cosmology and evolutionary biology, taking them to offer the best picture available at present of the way God's creative act unfolds. It sees this picture in relation to its own fundamental insight into creation: that God creates all things from nothing (*creatio ex nihilo*) and enables them to exist and to act at every point (*creatio continua*). All the entities and processes of the observable universe exist only because God is present to them, nearer to them than they are to themselves, as the constant source of their being and action. The Christian tradition sees the Creator not only as creating and sustaining but also as acting providentially in all things, bringing human beings and the universe and all it holds to their proper fulfillment.

This is already to say a great deal that is fundamental about God's action in creation. But far more can be said when a theology of creation takes its bearings from God's action in Christ. In the Christ-event, God is revealed as self-giving love: God bestows God's self to us in the Word made flesh and in the Spirit poured out. This can be taken as a shorthand but profoundly accurate description of what happens in the life, death, and resurrection of Jesus and the outpouring of the Holy Spirit. Because this is truly God's *self*-revelation, I will propose that divine self-bestowal can be taken as a proper description of God's action, not only in the incarnation but also in creation.

When we speak of divine action, it is fundamental to recognize that the word *action* is being used analogically when it is applied to God. We take something we know a little bit about—the way we human beings act—and apply it analogically to the way God achieves divine purposes with regard to creation. What needs to be remembered is the great difference between our acts and God's action. The difference is infinite, and we cannot pretend to comprehend the actions of God any more than we can comprehend God. We can speak of God only in terms taken from our human creaturely experience. It is important and right that we do, but we need to do so in awareness of the limits of our language.

In this chapter, I will explore a theology of creation as divine self-bestowal, building in part on insights from Karl Rahner's thought. I will argue that this divine self-bestowing love enables evolutionary emergence, creates through processes that involve chance and lawfulness, enables creaturely autonomy to flourish, is characterized by a divine love that accepts the limits of creaturely processes, and acts with regard to creation in a noninterventionist way. Before taking up this theology of creation, I will focus on the particularity and historicity of divine acts.

The Specific and Historical Character of Divine Acts

In the previous chapter, I considered divine action in the life of Jesus. This involved reflecting on some specific deeds and events: his proclaiming of the kingdom in parables like the Good Samaritan, his healing of individuals such as the blind Bartimaeus, his inclusive meals with particular people, his formation of a new community of the kingdom, his death on a Roman cross, and his resurrection appearances to individuals and small communities. Each of these, I proposed, can be seen as an anticipatory event of the kingdom, an experience of divine action. When Jesus brought healing and liberation to an oppressed individual, it was an act of a limited, human healer, but it was also an act of God: "But if it is by the finger of God that I cast out the demons, then the kingdom of God has come to you" (Luke 11:20). Jesus saw the God of the kingdom, the God who would act to bring all things to liberation and final fulfillment, as already acting in and through his own particular, finite, and limited actions. The Christian community has, ever since, seen God acting in Jesus, in his words and deeds, his death and resurrection in a way that is special, specific, and historical.

If the Christ-event is to be taken by Christians as revealing something about the way God acts in other contexts, as I have suggested, then it is significant that in this event, God's action always has a particular and historical character. The Gospels tell stories—the story of the liberation of this particular person from bondage, the story of a call to another individual to follow Jesus in the new way of life of the kingdom community. The experience of the Spirit today is also specific to particular persons and particular contexts. We always encounter grace in the particular and concrete circumstances of our lives. Liberation theologians, including Gustavo Gutierrez, have shown us how our specific acts aimed at authentic human liberation can be seen as real anticipations of and participation in God's eschatological saving action. We are confronted by this poor person before us. We are challenged to conversion by the recognition that we are participants in systems of injustice in our social and political world. Grace always has a historical character.

But what of God's action in the ongoing creation of the universe and its creatures? Is this simply to be thought of as a general overall act, or does it, too, have a specific character? In many discussions of divine action, God's creative act, the act by which God enables all things to exist and to act, is called general divine action. The question is then put: On top of this general divine action, are there also special divine acts in the history of the universe, in salvation history, and in our own lives? Recently, Niels Gregersen has challenged this way of thinking, arguing for the "ontological priority of special divine action."[1] He points to the sciences of complexity and to the example of a cell that emerges as a self-organizing and self-producing (autopoietic) system. Its emergence and operation involve a whole series of changes and responses to the operation of the system itself. In such a system, there is a "rewiring" that goes on from moment to moment, as a result of the system in relationship to it environment. This involves an enormous number of steps, which are not covered by any one scientific law but require a variety of interacting scientific explanations.

This suggests a theological conclusion to Gregersen. If God is engaged with every aspect of ongoing creation, then God's engagement must be with the particulars: "For if God is not in the particulars, God is not in the whole of reality either."[2] He sees God as involved in a kenotic way in all the particular details of self-organizing creation, "giving room—from moment to moment, from event to event—to the explorative capacities of God's creatures."[3] Gregersen offers a helpful insight here. He is right to insist that a theology of God as Creator can only mean that God's action must be in the historical and in the particular. In the evolution of the universe and in the emergence of life on Earth, divine action involves the historical, the unpredictable, and the specific.

Stuart Kauffman, among other specialists in the sciences of complexity, argues against all forms of reductionism for a scientific worldview of emergence, radical nonpredictability, and ceaseless creativity.[4] Kauffman's work supports the view that the patterns of self-organization at work in the universe—above all, in the emergence of life—involve the particular, the historical, and the new. With Gregersen, I think it is appropriate for a theology of divine action to give priority to the particular, to special divine action. I see this, however, as a priority in terms of the way we encounter divine action. We encounter it in and through events, processes, and entities at specific times and places. This suggests a kind of priority of the particular in the way God's action is experienced by human beings and takes effect in the wider creation (an epistemological priority).

But I would not want to claim for it an ontological priority, a priority at the level of being. Instead, at this level, the level of the divine being, God's action is to be thought of both as one and as intrinsically differentiated. The unity of the divine act is grounded in the unity of the divine being. But this one act of self-giving love always and everywhere affects creation in specific, historical, and finite ways.

A good, but obviously limited, analogy is found in the experience of diversity and unity in our own human actions. A man commits himself to a partner in marriage and lives this commitment until his death, embracing in this commitment not only his children but also a wider circle of family and friends. The act of committed love is in a very real sense one act, perhaps the defining act of the man's life. Yet this one act exists only in and through particular and "special" human acts: declaring love, taking the risk of saying yes to a lifelong commitment, giving priority to the partner in specific instances, finding ways to talk about what really matters, saying sorry, making decisions about work and home life that affect the partner, putting the other first in particular circumstances, and making space for the needs and priorities of the other.

Many other human acts are of this kind; writing a book or cooking a meal can rightly be thought of as one human act that takes effect only in a number of specific acts. This kind of human act is intrinsically both diverse and one. In a similar way, God's action, which we encounter only in diversity, in the specifics of time and place, can also be understood as one act—an act of faithful, creating, and redeeming love. I find the unity of this one differentiated act of God powerfully and beautifully expressed in Karl Rahner's notion of God's self-bestowal.

Creation as the Self-Bestowal of God

God chooses to give God's self in love to what is not divine, and so creation comes to be. This is the central insight in Rahner's theology of creation. Two fundamental assumptions are at work in this theology. The first is that God's action is not to be thought of only as a series of discrete and disconnected acts, but as one divine act. This one act involves all that we mean when we speak of creation, incarnation, the life of grace, and the final transformation of all things. While Rahner sees God's act as one, he also sees it is as intrinsically differentiated process.[5] There is a real distinction, for example, between God's act in creation and God's action in Jesus of Nazareth, and between grace at work in my own life and the final fulfillment of all things, but these distinctions exist within the one act of God. The unity of the act of God is grounded in the unity of the divine being. The differentiation within the one act comes from God relating in a differentiated way to created entities and processes. This one act has specific and diverse effects and outcomes in the created order. It is a Trinitarian act of self-bestowal: God gives God's self in the Word and the Spirit, in diverse ways, in creation, grace, incarnation, and final fulfillment.

A second assumption is that the incarnation is central to God's purpose in creating. While one tradition of Christian theology has assumed that the incarnation comes about as a remedy for sin, another has held that God's intention from the beginning was to give God's self to creation in the incarnation. This second tradition is associated with the Franciscan school of theology, exemplified in Duns Scotus (1266–1308). Taking up this tradition, Rahner holds that God freely chooses, from the beginning, to create a world in which the Word would be made flesh and the Spirit poured out. In this view, the Christ-event is not thought of as an addition to creation. It is not primarily a corrective for a creation that went wrong. It does not come about simply as a remedy for sin, although in the light of sin, it is certainly a radical act of forgiveness, healing, and liberation. In this theological approach, God's self-giving in the incarnation is the very purpose and meaning of creation.

For Rahner, the central insight of Christian revelation is that God gives God's self to us in the Word made flesh and in the Spirit poured out. This self-giving can be understood as defining every aspect of God's action in creation, redemption, and final fulfillment. In such a Christian vision, the story of the evolution of the universe, including everything that science can tell us about its long history, is part of a *larger* story, the story of divine self-bestowal. The creation of the universe is an element in the radical decision of God to give God's self in love to that which is not divine. This means that the story of salvation is the real ground of the history of nature, not simply something unfolding against the background of the natural world. The story of the universe exists within a larger vision of the divine purpose.[6] God wills to bestow God's self in love to creatures, and creation comes to be as the addressee of this self-bestowal. Creation, incarnation, and final fulfillment are united in one act of divine self-giving.

In one of his later essays, Rahner asks himself this question: What is most specific to the Christian view of God? The answer he finds is precisely this idea that God bestows God's very self to creation.[7] It is a view of God as one who creates creatures who are open to the infinite, and who without being consumed by the fire of the divine infinity, are able to receive God's life as their own fulfillment. Christianity, of course, maintains against pantheism that there is a real distinction between God and the world, but it does not see a distance between God and creatures. The transcendent Creator is understood as interiorly and intimately present to every creature.[8] What is truly characteristic of Christianity, Rahner claims, is that while it maintains this radical distinction between God and the world, it understands God's self-giving as the very core of the world's reality and the world as truly the fate of God. Rahner writes:

> God is not merely the one who as creator establishes a world distant from himself as something different, but rather he is the one who gives himself away to this world and who has his own fate in and with this world. God is not only himself the giver, but he is also the gift. For a pantheistic understanding of existence this statement may be completely obvious. For a Christian understanding of God, in which God and the world are not fused but remain separate for all eternity, this is the most tremendous statement that can be made about God at all. Only when this statement is made, when, within a concept of God that makes a radical distinction between God and the world, God himself is still the very core of the world's reality and the world is truly the fate of God himself, only then is the concept of God attained that is truly Christian.[9]

I find this an astounding claim. The idea that God is the "core" of the world's reality and that the world is the "fate" of God challenges many everyday assumptions about how God relates to creation. This claim is, however, fully justified by the gospel of Jesus Christ. It does no more than give expression to the good news that God really gives God's self to us in Jesus and in the Spirit, and that this is the meaning and purpose of the whole creation. The Word is made flesh, and flesh is irrevocably taken to God. The resurrection of the crucified means that the Word of God is forever flesh, forever a creature, forever part of a universe of creatures. In creation, incarnation, and its culmination in resurrection, God commits God's self to this world, to this universe and its creatures, and does this eternally. In the risen Jesus, part of this biological community of Earth, this evolutionary history, and this material universe is already forever with God, as the sign and promise of the future of all things in God. All of this is what Rahner means when he says that God's self-bestowal is the very core of the world's reality and the world is truly the fate of God.

Rahner offers a further way of pondering the divine action of creation as divine self-bestowal in his thoughts on the kind of causality at work in God's creative act. The common way of thinking about this has been through analogy with the way efficient causes function in our world. In an efficient cause, one thing causes another to exist or produces effects in another. A cook who makes a cake is the efficient cause of the cake. A person who turns on a tap is the efficient cause of water flowing. Rahner finds this insufficient as a model for understanding God's action in creation. It is based on the way a finite creature acts toward another and is not adequate for a God who creates through self-bestowal. Rahner suggests that a better analogy is found in the idea of formal causality. In Aristotelian philosophy, the form is the inner principle that makes a thing what it is.[10] In the theological tradition, the concept of formal causality has been used to describe what God does for us in the beatific vision. In this vision of God, we participate in the life of God in such a way that our being is transformed and fulfilled, because God communicates God's self to us. God gives God's self to us, and this self-giving makes us into something new. Yet God remains God, and we remain creatures.

Rahner has long argued that this self-communication of God happens not only after death, but begins now in the life of grace. In both grace and eternal life, we are transformed, in a kind of formal causality, by the indwelling God. In the image of Paul, we become adopted children of God (Gal 4:6; Rom 8:15). In the image of John, we are born again of the Spirit (John 1:13; 3:1-10). While remaining radically transcendent, God really determines our being, and we are transformed from within. We become a "new creation" (2 Cor 5:17). God freely gives God's self to us, and we are made "participants of the divine nature" (2 Pet 1:4). Because God is God and not a created cause, neither divine transcendence nor creaturely freedom is compromised.[11]

On the basis that creation is one, and that the whole history of the creation is directed to divine self-bestowal, Rahner proposes that the divine indwelling characteristic of grace is an appropriate analogy for the fundamental relationship that God has with the whole universe and all its creatures.[12] God is creatively present to every entity and process of the universe, in such a way that "the reality of God himself is imparted to the world as its supreme specification."[13] Creation is directed from within toward God's self-bestowal. And this very direction toward explicit self-bestowal in Christ, and to final fulfillment, itself springs from the God who is present in dynamic self-bestowing love. Self-bestowal is not only the goal of creation but also that which moves creation from within to the goal.

Creation does not mean only that God creates something other over against God's self, but also that God freely communicates God's own reality to the other. In this theological vision, the universe emerges, and life evolves on Earth, in the process of God's self-bestowal. God is never absent from this process, but is always immanent to the world in self-giving love. The self-bestowal of the transcendent God is "the most immanent factor in the creature."[14]

Again, it is worth stating that this act of God takes effect in diverse ways in specific creatures at specific times and places. Every galaxy, every insect in a rain forest, and in a unique way, every human person is a location where God is present in self-giving love. God, then, does not create simply by producing something different from God's self, as a carpenter makes a table. Rather God creates by communicating God's own divine reality and making it a constitutive element in the fulfillment of each creature.

Enabling and Empowering Evolutionary Emergence

The concept of divine self-bestowal describes the divine act of creation from the side of God, from the perspective of the divine purposes. A second fundamental concept looks at this same divine action from the perspective of its impact on creatures. It points to a fundamental effect of God's immanent presence: *creation has the capacity for self-transcendence.* Self-transcendence means that an entity is enabled to go beyond what it is and become something new. This theological idea is worked out in Rahner's anthropology and in his evolutionary Christology, but it functions throughout many aspects of his work.[15] The two concepts of divine self-bestowal and creaturely self-transcendence are interrelated: it is God's self-bestowal that enables and empowers creaturely self-transcendence.

Rahner takes up the traditional theology of creation, where God sustains all creatures in being (*conservatio*) and enables them to act (*concursus*), and transforms this into an evolutionary theology of becoming, a theology of self-transcendence. He considers the transitions to the new in the history of the universe, particularly when matter becomes life, and when life becomes self-conscious spirit. He argues that the emergence of the new requires explanation, not only at the level of science, but also at the level of theology. The traditional view, that God confers existence and the capacity to act on all things, needs to be developed to take account of the fact that we now know that God acts in and through an evolutionary universe. Rahner proposes a concept of the active self-transcendence of creation: there is an evolutionary dynamism that is truly intrinsic to creation but occurs through the creative power of the immanent God. The idea of *self*-transcendence indicates that at the empirical level of science, the emergence of the new is completely open to explanation. There is no need for a god of the gaps.

The Creator not only enables things to exist and act, but also enables them to become something radically new, as when life first appears in a lifeless universe. The immanent presence and "pressure" of the divine being enables creation to become more than it is in itself.[16] I think this act of God that enables evolutionary emergence can be understood, in relational and Trinitarian terms, as the interior, dynamic relationship of all things in the evolving universe to their Creator through the indwelling, life-giving Spirit.[17] This presence of the Spirit cannot, of course, be discerned by the natural sciences. But the Creator Spirit can be understood as enabling the new to emerge from within creation itself, by means of the processes, relationships, and causal connections that can be studied in the natural sciences.

Rahner proposes a large pattern of evolutionary self-transcendence, one that brings out the inner connection between evolution and Christology. The material universe transcends itself in the emergence of life, and life transcends itself in the human. In human beings, the universe becomes open to self-consciousness and freedom, and to a fully personal response to God's self-bestowal in grace. Within this context of an emergent and self-transcending universe, the Christ-event is the radical self-transcendence of the created universe into God. Jesus Christ is the culmination within our history of the dynamic movement of creation to God, but this will reach its fulfillment only when all things are finally taken up in Christ. Jesus in his life and death lives the radical "yes!" of creation to God's self-bestowal. In his humanity, he is, like us, part of the evolutionary history of life on Earth and a product of the long history of the universe, made of elements formed in its stars. Like us, he is the universe come to consciousness in a particular place and time. But unlike us, he is wholly open to God.

If the Christ-event is considered from below, it can be seen as the self-transcendence of the evolving universe into God. If it is considered from above, it can be seen as God's irreversible self-bestowal to creation. In this one person, Jesus Christ, we find the event of salvation: God's irreversible self-communication to creatures and the full creaturely acceptance of this self-bestowal.[18] Jesus, in his life, death, and resurrection, is the culmination of the process of evolutionary emergence, although one that has not yet reached its fulfillment.

In one of his essays, Rahner has said that in our time, God's presence and action in the world needs to be rethought in two ways, referring to the two aspects of divine action I have been discussing, God's self-bestowal and creation's self-transcendence.[19] It can be argued that, for Rahner, these are two consistent and fundamental characteristics of divine action. Together, they form the foundations for a truly Christian notion of divine action in creation, one that is firmly based on the Christ-event but is also informed by the scientific view of an evolving universe. As I have said, these two characteristics of divine action are mutually interrelated: God present in self-bestowal enables creaturely self-transcendence. Both divine self-bestowal and creaturely self-transcendence can be understood to characterize not only creation, but also grace, incarnation, and the final consummation of all things in Christ.

Noninterventionist Divine Action

Does God intervene in creation? Is divine action interventionist? Christians sometimes speak in ways that seem to assume God intervenes in creation from time to time. Many take it for granted that when someone is saved from tragedy or healed miraculously, God intervenes in the created order. It is important to question this commonsense view and argue for a noninterventionist view of divine action. It can be helpful to distinguish two possible meanings of *intervention*. The word can mean, first, the idea that at particular times, God acts from a heavenly realm beyond creation and breaks in upon creation from outside. A second possible meaning is that God acts in such a way as to overturn or disrupt or bypass the laws of nature. I will consider each of these in turn, and propose that God is not interventionist in either sense.

First, reflection on God's creative action as always present and ever immanent suggests that God does not intervene occasionally in creation from outside. If one accepts the idea that God is interiorly present to the whole creation and to every part of it, nearer to it than it is to itself, as the very ground and source of its existence, enabling and empowering it at every moment, then clearly God is never apart from or outside of creation. Divine transcendence does not make God distant. It enables God to be more interior to things than any creature could ever be. God never breaks in upon creation because God is already there. God never becomes present because God is not absent. God never comes from outside because God is always inside.

Perhaps the spatial idea of intervention from outside derives from the mental picture of a god acting like an individual human agent who sometimes steps in to modify or improve situations. But God is not an individual agent over against creation. God is intimately present to every dimension of creation, from the Andromeda galaxy to the unnamed insects of the Amazon rain forest, as a God of self-bestowing love. God is radically interior to every aspect of the universe from the very beginning by the very act of creation. And as Brian Davies says, God is wholly present in every place and in every thing; it is "the whole of God," not just a bit of God, who is actively present in all that exists.[20]

With regard to the second possible meaning of *intervention*, I am proposing that God is not to be thought of as interventionist in the sense of overturning or bypassing the laws of nature. God is precisely the one whose creative action enables the whole interacting network of creaturely causes and processes to exist and to interact. In the theological tradition, God has been called the primary cause, and this expression points to God's ongoing creative act, which confers existence on all natural processes. God does not need to compete with these processes, because God is always acting in and through them. Everything we see around us in the universe, every bit of empirical data, is created. It belongs to the world of interacting creaturely causes, which theology calls secondary causes. By definition, science is limited to the world of empirical reality, to this network of secondary causes. This world of secondary causes involves not only what science has already mapped with its laws and theories, but also aspects of the natural world that are not yet well modeled by the sciences.

Of course, it can be argued that a Creator is the best explanation for why the universe, its entities, and its processes exist. But this is the work of philosophy and theology rather than empirical science. Anything that can be discovered empirically through the natural sciences is a creature and not God. God is never found as a cause among other causes in the universe. When God's creative action is called primary causality, the concept of a cause is used of God only by way of analogy. God's act of conferring existence on all things is radically different from all created causes. There is an *infinite* difference between the divine act of creation and all the interactions of created entities.

While the Christian tradition, exemplified particularly in Aquinas, has held that God acts in the form of primary causality and this finds expression in, and is mediated through, a range of secondary, created causes, miracles have been seen as an exception, because in a miracle, God replaces the created cause. On this last point, I will respectfully disagree, but I will defer this discussion to chapter 5, where I will deal with miracles in some detail. And in the next chapter, I will say more about the approach to divine action through primary and secondary causality. What is intended here is simply to outline the broad lines of the noninterventionist theology of divine action that I will be arguing for and developing in the rest of this book. It will be noninterventionist in both senses discussed here: God does not intervene in the sense of acting to break into creation from outside, and God is not to be thought of as violating or undermining the laws of nature.

Enabling Creaturely Autonomy to Flourish

The relationship between God and God's creatures is absolutely unique. The divine act of creation is not like any other relationship. On the one hand, creation is a relationship of real dependence. The creature is always dependent on God for its existence and capacity to act. On the other hand, it is a relationship whereby God establishes the creature in genuine difference from God's self. Because of God's love and respect for creatures, this difference means that the creature has its own otherness, integrity, and proper autonomy. This difference, of course, does not imply distance between God and creatures.

A fundamental principle of the God–world relationship, grounded in the tradition of Aquinas and often repeated by Rahner, is expressed in the following axiom: radical dependence on God and the genuine autonomy of the creature are directly and not inversely related.[21] In ordinary experiences, it seems that the more one thing depends upon another, the less autonomy it has. The relationship of creation is exactly the opposite. It does not suppose a preexisting other but creates the other as other, constantly maintaining its existence and capacity to act, while setting it free in its own autonomy. In this relationship, dependence on God and creaturely freedom and autonomy exist in *direct* relationship to one another.

What this means is that the closer creatures are to God, the more they can be truly themselves. This claim is grounded for Rahner in the human experience of grace. Those who experience freedom and responsibility in the depth of their being and know themselves as grounded in God have some understanding of the relationship between God and creature. In the experience of grace, a person experiences freedom as "a freedom coming from God and a freedom for God."[22] The closer we are drawn into the love of God, the freer we are. In the experience of grace, we find that in relation to God, "radical dependence grounds autonomy."[23] Creaturely integrity is not diminished because a creature's existence is dependent on God, but flourishes precisely in this dependence.

In discussing this issue, Herbert McCabe reflects further on human freedom. He sees God as enabling us to act, and this means that our free acts are in this sense caused by God. Yet we think of ourselves as free precisely when our acts are caused by ourselves and not by anything else. So if God is enabling us to act, are we truly free? What needs remembering, McCabe notes in a typically succinct comment, is that *God is not anything else*. God is not an entity in the world. The creative power of God does not operate on me from outside, as an alternative to me. It is what makes me *me*.[24] God's action, God's causality, enables me to act in freedom as my most authentic self. McCabe sees something like this happening in the genuine experience of human love. He says that to love others is, in one sense, to give them the precious gift of nothing, space to be themselves, so they can grow and flourish. Love is a risking of self that another might be. McCabe sees God's act of creation as an act of love of this kind:

> But creation too is an act of love, it is a giving of a world in which things and ourselves can be. Creation too, as we saw, is not an interference with things. Any other kind of making, any making within the world changes things, but creation obviously does not change anything, or add anything to things; it makes things to be what they are, it does not make them any different. . . . Unless we grasp the truth that creation means leaving the world to be itself, to run itself by its own scientific laws so that things behave in accordance with their own natures and not at the arbitrary behest of some god, we shall never begin to understand that the Lord we worship is not a god, but the unknown reason why there is anything instead of nothing. [25]

I find this an insightful description of God's creative act: an act of love, of risk-taking love, that enables the universe to run itself by its own laws, with its own integrity, so things behave in accordance with their own natures. Of course, what McCabe is not emphasizing here, but certainly brings out in other places, is that God is not, as it were, sitting back and doing nothing. God is dynamically, creatively, and lovingly involved, always at work in and through created entities, relationships, and causes, and always respecting their independence and integrity. Through this whole range of creaturely causes, God not only makes things but also makes a difference to things. God enables, supports, and empowers creaturely processes and entities.

And as I argued in the previous chapter, God is not only actively present with every creature in the emergent universe, enabling and supporting each of them, empowering them to exist, to act, and to become, but also feels with each of them a transcendent capacity for empathy, sharing their joys and their sufferings with unthinkable and vulnerable divine love. In this way, too, God puts God's self at risk in creation. And, of course, this risk-taking God is also powerful and faithful, the God who brought Jesus from death to resurrection life as the promise and the beginning of fulfillment for all things.

Divine Action that Accepts the Limits of Creaturely Processes

The previous chapter proposed that what is revealed of God in Jesus' life, death, and resurrection will hold true in other aspects of divine action—in particular, in God's act of creating the universe and its creatures. In the Christ-event, the true nature of God is revealed as self-giving love. The incarnation and the cross reveal a God of divine vulnerability in love, while resurrection points to the power of this love to heal and save. In the extreme vulnerability of the cross, we do not find the loss of divinity or the absence of divinity, but the true revelation of God. The vulnerable self-giving love of Christ gives expression in our world to the divine nature. This self-bestowing love, revealed in the whole life and ministry of Jesus and culminating in his death, is the true icon of divine Trinitarian life.

If self-giving love is the way of God, if it is the way God is, then such a love will characterize the divine act of creation. If God's power is revealed in Christ as a power-in-love, then the divine power at work in the ongoing creation of all things can be understood as a power-in-love. In the preceding section, I proposed that divine love enables the flourishing of the integrity of natural processes and human freedom. What needs further emphasis is that a God whose nature is love accepts the limits of creaturely processes and actively waits upon creatures.[26] This is not a passive waiting, but the waiting upon another of a loving parent with a child, or a lover with the beloved—an active, nurturing, engaged love that enables the other to flourish in all her freedom and integrity. God's love and respect for creatures involve God freely embracing limits. God's freedom is not to be thought of as an absolute freedom to do anything at all, no matter how arbitrary. The love of the divine nature is such that God works with creaturely limits and waits upon them with infinite patience. By creating in love, God freely accepts limitations.

To say that God waits upon creatures is not to suggest that God is doing nothing or simply allowing things to run their course. Again, the best model we have of divine action is the Christ-event, culminating in the cross and resurrection of Jesus. God was not passive in the rejection, humiliation, and crucifixion of Jesus. God was with Jesus in his suffering, holding him in love, and acting powerfully in the Spirit, transforming his failure and death into the source of healing and liberation for the world, and raising Jesus up as the beginning of life for the whole creation. God's way is not the way of an intervention that would overturn the laws of nature or human freedom to save Jesus from what looked like the total failure of his mission and from a brutal death. God's way is revealed as that of accompaniment in love, transformation in the Spirit, and resurrection life. It appears from the Christ-event that God's way is that of being committed to allowing events to unfold, even when they are radically opposed to the divine will, and to bring healing and liberation in and through them.

It makes an enormous difference whether one thinks of God as able to do absolutely anything or as acting in a way that lovingly respects and accepts the limits of finite processes and entities. Based on what we know to be the true nature of God revealed in Christ, we can say that in creation, too, God's love is of a kind that respects and works with the limits of creaturely processes. Christian theology has always understood that God can act only in accordance with the divine nature. This nature is revealed in the Christ-event as radical self-giving love. This is a divine and transcendent love, a love that has an unimaginable capacity to respect the autonomy and independence of creatures, to work with them patiently, and to bring all things to their fulfillment.

This divine capacity to wait upon the processes of nature becomes evident when we ponder what science teaches us about our own origins as human beings. If one thinks, as Christians do, that the divine purposes include the emergence of human beings, then the divine purposes are achieved with extraordinary patience, as God waits upon, empowers, and enables the 3.7-billion-year history of life on Earth, with modern human beings appearing only in the last 200,000 years. The emergence of life on our planet depends upon the forging of elements like carbon in stars over billions of years. The existence of stars and galaxies depends upon the fine-tuning of the universe from its origins 13.7 billion years ago. All of this suggests that the God of creation is a God who loves to create through processes that involve emergence and increasing complexity and who is a God of immense patience.

If divine love involves divine respect for and patience with created processes as well as human freedom, this means that God is not *absolutely* unlimited in freedom and power to achieve the divine purposes. There may be circumstances, and very many of them, when God embraces limits in God's love and respect for finite creatures. God's nature, as lovingly respectful of both human freedom and the finite limits and autonomy of natural processes, may involve limitations on divine action in particular circumstances. But as the resurrection of Jesus promises, God will bring good out of evil, glory out of failure, and life out of death, and do this faithfully and unfailingly. God will achieve the divine purposes, but not in ways that override the proper autonomy of creaturely processes. The love that defines the divine nature is a love that lives with the process, a love that accompanies creation, delighting in its beauty and its diversity, suffering with it with the divine capacity for love, responding to it creatively, and bringing all to liberation and healing in Christ.

Creating through Chance and Lawfulness

In the first chapter, I pointed to the role that chance plays in evolutionary history. Genetic mutations that arise randomly can have disastrous consequences for organisms, but they can also give rise to better adaptation to an environment and to new evolutionary developments. I am using the word *randomness* in the way it is commonly understood, as another way of speaking about chance, rather than as a precise mathematical concept. Random mutations function as a source of novelty for natural selection in the evolution of life. Chance events, such as a comet colliding with Earth, have had deadly effects on some species and provided new opportunities for others. The discovery by science of the fundamental role of chance in evolutionary history led Jacques Monod to claim that "the stupendous edifice of evolution" is based on "pure chance."[27] Because he saw everything as dependent on pure chance, Monod saw no place for purpose or meaning in the evolution of life.

Monod's claim amounted to a serious challenge to belief in a Creator and to religious faith. Arthur Peacocke responded to this challenge in a number of publications and ultimately with his life's work in science and religion.[28] He was joined by D. J. Bartholomew, among others.[29] They argued that there is no necessary conflict between the idea of chance operating within a framework of lawfulness and the idea of a Creator working in and through the whole process. They went further and argued that there is good reason to think of the Creator as choosing to create, in part, precisely through randomness and lawfulness working together.

Peacocke points out that randomness at the level of mutation in DNA does not preclude regular trends and inbuilt tendencies at the higher level of organisms, populations, and ecosystems. He argued that randomness at the molecular level seems essential if the Creator is to explore the full gamut of potentialities of life. It is chance and law together that allow for the thorough exploration of living and nonliving forms of organization. As Bartholomew puts it, chance offers a way of creating a richer environment than would otherwise be possible: "Chance offers the potential Creator many advantages which it is difficult to envisage being obtained in any other way."[30]

Randomness occurs within the context of an evolving universe that has particular laws, relationships, entities, structures, and processes. Peacocke points out that this givenness of the universe and its laws is, for a theist, God given. The role of chance within this framework is to elicit potentialities that are written into creation by the Creator's intention. The Creator, Peacocke argues, is to be seen as the ultimate ground and source of both law and chance.[31] He sees God as genuinely innovative and responsive to the evolving universe, constantly involved in exploring new possibilities, and working with the propensities built into the universe from the beginning. The Creator is "an Improvisor of unsurpassed ingenuity."[32] God responds to and improvises on what is happening in the emergent universe and in the evolution of life, as a great musician like Johann Sebastian Bach improvised on a theme given to him with a brilliant three-part fugue, or as jazz musicians of today respond creatively not only to a melody but to the improvisations of each other.

Although Aquinas never had a chance to consider the place of random mutation in biological evolution, his system of thought can easily accommodate it. He certainly did consider contingent events and had already integrated contingency and chance into his thought: "Contingency is not incompatible with providence, nor are chance or fortune or voluntary action."[33] For Aquinas, contingency, chance, and human freedom are secondary causes through which God acts. He believed that divine providence has no need to impose necessity upon human beings or the rest of creation, but is able to work creatively through both contingent events and human freedom.[34] In a contemporary account that builds on Aquinas, Elizabeth Johnson reflects on the way chance and law can be understood as mutually interrelated:

> If *this* is the kind of universe created by Holy Mystery who is God, then faith can affirm that God works not only through the deep regularities of the laws of nature but also through chance occurrence which has its own, genuinely random integrity. God uses chance, so to speak, to ensure variety, resilience, novelty, and freedom in the universe, right up to humanity itself. Absolute Holy Mystery dwells within, encompasses, empowers the evolutionary process, making the world through the process of things being themselves, thus making the world through chance and its genuinely irregular character.[35]

Chance can be thought of as an expression of divine creativity. God acts through random events as God works through the laws of nature, and both are secondary causes that God respects. Johnson insists, as does Peacocke, that randomness is real.[36] God takes risks in creating. It is not simply that God manipulates events in a way that looks random. Rather, the love of the divine nature is such that God respects the real randomness of nature. Through dynamic and responsive engagement that always involves created realities possessing their own integrity as agents, God achieves the divine purposes. This requires that the Creator be seen as less like a monarch who controls every aspect of the history of the universe according to some preexisting blueprint and more like an artist exploring in creation, responding in spontaneity and freedom to what is given. God acts dynamically, responsively, respectfully, and lovingly in and through a whole variety of secondary causes, including the chance and the lawfulness of the natural world.

By way of conclusion to this chapter and of preparation for considering special divine acts in the next chapter, it may be helpful to sum up briefly the approach to divine action that has been outlined here:

1. *God's actions in creation, in the history of salvation, and in the life of grace are specific and historical, occurring for specific creatures in particular contexts.* In this sense, they have the character of diverse but special divine acts. God's action is to be thought of both as

intrinsically differentiated and also as *one*. This one act of God finds expression in our universe in particular and "special" human acts.

2. *Creation is an act of divine self-bestowal.* For Christian theology, God's act of creation is to be understood from the perspective of Christ. Incarnation is its very purpose and meaning. God gives God's self to us in the Word made flesh and in the Spirit poured out. Divine action is *one* act, a differentiated act, involving creation, salvation, and final fulfillment, rather than a number of separate acts. The unity of the divine act springs from the unity of divine nature. Its differentiation comes from its distinct outcomes in the created order.

3. *God's creative act enables evolutionary emergence.* It is God present in self-bestowing love who enables creaturely self-transcendence and emergence. Both divine self-bestowal and creaturely self-transcendence can be understood to characterize not only creation, but also grace, incarnation, and the final consummation of all things in Christ.

4. *God creates through a range of creaturely processes that involve chance and lawfulness working together.* The Creator works not only through the regularities of the laws of nature but also through chance, exploring the potentialities inherent in the natural world and enabling the new to emerge.

5. *God's creative act enables creaturely integrity and autonomy to exist and flourish.* In creation, God establishes the creature in its own otherness, integrity, and proper autonomy. Dependence on God and creaturely autonomy are directly related, not inversely related.

6. *Divine action is constrained by love, the love of the divine nature.* God's power is a power-in-love, a love that waits with infinite patience on creaturely integrity and human freedom in achieving the divine saving purposes.

7. *Divine action is noninterventionist.* This divine action is present and interior to every aspect of the emergent universe and all its creatures. It works in and through the laws of nature rather than by violating, suspending, or bypassing them. God acts through created processes and entities..

4

Special Divine A[...]

In the previous chapter, I proposed that God's action with regard to creation is both one and diverse. It is one act of self-giving love. But this one act issues forth in creation in a range of particular acts. God's acts with regard to creation are plural because they take effect in specific circumstances and in particular times and places, in a range of particular creaturely processes and entities. In this chapter, I will explore how this approach can help in understanding what have often been called *special divine acts*. The Christian tradition has understood God to act in special ways, such as in the emergence of human beings, the call of a prophet, the experience of personal providence, and the life and ministry of Jesus. I will suggest that such special divine acts can be understood as particular instances in which God's free self-giving love comes to expression in a diverse range of particular events in the history of the universe and of our life on Earth.

In this approach, special divine acts are intrinsic to the way God acts. I am not, then, doing what is often done: starting from an assumption of general divine action in the ongoing creation of all things and then asking whether there are also special divine acts on top of this general notion of divine action. General divine action is accomplished through particular divine acts. The proposal here is that divine acts are always specific to the particular entity or process. In this sense, they are always special. I understand these acts as objectively special, in the sense that they have objective

God given. This, of course,
...ne. God's presence and action with
regard to an individual sparrow (Luke 12:6) is not the same as God's presence and action in Jesus of Nazareth. But I would want to hold that they both are particular, historical, and special divine acts.

To say that God acts in special ways is not to say that God intervenes in such a way as to overturn or suspend the laws of nature. In this chapter, I will explore a noninterventionist theology of special divine acts, proposing that in such acts, God can be thought of as acting and bringing about specific effects in and through the laws and contingencies of the natural world. The proposal is that God acts in special ways through created causes. I will begin by focusing on God's acts in the providential guidance of creation, then turn to grace at work in the life of human persons, and finally consider special divine acts in the history of salvation.

Special Acts in the Providential Guidance of Creation

God's creative action involves not only original creation but also continuing creation, by which God enables all things to exist and to act, and God's providential guidance of the universe and all its creatures. It is important to insist that God is involved in all the specifics of the emergence of the universe over its 13.7-billion-year history. Thomas Aquinas long ago showed how God is to be understood as intimately present as creative agent to absolutely all things. God causes all particular things to be and enables them to interact. God is interior to every creature of the universe and confers existence on each entity and process.[1] This includes the nuclei of hydrogen formed in the first seconds of the life of the universe, the first stars that lit up the early universe, the development of the planet Earth from the matter circling the young Sun, the emergence of the first forms of microbial life on our planet 3.7 billion years ago, and the arrival of modern humans 200,000 years ago. God is present and acting in all of these events and in all that constitutes them. Divine action involves every form of life. God is present and acting in all Earth's living creatures—in the lives of ants, salmon, parrots, dogs, kangaroos, and human beings. God's special acts are beyond counting. As the psalmist sings to the Creator, "O LORD, how manifold are your works! / In wisdom you have made them all" (Ps 104:24). Before exploring these special divine acts in the history of the universe further, I will situate my own approach to divine action in the context of some other approaches.

Approaches to Special Divine Acts

Not all theologians support the idea that there are special divine acts. Maurice Wiles, for example, argues that divine action is to be understood simply as the one act of continuous creation: he sees "the whole continuing creation of the world as God's one act." In this view, what traditionally have been understood as specific divine acts are subsumed within this one creative act. There is no place for special acts of providence. For Wiles, God's ongoing act of creation is "incompatible with the assertion of further particular divinely initiated acts within the developing history of the world." Likewise, events in the biblical story of salvation, including the incarnation and redemption, are not to be seen as special divine acts. They are aspects of the one divine act of creation. They can be seen, Wiles tells us, as "specially significant aspects of divine activity, but not as specific, identifiable acts of God."[2]

My approach differs from his in two fundamental respects. First, Wiles's theology of divine action begins from a theology of creation and then interprets everything else, including the incarnation and redemption, as aspects of creation. The approach I am taking begins from the Christ-event as the act of divine self-bestowal and then seeks to understand creation in terms of Christ. Second, unlike Wiles, I defend the idea that God does act in specific and special ways.

Keith Ward is an example of a theologian who takes a very different approach to Wiles. He sees God as acting in special ways in the lives of human beings and in the evolution of the physical universe as well as in the history of salvation. These special acts of God are both creative and responsive to creatures. Ward argues that God can be thought of as working providentially in the openness that contemporary science finds in the universe, exemplified in chaos theory and quantum mechanics, to achieve the divine purposes.[3] God's special providential acts, he suggests, account for the bias in evolution toward complex and sentient life-forms: "It is the being of God, which alone sustains the universe, that exercises a constant 'top-down' influence on the processes of mutation and natural selection, and guides them towards generating sentience and the creation and apprehension of intrinsic value."[4]

In his further reflection on Darwinian evolution, Ward gives the impression that he is placing the scientific theory of natural selection and the causal influence of God as explanations *at the same level*. He argues, against Richard Dawkins, that natural selection is insufficient as an explanation for the purposive nature of evolution, insisting that the additional explanation of God's action is required.[5] I have reservations about this strategy. Of course, in the approach I am taking, God's creative act is needed as an explanation at the metaphysical level. It is God who enables evolutionary processes to exist and to act with their own independence. But as I have argued in the first two chapters, it is important for theology to recognize the integrity of scientific explanation at its own level, that of empirical reality. It may well be that science will come to a better or fuller explanation of evolutionary emergence in strictly scientific terms. In this, theology should cheer science on. With Ward, I believe that God is involved purposefully in the process of evolution. But I think we need to see God as achieving the divine purposes in and through creaturely processes and causes, all of which are in principle open to scientific investigation. I am arguing for a theology of special divine acts that fully respects the integrity of secondary causes, including all the processes that drive biological evolution. In such a theology, these processes are seen as the proper domain of science.

In recent years, divine action has been studied by philosophers, theologians, and scientists working together in a collaborative and intensive way. During the 1990s, the Center for Theology and the Natural Sciences at Berkeley cosponsored, with the Vatican Observatory, a series of research conferences and publications on the theme of divine action, exploring it in relation to quantum cosmology, chaos and complexity, evolutionary and molecular biology, neuroscience and the person, and quantum mechanics.[6] There was broad agreement on a concept of divine action that includes not only God's continuous creative act, but also special and objective divine acts. Over the series of conferences, a consensus emerged around an approach to divine action that was special and objective but noninterventionist.[7] A noninterventionist view of divine action was taken *noninterventionist:*

to mean that God acts in nature without breaking or suspending the laws of nature. The "laws of nature" can be understood in various ways, and this is something I will take up in the next chapter.

Within this consensus about divine action as special, objective, but noninterventionist, five different approaches emerged. They can be seen as five distinct but related theological research programs in special divine action. First, Ian Barbour (with Charles Birch and John Haught on occasions) represented the perspective of process theology, understanding divine action as the inviting lure of God, which is operative in every actual occasion, but which does not determine the outcome in an exclusive way. Second, a significant group, including Robert John Russell, Nancey Murphy, George Ellis, and Thomas Tracy, explored the idea that God acts in the indeterminacy of quantum events to bring about particular outcomes.[8] Third, John Polkinghorne saw God as acting in the openness of nature, which he finds represented in chaotic and complex systems, to bring about outcomes through the top-down imparting of information. Fourth, Arthur Peacocke saw God as acting in and through and under every aspect of nature, acting on the system as a whole, by way of analogy with a "top-down" or "whole-part" cause in nature. Finally, William Stoeger and Stephen Happel worked consistently with Aquinas's distinction between primary and secondary causality, and understood God as acting in the world through a whole range of secondary causes.

Since then, various scholars have built upon one or another of these positions. Robert John Russell, for example, has worked to refine and develop the notion of God acting in and through the indeterminacy of the quantum level of reality.[9] Philip Clayton has engaged with process theology in a panentheistic and emergentist theology of divine action.[10] While owing a debt of gratitude to all these positions, I am attempting further exploration of the last of the five. Stoeger's position is that God acts in the whole of the natural world, by God's immanent and differentiated presence to all things, not only through the laws of nature of which we have a partial understanding, but also through those processes and regularities of nature that are still unknown to us. I see myself as attempting to build on this approach in a theology of special divine action that takes effect through a variety of created causes.

Divine Action through Secondary Causes

The collaborative discussion of divine action that I have just described has been fruitful, and each of the five approaches contributes important insights to our understanding of divine action. In particular, the approach associated with Robert John Russell and others, where God's action is explored in terms of quantum mechanics, has highlighted the indeterminacy and openness of our universe at this fundamental level of physics, and brought out the importance of this openness for all contemporary discussions between science and theology. There is no doubt that the openness of physics, articulated by Russell and others, creates space for a healthy dialogue between science and religion.

Why, then, opt for the approach to divine action in which the Creator is thought of as acting through secondary causes? Fundamentally, I embrace this approach because it represents a foundational metaphysical understanding of the God–world relationship, which is at the heart of the Christian tradition and which I find intellectually coherent and religiously meaningful. At its center is the idea that the Creator is present to all creatures, closer to them than they are to themselves, conferring existence and the capacity to act on every entity and every process. God does this always and everywhere in our universe. And at the heart of this approach is the idea that God gives creatures independence and integrity, including the capacity to act as real causes. In this view, God consistently respects the proper autonomy of creation. The only viable alternative I see to this position is another metaphysical position, such as Whiteheadian process theology.[11] While I have learned from process theology, I take a different approach because of my commitment to divine transcendence, among other things.

The position I am taking, that God works consistently through secondary causes, is based upon a strong notion of both God's transcendence and creaturely autonomy. It is an understanding of the God–world relationship that operates at a different and more fundamental level than some of the specific proposals just mentioned, such as that of divine action operating at the quantum level. It is not necessarily opposed to such proposals but puts critical theological questions to them about the radical mystery and transcendence of God and the integrity and autonomy of the natural world.

doesn't reduce God to 1 cause among many,
autonomy to creatures respects natural science,
less likely to have a problem w/ suffering

There are three reasons why I choose to give primary place to this way of understanding special divine acts. First, it upholds the absolute mystery and transcendence of the Creator and resists any tendency to see God as one cause among others in the world. Second, this view gives proper autonomy and independence to creaturely causes and processes, and fully respects the integrity of the natural sciences. Third, this approach is less likely than some other options to exacerbate the theological problem of suffering. At least in the way I am proposing it, the approach to divine action through secondary causes means that God may be understood as accepting the limits of created processes. Alternative approaches to divine action, which suggest that God can freely change things, face more difficulties with the always difficult issue of the suffering of creation.[12]

A common objection to the idea that God acts through secondary causes is that it does not tell us *how* God acts through them. In response, it is important to say that from a theological perspective, we do not know *how* God's creative act works. What we know is the result of this act but not the act itself. God's creative act is what I am calling, with Aquinas, primary causality. It is an instance, one of many, where theology has to face up to and insist on what human beings cannot know. The incomprehensible God is, by definition, the one beyond our knowing. Whatever we can comprehend is not God, but a construct of our minds. One of the most important tasks of theology is to point to the limits of our concepts and our speech about God. For this reason, Eastern Christianity has a long tradition of apophatic theology (a theology of unknowing), and the West has the similar concept of *docta ignorantia* (learned unknowing).

There is a very good reason for an apophatic stance in relation to God's creative act. God's creative act *is* God. Whatever we see, whatever science studies, is not God. We have no direct access to God's creative act, only to its effects: the universe of creatures we find around us, with the relationships between them and the laws that govern them. We never find any particular point of intersection (the "causal joint") between God and creatures, because we have no empirical access to God. In a sense, of course, every creature in the universe is this point of intersection, but what we have empirical access to is simply the creature. So a theology of divine action not only should not spell out how God acts, but should insist that this is something we cannot know.[13]

A second objection to this approach to divine action through secondary causes is that it does not point to any one particular place where science and theology might collaborate to better describe divine action. It has little to say to science. In response, it is important to note that this approach not only does not exclude detailed discussion between science and theology on particular issues, but encourages and undergirds them by providing clear ground rules. Within this perspective, it is perfectly appropriate to discuss divine action through focusing on one aspect of science, such as quantum mechanics. But divine action would be seen as involving not only the quantum level but every level, every entity and process of the observable universe, at every point of its evolution. In this approach, divine action cannot be located *only* in any one area of scientific research or human experience. It is always understood from the perspective of a Creator who is present and acting in and through every entity and every process.

There is a great deal that can be said about special divine acts, and I am trying to say some important things about them in this chapter. But it is inappropriate to think we can describe the nature of divine action, because to do so would be to describe the nature of God. What we know about the nature of God comes from the Christ-event, and on this basis, I have been proposing that it can be understood as divine self-bestowal, as a radical act of love, and I will seek to fill out this description in what follows. We have good reason to attempt to describe divine acts in the light of God's act for us in Christ. But I do not think we can comprehend the nature of God's act any more than we can comprehend the divine essence.

God's Special Acts in Evolutionary Emergence

How, then, might we speak about God's action in, for example, the emergence of life on our planet 3.7 billion years ago? In the approach I am advocating, this can be seen as a special act of God in the sense that God chooses, eternally, that the universe would bring forth biological life on our Earth by means of emergence and increasing complexity. What makes this act special is that (1) this action of God has a specific effect in creaturely history, the emergence of life in the universe, and (2) this specific effect is intended by God. Through the creative act of God in the eternal Word and through the immanent Spirit, inert matter becomes something new. God's one act of self-bestowing love is expressed in the specific and special act of the emergence of life on Earth.

This act of God takes effect in and through all the regularities and constraints of nature, including chance events occurring within the structure provided by the laws of nature. It involves a whole series of events in the 13.7-billion-year history of the universe, particularly the formation of stars, in which carbon and other elements so necessary for life on Earth can be synthesized. It involves particular features of our planet, including its placement at the right distance from the Sun, its formation from the molecules that are the raw materials of life from the matter surrounding the Sun, the continual bombardment of the young Earth by ice-bearing comets, the formation of a first atmosphere, and many other factors studied in the sciences. In all of these events, God is acting in specific and special ways. And all of this and a great deal more are part of that special act by which God brings life to Earth.

As is well known, science cannot yet offer anything like a full explanation of the origin of life. What I am proposing is that, in principle, it is the role of science to explain everything possible about this event. There are no gaps in the causal explanation at the empirical level that theology should fill. In the divine act that brings forth life on Earth, God acts in and through secondary causes, through the natural world, and the regularities, contingencies, processes, and laws studied by the sciences. These are the expression of God's creative act. God acts powerfully, creatively, and dynamically, not in a way that overrides the processes of nature, but precisely in and through them.

The Dynamism and the Creaturely Limits of Special Divine Acts

This conception of special divine action involves a dynamic understanding of God's engagement with every aspect of the expanding and evolving universe, and with the whole process of the evolution of life in all its complexity, including that of human beings. God wants a world of diverse living creatures to evolve on our planet and acts in all the regularities and contingencies of the natural world to bring this about. God is always present, in the Word and in the Spirit, always breathing life into the process, always engaged, always responsive, and always achieving the divine purpose of creating a world of creatures to which God will give God's self in love.

But this dynamic presence of God in the Word and in the creative Spirit to all things is precisely a presence in love. It is the love exemplified in a staggering way in the cross of Jesus. Creation is an act of self-giving love. And divine love involves divine respect for the independence and integrity of the creature and the creaturely processes involved in the emergence of life on Earth. God does not override the process, nor bypass the laws of nature. God accepts and works creatively with the limits of creaturely processes, lovingly respecting the integrity of creatures, and allows things to unfold in a finite way that involves enormous lengths of time. God works with the process and waits upon its unfolding.

I have already pointed out that in order to have human beings and koalas, you need to have carbon. Carbon exists only because of the formation of galaxies and stars in the expanding universe. The production of the carbon and the other elements that make up human beings and koalas takes billions of years of star burning. God creates with infinite patience and with a divine capacity to wait upon the emergence of all that is needed for the evolution of life. These processes involve false starts and setbacks and the exploration of new directions. God works creatively, dynamically, and responsively, loving the process, delighting in the emergence of a world of creatures with their own independence and integrity.

Special Divine Acts in the Life of Grace

How do we think of God acting in our own personal lives? According to the long tradition of Christian faith, there are times when we can experience the Holy Spirit in moments of profound grace. And according to this same tradition, God acts providentially and personally in lives. I will consider each of these briefly as instances of special divine action.

Experiences of the Holy Spirit

Do we experience the Spirit of God? Does God break in upon our day-to-day lives, addressing us, calling us, challenging us, inviting us, loving us? I am convinced that the answer to these questions can only be yes.[14] Of course, cultural and psychological factors play a role in the interpretation of all of our experiences, and this suggests a cautious and critical approach to claims about the experience of the Holy Spirit. What is claimed to come from the Spirit will *always* be, at least in part, the product of a human imagination. It will always be interpreted with the aid of preexisting images, language, and concepts.

Granted this, I believe we can claim with Rahner and others that we do experience the Spirit and that this occurs in ordinary human experience of the world.[15] This experience of God's Spirit is not of the same order as the experience of a created object, such as a tree or a human being. It is an experience of openness to mystery that occurs in our encounters with other persons and other creatures in our world. When we form a concept of a specific person or object in our world, there is always openness to more, to the unlimited range of possible knowing. And when we ask questions, they always open us up to further questions. Our minds are never satisfied. The horizon of our knowing reaches toward the infinite. It continually opens out toward what is boundless. Rahner calls this the experience of mystery that accompanies all our knowing. The experience of mystery is not simply the experience of something we do not know or do not understand. It is more the experience of the inexhaustible depths of reality.

This experience of mystery occurs not only in our knowing, but also in our free acts of love. These particular acts can contain an implicit invitation to give ourselves into a love that is unconditioned. The partial fulfillment we experience in our love and commitment to others in our world can open out toward a love that has no limits. There is a boundless expanse to the human mind and heart, and this boundless expanse is always there as the context of ordinary knowledge and love. On the basis of Christian revelation, which tells us that "God's love has been poured into our hearts through the Holy Spirit that has been given to us" (Rom 5:5), this dynamic openness of the human person can be understood as an openness toward the Spirit of God present to us by grace in self-offering love.

There are moments of special grace in our lives, when the experience of the Spirit is brought more clearly to the forefront of conscious experience. These can be positive experiences: when we are caught up in the exuberance of life in a rain forest, when we ponder and are deeply touched by the absolute gift of mutual friendship, when the birth of a child fills us with awe. There are also negative and extremely painful moments that lead us into mystery: when loneliness takes hold in our hearts, when we face failure in our projects, when grief seems unendurable, yet we come to know that we have been lovingly held in what seemed hopelessness, emptiness, and pain.

Grace can come to us in any moment. We are challenged by an encounter with a homeless person and forced to ask hard questions about our use of wealth and our collusion in systems that damage people. We are entranced by the song of a single bird and led beyond it for a moment to the Source of all music. In a quiet moment in the celebration of the Eucharist, we are led to stillness before God. The experience of the Spirit can be an experience of radical intimacy or disruption, but in either case, it is an experience mediated by our engagement with created words, events, and persons. Experiences of grace are mediated by secondary causes: we encounter others in our world and find in these encounters an openness to a Holy Other, present in a mysterious way beyond concepts and words.

all experiences w/ the Spirit happen through the created world

Personal Providence

What of God's day-to-day care of us? Are we right to find God at work providentially in the small as well as the large events of our lives? With many others in the Christian tradition, I am convinced that personal providence is a central dimension of Christian faith and fundamental to a gospel way of life: "Look at the birds of the air; they neither sow nor reap nor gather into barns, and yet your heavenly Father feeds them. Are you not of more value than they?" (Matt 6:26). Jesus tells his disciples that there is no need to worry. They are to set their hearts on the kingdom of God, and what they need will be provided (Matt 6:33).

Two ideas seem linked in this Christian notion of personal providence: (1) the conviction that God does things for us, and (2) the understanding that God's doing of things for us is personal. God does things for us as persons. Providence involves the idea that we are being cared for. Events occur that we take as a gift. It is important to note that understanding life in this way does not necessarily involve the idea of God acting in an interventionist way. It can also be understood within a noninterventionist theology of God acting through secondary causes. It is possible to hold a strong notion of providence together with the idea of a God who does not overrule creaturely cause and effect, but acts in and through them. In this view, God really comes to us, responds to us, and provides for us through secondary causes.

Karl Rahner offers a simple, everyday example of a special providential act.[16] I have a good idea that proves to be effective and important, and I think of it as a gift of God. Am I right to think of it in this way? Can this good idea be understood as providential? There may be natural explanations for this good idea coming upon me, but this does not rule out the interpretation of it as an act of God. If, in fact, I do experience the good idea as a place of encounter with the living God, then I am surely right to think that the God who is present as Source of All in every aspect of creation is now really mediated to me in this event of a good idea. It is appropriate, then, to see this good idea as willed by God, as given by God, and thus as a genuine experience of God's special providence. There are many such experiences in daily life, in our relationships, and in our actions. As saints such as Ignatius of Loyola have taught us, the spiritual journey is a continual learning to find God in all things, and this is based on the conviction that God is there *for us* in all things.

The claim that God cares for us and that we experience God's providence in a personal way does not mean that our lives will be without pain, failure, grief, and death. The Christian assertion of a God who cares for us can be made with integrity only when the hunger, cruelty, and violence of our world are fully acknowledged. The kind of theology of providence I am advocating does not mean that God is thought of as intervening in the order of nature to make my life pain free. It proposes, rather, that the God who provides for me through secondary causes may also respect the proper autonomy of the created order. This means that while God can be seen as acting in secondary causes for my well-being, God may not be free to intervene in the functioning of secondary causes in a way that overturns the laws of nature in order to preserve me from suffering. In his life and ministry, Jesus found God in all things. He had a profound belief in divine providence. But God did not respond to Jesus' cry "Abba, Father, for you all things are possible; remove this cup from me" (Mark 14:36) by intervening miraculously to save Jesus from suffering and death. The divine response was to be with Jesus in suffering and death, transforming it in the power of the Spirit into resurrection life and salvation for the world.

We can and do experience God's providential care, but we also experience life as painful and, for some of us, as unbearably cruel. The sense of providence in some aspects of life can be accompanied by experiences of suffering. Providence does not mean that I will not suffer cancer. It clearly does not mean that I will not die. But it means that God will be with me in my illness and that when I die, I die in Christ. In this view of providence, then, it is appropriate to think of God as doing things for me. It is appropriate to think of some events as a gift given to me. But it does *not* follow, as it may seem to at first sight, that when I am diagnosed with a serious illness, I am to see this as something God is sending to me. When tragedy strikes me or someone I love, it is not God who is doing it to me, except in the broad sense that God is creating and sustaining a world that unfolds according to its own patterns, and these patterns involve illness and death. God wants our life. God does not want our suffering. God does not send us suffering and grief.

Great suffering can befall us. Providence means that even here, God is not absent but with us. God does not send us suffering, but the cross reveals that suffering *is* the place of God. Even when we cry out, like Jesus, "My God, my God, why have you forsaken me?" (Mark 15:34), we are not abandoned. God is the faithful companion in our suffering, profoundly with us in love, feeling for us with the divine capacity to be with others in their pain, and taking us into life. There are times, even in great suffering, when we can come to know, perhaps only in retrospect, that we were held and loved even in what seemed utterly unbearable.

Suffering and grief are built into the kind of world in which we live, a world of natural process and human freedom. God is made flesh in this world in Jesus of Nazareth, embracing the flesh that is subject to suffering and death and the humanity distorted by human sin. Suffering flesh is taken into God, forever. Providence does not take suffering from our world. It assures us of a God who is with us as the faithful companion of our lives and deaths, with us in it all, leading us into resurrection life.

Disruptive Grace

The relationship with God in the Spirit can be an experience of great consolation but also one of disruption and challenge. Two incidents in the life of Francis of Assisi show divine action functioning in disruptive ways. When Francis was praying in the little church of San Damiano before the image of Christ crucified, he heard these words: "Francis, Go and repair my house which, as you see, is falling into ruins." Francis took this literally; he set about rebuilding San Damiano, selling his horse and some goods of his father. This led to a rupture with his family and his former lifestyle and the beginning of a new way of life. Later, in a Eucharist celebrated in another little church he restored and loved, the Porziuncola, Francis heard the priest read Matt 10:5-13, where Jesus tells his disciples to go out to proclaim the gospel without money, staff, bag, sandals, or spare tunic. Hearing these words changed Francis for good. He embraced poverty, began his preaching mission, and was soon joined by a first band of followers.

These are experiences of a great saint. Similar stories are told about other saints, and it can be argued that these kinds of experiences occur in some way in every life. Some words can form in our minds in a moment of stillness or of prayer, perhaps when, like Francis, we are before an icon of the crucified one. They may be words we have come across in reading or heard from someone else. But they come to us in this moment as a word of God, as a word of invitation and call. These words are not direct revelations from God, but divine action mediated through our own consciousness, our imaginations, our memories, and the prompting of circumstances. Or a word of Scripture proclaimed in the community hits us with the force of revelation. It may well be a text we have heard many times before, but it comes to us now as a word of challenge and grace, a word of God that demands a response.

Grace breaks in upon us in many ways. A friend or spouse may challenge us about an aspect of our behavior. We may find ourselves consumed with hurt and resentment toward another and know the call to forgiveness and freedom in Christ. We may find ourselves caught up in a work life of increasing demands and find an invitation to consider what really matters before God. We may be confronted by a person in real need and, perhaps, feel the burden that person places upon us, but come to know this as the invitation of grace. Divine action is always at work in new ways in our lives. God engages with us in the day-to-day, inviting, luring, challenging, loving, responding to our choices, concerns, moods, failures, and hopes. God comes to us through the mediation of creatures, not only through the biblical word and the liturgical life of the church, but also through other persons, animals, special places, words, events, and the workings of our own imaginations, memories, and thoughts.

Special Divine Acts in the History of Salvation

Christian faith sees God acting freely in special ways that include Israel's experience of the Mosaic covenant; the words of the prophet Isaiah; the life, death, and resurrection of Jesus of Nazareth; and the Spirit poured out at Pentecost. A little reflection makes it clear that in each of these cases, God is not becoming present where God was formerly absent. God was *totally* with Israel before the covenant. God was fully present to every part of the universe, including all flesh, before the incarnation. The Holy Spirit was present in the world as Breath of Life, breathing life into all things as the Creator Spirit, long before Pentecost. How, then, can we think about special divine acts in relationship to God's abiding, enabling, interior presence with all things?

Mediation by Created Realities

In a special divine act, a creaturely reality expresses and mediates God's self-giving love. We encounter God in and through the mediations of the natural world. In a special divine act, a particular event or person can be understood as God freely bringing to particular and historical expression the act of self-giving love by which God has been immanent to creation from the beginning. As Rahner says, God is never simply one object among others in our world, but is "embedded" in this world from the very beginning.[17] A special act of God in the history of salvation, then, is the expression in particular persons and events of God's one act of divine self-bestowal. A created reality expresses and mediates the immanent presence and action of God. In something of a similar way, cooking a meal for a human beloved can be a special act that embodies and brings to concrete expression the lifelong act of committed love.

In what Christians see as God's uniquely special act in our history, God acts in and through the mediation of the humanity of Jesus. He is the unique historical expression of the love that is already interior to all the entities, processes, and persons that make up our universe. As John's Gospel tells us, the Word "was in the world, and the world came into being through him; yet the world did not know him," so "the Word became flesh and lived among us and we have seen his glory" (John 1:10, 14). As Rahner has noted, traditional theology tended to see events like the incarnation according to a model of divine intervention. In Christian history, this interventionist model has coexisted with a more universal view of God as the "deepest energy of the world."[18] The universal and interventionist models of divine action were never completely reconciled. What is needed today, Rahner says, is the emergence of a "universalist basic model in which God in his free grace, from the very beginning and always and everywhere, has communicated himself to his creation as its innermost energy and works in the world from the inside out."[19] It is, of course, precisely this model that I am seeking to advance in these pages.

Rahner

In a theology of divine action understood as self-bestowal, the incarnation governs creation from the beginning. I have been proposing that Jesus Christ, the Word made flesh, can be seen in a noninterventionist way as the particular, unique, and historical expression of the divine self-giving that is always at work in every aspect of creation, redemption, and final fulfillment. Jesus in his created humanity makes God's self-bestowing love and promise of fulfillment historically accessible and tangible. His is the human face of divine love in our history. The divine self-bestowal always and everywhere at work in particular ways in all things finds its radical expression in our history in the words, deeds, death, and resurrection of Jesus of Nazareth.[20]

Sacramental Structure of Special Divine Acts

When God's grace is not only expressed but also communicated through the mediation of a creaturely reality, Christian theology sees this in sacramental terms. A sacrament is a visible sign and agent of divine self-bestowal. The prime instances of this in the life of the Christian community are sacramental celebrations, like baptism and the Eucharist. But as a great deal of twentieth-century theology and church teaching has made clear, these sacraments reflect the fact that the church itself has a sacramental nature. It is a sign and agent of communion with God and of human community, called to be the universal sacrament of salvation.[21]

At a more fundamental level still, Jesus of Nazareth is the fundamental and primary sacrament of God in the world.[22] He is the radical expression of, and mediation of, divine self-bestowal. As the incarnate Word and Wisdom of God, he is the sacrament of divine self-bestowal in the world. He is the real symbol of God, in which God is manifested and acts in a world of matter and flesh. It is fundamental to note, of course, that Jesus' humanity is created and part of the network of secondary causes that make up creation. Like us, Jesus is part of evolutionary history, dependent on the hydrogen that formed in the beginning of the universe, on the carbon and the other elements synthesized in stars, and on the long history of evolutionary emergence on Earth. Precisely as created, and as interconnected with evolutionary history, with all flesh, Jesus is the irreversible historical expression of God's self-bestowal and the sacrament of salvation for our world. In Jesus Christ, and in the life of the church, we find that the economy of God, the structure of revelation and salvation, has a sacramental structure. This, of course, is another way of saying that God acts in our world through the mediation of creatures, through secondary causes.

This leads to a further proposal: that divine action as such has a sacramental nature. The sacramental character of divine action is not limited to Jesus as the fundamental sacrament of God, or to the communion of the church and its sacramental celebrations. Every experience of divine action, each in its own different way, has a sacramental structure: God's one act that embraces creation, salvation, and final fulfillment finds sacramental expression in our history in particular events, words, and persons. A diverse range of creatures become mediations of the divine, sacraments of divine action. Such sacramental mediations are differentiated in the way they participate in and mediate the one act of divine self-bestowal. Their variety comes from the various created realities that mediate the divine in our history. Based on revelation in Christ and led by the Spirit, Christians discern what is truly of God. For them, the various sacramental mediations of the one divine act find their central focus and basis for interpretation in the Word made flesh.

Conclusion

I have proposed in this chapter that there are special acts of God, and that these include God's creative and providential action in evolutionary emergence, God's personal action in the life of grace and in the experience of personal providence, and God's action in the history of salvation, particularly the Christ-event. These special acts are not interventions that overturn or bypass the laws of nature, but are acts of God in and through the mediation of the natural world, its regularities and contingencies. These special acts of God are intrinsic to divine action because God's one act of self-giving takes effect in the created order in ways that are limited, specific, and historical. They are not uniform but wonderfully diverse. Some are certainly more central than others, and God's act in Christ is the most central and most special to any Christian theology of special divine acts.

But these acts are not special because God acts in them in a more interventionist way than in other cases. They are special because of the special nature of the mediation involved. Ultimately, these mediations involve the whole of the natural world. But God acts in particular and distinctive ways, in and through, for example, all that enables life to emerge on Earth, and through the life and work of a prophet or saint, and in a unique and radical way, through the Word made flesh. There is an enormous variety of mediations of God's action, because God is always acting in the particular and the historical of the universe and its living creatures. In the next chapter, I will take up the issue of miracles, focusing on the miracles of Jesus, and then in the following chapter, turn to the resurrection as the central act of God in our history.

5

Miracles and the Laws of Nature

Any Christian theology of divine action needs to discuss miracles, above all because they are central to the ministry of Jesus. Throughout this book, I have been proposing that God can be thought of as consistently working through the processes of the natural world. Are miracles an exception to this? Is a miracle an instance where God overturns or bypasses the laws of nature? If so, then why would God intervene in the natural order at some times and not at others? Why would God save some from harm and not others?

Some of the pastoral practice of the church seems to be based on an assumption that, in miracles, God intervenes in a way that suspends or bypasses the laws of nature. An alternative theology of miracles is needed, and I will propose a theology of miracles in noninterventionist terms: as wonders of God that take place through natural causes. An important part of this discussion will involve clarifying that these natural causes involve not just the laws of nature that we already know, but also many aspects of the natural world that are not yet well modeled in our scientific theories and laws.

The miracles that are crucial to the Christian tradition are those connected with Jesus. Because of this, I will begin with a brief exploration of miracles in the life of Jesus, making use of the historical work of biblical scholar John Meier. Then I will turn to the classical treatment of miracles in the work of Aquinas. This will be followed by a discussion of the laws of nature, taking up the ideas of William Stoeger. Finally, I will suggest a theology of miracles as wonderful manifestations of grace that occur in and through secondary causes.

The Miracles of Jesus

It is obvious from any reading of the Gospels that the four evangelists see Jesus as a wonder-worker. Alan Richardson long ago pointed out that in Mark's Gospel, 209 verses out of a total of 666 deal directly or indirectly with miracles.[1] While some scholars involved in the historical study of Jesus have little to say about his miracles, John P. Meier devotes 529 closely argued pages to them in the second volume of his *A Marginal Jew*.[2] I will take Meier as a helpful guide to the historicity of the miracles, focusing first on his findings on the general question of Jesus as a miracle worker, and then pointing very briefly to his conclusions concerning three particular incidents: the healing of Bartimaeus, the raising of Lazarus, and the walking on the water.

Before he takes up individual miracle stories, Meier addresses this global question: Did Jesus perform extraordinary deeds that were considered by himself and by others as miracles? Meier's response is governed by criteria that he uses throughout his work on the historical Jesus:

- The miracles are very *widely attested to* in the sources we have for Jesus' ministry. Every Gospel source, including Mark, Q (the non-Markan material common to Matthew and Luke), the material found only in Matthew, that found only in Luke, and John, as well as every evangelist in editorial summaries, and the Jewish writer Josephus all witness to Jesus as a miracle worker. Jesus' miracles are attested to, as well, in different kinds of literary forms: in exorcism stories, healing stories, nature miracles, summary statements, parables, dispute stories, and Jesus' mandate to his disciples instructing them to heal. This level of attestation is a powerful argument for historicity.

- On top of this, the criterion of *coherence* supports the argument that Jesus was seen as a miracle worker. There is coherence between Jesus' exorcisms and his sayings, between his healings and sayings, and between the signs and the discourses in John's Gospel. In a more general way, Jesus' miracles are coherent with the picture of one who gained a large number of disciples and aroused much interest.

- It cannot be argued that Jesus' miracles stand out as unique to him (the criterion of *discontinuity*), since there are accounts of other miracle workers, both Jewish and Christian. Meier points out that what is distinctive to Jesus is the picture of one who not only preached in parables proclaiming the kingdom of God, but also worked miracles that actualized his own proclamation.

- The criterion of *embarrassment* comes into play in material that the Christian community would have found awkward and therefore was unlikely to have introduced. This criterion has a limited application in the Beelzebul incident, where Jesus' exorcisms lead to the charge that he is in league with the devil (Mark 3:20-30; Matt 12:22-32).

- Meier finds that the miracles fit coherently with the criterion of his *death on a cross*, in that they would have stirred up excitement and energy and been an aggravating circumstance contributing to his death.

The careful application of these criteria to the general question of whether Jesus was seen and saw himself as a miracle worker leads Meier to the unambiguous conclusion that Jesus was understood by others and by himself as a miracle worker: "Viewed globally, the tradition of Jesus' miracles is more firmly supported by the criteria of historicity than are a number of other well-known and readily accepted traditions about his life and ministry. . . . If the miracle tradition from Jesus' public ministry were to be rejected *in toto* as unhistorical, so should every other Gospel tradition about him."[3] Meier is left in no doubt that Jesus was seen as a wonder-worker and that he saw himself as healing in the cause of the reign of God.

Meier's detailed discussion of the healing of the blindness of Bartimaeus leads him to conclude that this story is one of the strongest candidates for a specific miracle story that goes back to the historical Jesus.[4] This story has a good claim to historicity. His analysis of the raising of

Lazarus, told in John's Gospel, leads him to think that this story reflects early material and that it is likely that the story "goes back ultimately to some event involving Lazarus, a disciple of Jesus, and that this event was believed by Jesus' disciples even during his lifetime to be a miracle of raising the dead."[5] He notes that, at this distance from the event, it is impossible to know whether Lazarus was clinically dead. His examination of the story of Jesus walking on the water leads him to believe that "the walking on the water is most likely from start to finish a creation of the early church, a christological confession in narrative form."[6] Meier argues that the walking on the water is a narrative comment on the feeding of the five thousand, which symbolizes the eucharistic experience of the early Christians: "What I am suggesting is that, to a small church struggling in the night of a hostile world and feeling bereft of Christ's presence, the walking on the water likewise symbolized the experience of Christ in the eucharist."[7]

This sample of some of Meier's conclusions does not reflect the subtlety of his arguments or the breadth of his discussion, and it represents the views of only one scholar. But it offers a sketch for a tentative overview of Jesus as a miracle worker, which can give direction to my further exploration here: Jesus was a miracle worker, and his healing ministry proclaimed and anticipated the coming reign of God; he brought healing to individuals like Bartimaeus; it is probable that, during his lifetime, he was thought of as restoring Lazarus to life; the walking on the water can be seen as giving expression to the presence and action of the risen Christ in the eucharistic experience of the early church. I will take this as a reasonable working assessment of the kind of data that a theology of miracles needs to address and, with this in mind, will turn to insights from one of the greatest theologians of the Christian tradition, Thomas Aquinas (c. 1225–1274).

Aquinas on the Dignity of Secondary Causes

Aquinas insisted that, unlike all creatures, God's very nature is to exist. And God causes existence (*esse*) in all other things. God causes this effect in creatures not only when they begin to exist, but also at every moment in which they are maintained in existence. Nothing is more deeply interior to an entity than its existence. God is present to all things at this most interior level, enabling them to exist and to act at every moment.[8] All things exist only as created by God ex nihilo at every moment. All things depend on God entirely for their existence and action at every point. They find in God not only the cause of their being (efficient cause), but also their final end (final cause). God's providence governs all creatures toward their end, which is participation in the goodness of God.

Aquinas calls all the interacting causes we find at work in the empirical world, absolutely all created causes, *secondary*. He sees God as the *primary* cause, who is always providentially at work in all created causes. It is by God's power that every other power acts.[9] It is through created causes that God cares for creation. It is important to note the infinite difference between primary and secondary causality. What Aquinas calls secondary causality includes absolutely all the patterns of relationship we find in the natural world, everything studied by the sciences, and everything that could ever be studied by the sciences. When God is described as the primary cause, the word *cause* is being used only by way of analogy. God is not a cause like other causes in the world. God is never one among other causes. In this context, the word *cause* refers to the absolutely unique relationship between Creator and creatures, by which God confers existence on all things and enables them to be, to act, and to become.

Aquinas insists that God acts in and through creatures that are themselves truly causal. He writes: "Divine Providence works through intermediaries. For God governs the lower through the higher, not from any impotence on his part, but from the abundance of his goodness imparting to creatures the dignity of causing."[10] I find this a remarkable statement. God so loves and respects the dignity of creatures that God wants them to be fully causal. God fully respects their integrity, their dignity, and their proper autonomy.

Aquinas thus opposes the view, sometimes called occasionalism, that sees God constantly intervening and acting as the only real cause at work in the universe. He is also opposed to what is later called Deism, the idea that God is involved in creating things at the beginning but takes no further part in the functioning of the universe. For Aquinas, providence and God's government are always and everywhere at work, taking effect through the range of secondary causes. He challenges those who would say that God acts alone and without intermediaries:

But this is impossible, and first because it would deprive creation of its pattern of cause and effect, which in turn would imply lack of power in the creator, since an agent's power is the source of its giving an effect a causative capability. It is impossible, secondly, because if the active powers that are observed in creatures accomplished nothing, there would be no point to their having received such powers. Indeed if all creatures are utterly devoid of any activity of their own, then they themselves would seem to have a pointless existence, since everything exists for the sake of its operation.[11]

There are three lines of thought at work in this text. First, God's love and respect for creation is such that God wants creation to have its own pattern of cause and effect. Second, God's creative power is all the more wonderful insofar as it enables creatures to genuinely participate in causing. It reflects all the greater glory on God that God creates in such a way as to enable creatures to be genuine causes. Third, if created causative powers did not genuinely accomplish their operations, they would have a pointless existence. They would lack meaning and integrity.

These arguments can be brought to bear on contemporary controversies. The proponents of "intelligent design," for example, seek to show that there are instances of "irreducible complexity" in the natural world that cannot be accounted for by Darwinian evolution and that require the intervention of a designer.[12] It seems to me that one who thinks like Aquinas would not be inclined to support this line of thought. Aquinas would find no need to search for a place where a designer intervenes, because God is found in every dimension of creation: God "acts interiorly in all things," because "God is the cause of *esse,* which is innermost in all things."[13]

In today's context, it would be consistent with Aquinas to see God's creative action as finding its most profound expression in evolutionary history, by enabling creaturely processes to have their own dignity and integrity as genuine causes of novelty in the world.[14] For Aquinas, it would reflect all the more glory to God if God enables life to evolve through natural processes, which can be accounted for empirically by the natural sciences, including Darwinian evolutionary theory.

How does Aquinas think about miracles? He tells us that miracles have as their purpose the manifestation of God's grace.[15] They are signs of grace and manifestations of the Spirit (1 Cor 12:7). Like most people of faith of the thirteenth century, he takes it for granted that miracles occur. He notes that the word *miracle* comes from the Latin word *admiratio*, suggesting the wonder that accompanies the experience of something whose cause is hidden from us.[16]

A real miracle, he says, has its cause hidden, because its cause is God. This is because, in a miracle, the action of God replaces secondary causes. Miracles are "exceptions to the pattern in nature."[17] They occur in a manner that "surpasses the capabilities of nature."[18] They can exceed the capability of nature in three ways: in the kind of thing done, in the person who does it, and in the manner and order in which it is done.[19] A miracle is an event that occurs *only* through God's action and without a secondary cause:

> But if we take the order in things as it depends upon any of the secondary causes, then God can act apart from it; he is not subject to that order but rather it is subject to him, as issuing from him not out of necessity of nature, but the decision of his will. He could in fact have established another sort of pattern in the world; hence when he so wills, he can act apart from the given order, producing, for example, the effects of secondary causes without them or some effects that surpass the powers of these causes.[20]

Brian Davies points out that, for Aquinas, a miracle occurs because of what is *not* present—namely, a secondary cause.[21] Davies finds two theses flowing from Aquinas's view of miracles. First, no one but God can work a miracle. Insofar as holy people are involved, it is not that they work miracles but that God brings about miracles at their request.[22] Second, in working miracles, God does not do violence to the natural order. All the events that occur in the universe are the effect of God's will. If God brings about something miraculous in the natural order, this is no more a violation of the natural order than the fact that the order exists in the first place.[23] I think Davies is right to insist that, for Aquinas, God's miracles surpass the natural order but do not do violence to it. What is not explored by Aquinas, however, is the possibility that God may so respect the unfolding of the processes of the natural order that even in miracles, God works in and through the laws of nature. What if God, out of loving fidelity to creatures, works *consistently* through secondary causes?

I find Aquinas's concept of primary and secondary causality indispensable and foundational in the current dialogue between science and theology, and the same is true of his view of God's respect for the integrity of secondary causes. I also embrace his view of miracles as wonderful manifestations of the Spirit. But I will depart from his view that in miracles, God replaces secondary causes, to propose the idea that miracles can be seen as wonderful manifestations of the Spirit that occur *through* secondary causes. God's respect for the integrity of secondary causes, so clearly defended by Aquinas, may mean that even in miracles, God acts in and through the known and unknown laws of nature. Taking this proposal further will mean attempting to clarify what is meant by the laws of nature.

The Laws of Nature

In a series of articles, William Stoeger has explored the meaning and ontological status of the laws of nature.[24] I will focus on three questions that he addresses in this body of work. The first asks: To what extent do well-confirmed scientific theories, and the laws of nature they embody, describe what occurs in reality? Stoeger begins by discussing scientific theories that are highly successful and, because of this success, have the status of laws. They offer a detailed model of fundamental patterns of order and causal influence that we observe in the physical and chemical world. Such theories have been molded, modified, and refined through continual observation and experiment. Stoeger sees such theories and their laws as having a "very strong basis" in observed reality, but he points out that even in these cases, our observations do not reveal the whole of the reality under scrutiny.[25] Some aspects, even some of the most fundamental, remain hidden. Science focuses on stable and characteristic features that are accessible to it. It seeks what is universalizable and what is relevant to the questions of the scientist. Science isolates and simplifies aspects of reality and models them with concepts such as mass and velocity. And the design of a research program and the interpretation of its results are limited by the heuristic anticipation of the researcher. All of this means that much of the reality of the matter under observation is missed.

Even in the many cases at the physical level, where scientific laws have been confirmed as modeling reality effectively, it is still important, when speaking of laws of nature, to distinguish between scientific theories and the relationships, processes, and causal interconnections of the natural world itself. Our theories are not to be confused with nature. Even at the level of physics, where reality often seems very well modeled by our laws, there is much that escapes our comprehension, including aspects of the quantum level of reality and the physics of complex systems, where "order and chaos nourish one another with a strange reciprocity."[26] The turbulence of flowing fluids is but one example of physical reality that is difficult to model in detail or to compress algorithmically. These difficulties only increase in biology, neurophysiology, psychology, economics, politics, and sociology, where the reality we encounter escapes attempts to describe it in the law-like and rigidly predictable ways of physics and mathematics.

A second, related question concerns the function of the laws of nature: Do they *prescribe* the way reality behaves or merely describe it? They certainly do describe the behavior of the natural world in certain circumstances and attribute this behavior to particular causes and influences. But do the laws force or constrain the behavior? While it is common to assume that they do, Stoeger argues that the laws cannot be said to be the source of the behavior. Rather, they simply model or describe it. Of course, one reason why the laws of nature were long ago assumed to be prescriptive is that they were thought of as God's laws, governing the physical world as God's commandments governed human conduct. Stoeger sees the laws of nature as human descriptions of observed regularities: "In a way, saying that something is a 'law of nature' is simply a way of indicating that it is so fundamental to the description of the detailed workings of physical, chemical or biological systems that it never is observed not to hold when those systems are properly isolated and simplified and certain conditions are fulfilled."[27] There is no reason to assume that the law is the cause of the regularity that is observed. It is a description of the regularity and of its fundamental character.

There are times when a source of behavior at one level is found to be grounded in the next level of physical process and structure, as when the laws of chemical reactions are explained at the level of atomic structure. These deeper explanatory connections provide intermediate, detailed descriptions that causally link phenomena that had seemed unconnected, but they never explain completely why reality is the way it is: "Rather, they explain that, since it is this way, it has to have these relationships with what appear to be more fundamental realities."[28] The models give the appearance of imparting necessity, but this apparent necessity does not come from the models; rather, it is hidden in the observed entities and their regularities. The ultimate source of the regularity we observe is not the model we articulate. The model itself does not tell us why this model holds and not some other. While the theories and laws of nature can describe reality well and point to intermediate causal connections between different levels of reality, they do not prescribe reality. They do not cause it to be the way it is.

The third question concerns the independent existence of our models and laws: Do they have an existence outside our minds? Are they more than our approximations of what is manifest in the physical phenomena being observed? Stoeger opposes the Platonic view that would give these laws an independent and preexisting reality. He finds no scientific or philosophical reason to see the laws of nature as constituting an underlying plan or pattern of physical reality: "The most we can say is that there are regularities and interrelationships in reality as it is in itself—a fundamental order—which are imperfectly reflected in our models and laws."[29] Even when these models are highly successful, they remain imperfect and limited. The models represent in an idealized way the structures and relationships between the phenomena under study, but they always leave a great deal out: "It is an illusion to believe that these incredibly rich representations of the phenomena are unconstructed isomorphisms we merely *discover* in the real world. Instead they are *constructed*—painstakingly so—and there is no evidence that they are isomorphic with structures in the real world as it is in itself."[30] Our scientific models are the result of imaginative and conceptual abstraction guided by continued observation and experiment. There is no justification for the idea that they correspond in a direct way to the entities, structures, and relationships of physical reality as it is in itself.

This whole line of argument suggests that in using the language of "laws of nature," there is a need to distinguish between two possible meanings: "We may mean the regularities, relationships, processes and structures in nature: (1) *as we know, understand and model them*; or (2) *as they actually function in reality,* which is much, much more than we know, understand or have adequately modeled."[31] The laws of nature as we know them are provisional, imperfect and limited, and not well equipped to deal with important areas of life, including not only the metaphysical, but also the mental, the ethical, the interpersonal, the aesthetic, and the religious. The existence of parts of reality that defy scientific analysis, such as personal relationships or deeply held values, is an indication not that these phenomena are illusory but that the laws of nature, meaning the natural sciences as we know them, do not model or describe central aspects of reality.[32]

This clarification has important consequences for a theology of miracles. It suggests that a marvelous manifestation of the Spirit, such as an act of healing, may take us beyond the laws of nature understood in the first sense—as our limited models of reality. But it may not be beyond the laws of nature understood in the second sense—as the relationships and processes that function in reality, which are more than we have fully understood or adequately modeled. And, of course, all of these patterns of relationship and causality that escape our present models are, theologically, secondary causes. This opens up the possibility that miracles may occur through a whole range of secondary causes that our current science cannot yet model or cannot yet model well.

A Theological Approach

In the gospel tradition, the miracles of Jesus function as signs and mediations of the coming reign of God. They are presented not as the reports of detached observers, but as the testimony of believers. They are of their very nature signs, signs that bear on salvation. They are signs that summon a person to conversion and commitment to the way of the reign of God.

Karl Rahner sees miracles as signs and manifestation of God's saving action. They are manifestations of grace in the midst of life. They are always directed toward persons in particular contexts, and always involve personal faith: "They are not *facta bruta* but an address to a knowing subject in a quite definitive historical situation."[33] In Rahner's theological understanding, a miracle occurs when a person experiences God's self-communication in a particular configuration of events, in such a way that God's self-communication participates immediately in the event. God is experienced with a kind of immediacy, in and through the event. A miracle is a call of God in and through specific events that calls us to wonder. In such a miraculous event, God's self-communication comes to appearance and witnesses to itself.[34]

To experience the miraculous, a person is needed who is "willing to allow himself to be called in the depths of his existence, who is free and open to the singularly wonder-full in his life."[35] The recipient needs a willingness to believe, to have eyes to see and ears to hear. Such a person keeps alive a humble and receptive wonder in the concrete events of her existence. She can find in historical events a call from God and be empowered and obligated by these events to a historical dialogue with God. This is, after all, the Gospel presupposition for a miracle: "Daughter, your faith has made you well; go in peace, and be healed of your disease" (Mark 5:34).

Rahner suggests the idea I have been developing in this chapter—that we can do without the notion of miracles interrupting the laws of nature and think of miracles as occurring in and through the mediations of creation. He points to the multilayered nature of our everyday experience of the world, where fundamental levels of reality are subsumed into the higher without violating what is proper to the lower but become something new. So the physical is subsumed into the chemical and the biological, and in us, the material, chemical, and biological are subsumed into human freedom, without losing the integrity of the lower levels. Rahner finds something analogous happening with regard to God's action in the world. The natural world, with its processes and laws, is created by God as part of the process of God's self-bestowal to the world. The miraculous and wonderful self-giving of God is experienced in and through the natural world.

It is not that God creates a world that is distant from God so that, in order to communicate, God needs to intervene in the world from time to time. Rather, the natural world, with its processes and laws, exists within God's one act of self-bestowal. The laws of nature are part of God's own self-giving. They are an element within grace.[36] God does not need to break these laws or overturn them or interrupt them in order to communicate to human persons in specific circumstances. The natural world with its laws is the means of God's self-revelation. God can give marvelous signs of grace to God's people without violating natural laws.

Rahner's thought can be developed by the distinction Stoeger makes between the two meanings of the laws of nature. The vehicle for God's self-communication is not simply the natural world as our theories model it. Instead, the vehicle of God's self-manifestations is the far more mysterious world of nature itself, much of which is beyond our present understanding and modeling. And, in terms of Aquinas's theology, this is the world of secondary causes. If a miracle is a wonderful manifestation and sign of God's grace, there is every reason to think it can take effect in the natural world, some of which is beyond our modeling, but which has its own God-given integrity as a world of interacting secondary causes. God's grace can be understood as taking effect in a way that fully respects the integrity of nature at the physical and biological level as well as at the level of human freedom.

This line of thought suggests that some miracles, experienced as marvels of God's gracious self-communication, may occur at levels beyond the laws we know at present that govern physics, chemistry, and biology. A person suffering from cancer might pray with her community for healing from the cancer and find herself miraculously restored to health. According to the line of thought developed here, this need not be taken as God acting without secondary causes. It may well be that God is acting in and through secondary causes that we do not fully understand. It may be that science will one day understand more clearly how prayer, human solidarity, love, or faith can contribute to biological healing. Some other miracles may occur in ways that are consistent with contemporary science. A person who is cured from illness in a way that science can explain, and who finds God providentially at work in this cure, so that it becomes for her a call and address by God, might well see this as a miracle, a wonderful manifestation and sign of the Spirit of God. A person might receive, as a gift, the capacity to make peace in a damaged relationship and experience this as a miracle of grace. Such events do not affect any known law of nature, but they are marvelous manifestations of the Spirit.

The proposal I have made is to extend Aquinas's view that God respects secondary causes, in the light of Stoeger's insights concerning the laws of nature, so that we think of God working consistently through secondary causes. This, perhaps, puts me in the company of Pope John XXII. When Thomas Aquinas's canonization was being discussed, the paucity of miracles was raised as an objection, and the pope is said to have replied that every question Thomas Aquinas answered was a miracle.[37] Certainly, Aquinas's body of work, the Spirit-led expression of his faith, hope, and love and the integrity of his commitment to truth, could constitute a miracle in the sense proposed here, as a marvelous manifestation of the Spirit.

6

The Divine Act of Resurrection

Throughout this book, I have been proposing a noninterventionist view of divine action where God is understood as acting in self-bestowing love, and this act of self-bestowing love takes effect in the whole range of created, secondary causes, including persons, words, and deeds. Even the incarnation can be understood in noninterventionist terms as the divine act by which the eternal Word of God is made flesh in the secondary cause that is the created humanity of Jesus of Nazareth. In the previous chapter, I proposed that the miracles of Jesus might be understood as wonderful acts of God that take place through the mediation of secondary causes. Now the question of the resurrection must be addressed. Is the resurrection an exception to this pattern? Is this an instance where God intervenes in such a way as to overturn, bypass, or change the laws of nature?

Many would think of the resurrection as the hardest case for a non-interventionist theology of divine action. Certainly, the resurrection is, for Christian believers, the central and absolutely unique act of God in our history. It cannot be fitted into any pattern or preexisting category. It is that which determines all other things. It is the resurrection that reveals God's meaning and purpose in creation and redemption. I will maintain this view of the resurrection as the central act of God that shapes the history of the universe but will suggest, tentatively, that here, too, God can be thought of as acting in a noninterventionist way, in the sense of acting in and through created causes.

A theology that can offer some response to the suffering of creation must be more than noninterventionist. It must also offer hope of the final liberation and fulfillment of creation in God. It needs to be a powerful theology of transformation. With Robert John Russell and others in the science–theology dialogue, I hold that a theological response to the costs of evolution must involve eschatology, even though the claims of Christian eschatology exist in some tension with the predictions of scientific cosmology.[1] What is needed is an objective and powerful theology of resurrection that promises the final healing of creation. A merely psychological or subjective theology of the resurrection cannot offer hope to creation. Only a theology of resurrection that is eschatologically transformative can begin to respond to the suffering that is built into an evolutionary universe.

In this chapter, I explore the idea of the resurrection as an act of God that is objective and powerfully transformative but also noninterventionist in three steps, proposing that: (1) the resurrection can be seen as a free act of God that comes from within creation and gives creation its deepest meaning, (2) it is to be understood as an ontological transformation of reality, and (3) it is an act of God that finds expression in secondary causes.

Resurrection: A Free Act of God from within Creation That Gives Creation Its Deepest Meaning

To say that the resurrection of the crucified Jesus is a unique and objective act of God is not to say that it is an intervention in the universe from without. I will propose that the resurrection is the unique and objective act of the God who is already present in all aspects of the history of the universe. To explore this proposal, I will show how it is supported by three lines of thought found in Rahner's theology: the resurrection is the central expression of God's one differentiated divine act; it is the culmination of an evolutionary Christology; it is the sacrament of the salvation of the world.

Central Expression of Divine Self-Bestowal

In chapters 3 and 4, I discussed and adopted a theology where God's action in creation, redemption, and final fulfillment is understood as one differentiated act of divine self-bestowal. In this view, creation is always directed toward the Christ-event and, in and through the Christ-event, to the fulfillment of creatures in the Trinitarian life of God. God creates because God wants to give God's self in love to creatures in the Word made flesh and in the Spirit poured out in grace. The incarnation and the gift of the Spirit are directed to the completion of all things in God. Creation from the very beginning is energized from within by the God of self-bestowing love. Every aspect of the history of salvation, and every experience of providence and grace, is an experience of the God of self-bestowing love.

The self-bestowal of God finds its ultimate and radical human expression in Jesus, in his words and deeds, his death and resurrection. The resurrection represents something completely unpredictable and new. While many human beings long for life beyond death, and while some faithful Jews had put their hope in general resurrection, the resurrection of the crucified one was beyond all human expectation. It is an unimaginable and amazing act of God in our history. It constitutes a promise that human beings and with them the whole creation will be transfigured in Christ. It contains a claim that the final transformation of all things has already begun in Jesus and is at work in the universe.

But in the light of the resurrection and with the gift of the Spirit, the early Christian community could begin to see that this had always been the divine plan: "With all wisdom and insight he has made known to us the mystery of his will, according to his good pleasure that he set forth in Christ, as a plan for the fullness of time, *to gather up all things in him, things in heaven and things on earth*" (Eph 1:8-10; emphasis added). The resurrection is not only the culmination of the life and death of Jesus, but also the inner meaning of creation. The God who creates is the God who raises Jesus from the dead. In this sense, the resurrection is the central expression in our history of the self-giving love of the God who is present in every ancient oak tree, every ant, and every kangaroo, closer than they are to themselves, as the source of their being and the enabler of their action.

This view of God's acting in one differentiated act of self-bestowal constitutes a first line of thought that can build toward a noninterventionist theology of resurrection. The resurrection is not seen as an act of God *revelation of DSB* [handwritten annotation]

from without, but the revelation of that divine act of self-bestowal that is already at work in every aspect of our universe. Self-bestowing love is what characterizes the divine act of creation, and it is this same self-bestowing love that is revealed with the fullness of its promise in the resurrection of Jesus. The resurrection is not an intervention of God from without, but the central revelation in our history of the act by which God creates, saves, and brings all to fulfillment.

Evolutionary Christology

Christ is undeserved, unpredicted, but all things were directed towards him [handwritten annotation]

A second contribution to a theology that sees the resurrection as a divine act from within creation that gives creation its meaning comes from evolutionary Christology, which I discussed briefly in chapter 3. This kind of evolutionary Christology does not see the Christ-event as simply the outcome of nature or history. On the contrary, it sees God with us in Christ as an unpredictable, undeserved, and gratuitous divine act of self-bestowing love. But in the light of this free act of divine self-bestowal, it looks back at the whole history of the universe and sees it and every entity in it as created and sustained by the God who gives God's self to us in Christ. It sees the whole universe as directed to Christ: "through whom are all things, and through whom we exist" (1 Cor 8:6); "for in him all things in heaven and earth were created" (Col 1:16).

All of creation is united in its one origin in God, in its self-realization as one united world, and in its one future in God. Within this unity, there are transitions to the new in the history of the universe, particularly when matter becomes life and when life becomes self-conscious. It is God's creative presence in the Spirit that enables the active self-transcendence of creation. The material universe transcends itself in the emergence of life, and life transcends itself in the human. In human beings, the universe becomes open to self-consciousness and freedom and to a personal relationship with God in grace. In this history of self-transcendence, Jesus, a product of evolutionary history, can be understood as the radical self-transcendence of the created universe into God.[2] In Jesus, a part of creation is completely and uniquely open to the divine self-bestowal. And in Jesus, God gives God's self radically to creation in the Word made flesh.

Jesus' life of self-giving love culminates in his death as a radical act of love for God and for others. In Jesus' act of self-giving in death, he falls into the arms of God and is raised up and transformed in the life-giving Spirit. Jesus, in all his bodily creatureliness, is taken eternally to God's self. The life, death, and resurrection of Christ are always to be seen together. In this paschal event, part of evolutionary history gives itself completely into God and is taken up and transformed in God, as the beginning of the reconciliation and transformation of all things (Col 1:20).

The resurrection is the culminating moment of the self-transcendence of creation to God and the irreversible self-bestowal of God to creation. It is not an intervention from without, but the manifestation of the free divine self-bestowal to the world that has been immanent in creation from the very beginning. The God of resurrection is the God of creation and of grace. The God of resurrection is the God who is present, in the life-giving Spirit, in the events of the big bang, in the stars that lit up the early universe, in the first bacterial life on Earth, in the lives of the first human beings, in the history of Israel, and in the life and death of Jesus.

Sacrament of Salvation

A third theological idea that can support the idea that resurrection is an act of God that occurs from within creation and gives creation its meaning is that of the Christ-event as the sacramental cause of our salvation. The Christian tradition has always claimed that Jesus died and was raised up "for us." Rahner asks how this is to be understood. In what sense is the paschal event the cause of our salvation? He is convinced that a fundamental requirement for a contemporary theology of salvation would be that it shows clearly that God is the cause of salvation. What is to be avoided is any suggestion that the cross changes God from being a God of wrath to a God of grace. Christ's death and resurrection do not cause God to begin to love us sinners. They are the expression and consequence of God's divine love. They give expression to God's eternal will to save.

Rahner suggests a theology of salvation in which the Christ-event is the sacrament of the salvation of the world.[3] The life, death, and resurrection taken together can be seen as the sacramental sign or real symbol in which God's saving will reaches its full and irrevocable realization and

[handwritten margin note: R does not change God's attitude towards us]

manifestation in the world. Rahner's concept of this sacramental causality is a strong one. It involves not only the revelation of salvation but also its accomplishment. Jesus' life finds its climax in the surrender to God in his death and in God's acceptance of this in the resurrection. This is both the visible symbolic expression of God's saving will in our history and its radical accomplishment.

Jesus, who is one of us, who has given himself in death to God, is raised up by God. This is the irreversible manifestation of God's saving love. In the Christ-event, God's salvific will is made present in the world "historically, really and irrevocably."[4] But God's saving grace was at work in the world long before the time of Jesus. By grace, God has been present in self-offering love from the very beginning. The universal experience of the Spirit in grace is always ordered to the Word made flesh, to Jesus' life, death, and resurrection. The grace of the Spirit is always the grace of Christ. In this sense, Christ is the final cause of the Spirit, and the Spirit is always the Spirit of Jesus Christ.[5]

In this theological framework, the resurrection is not an event that comes from outside, but the expression in history of God's will to save, which has been operative in creation from the beginning and will find its fulfillment in the transformation of the whole creation. Of course, from the more narrow perspective of empirical science, the resurrection can appear as something that comes from beyond the natural world. But from a theological perspective, it is an unpredictable and free act of God that comes from the God who has bestowed God's self upon creation from the very beginning. The resurrection is both the ultimate expression of the promise of God and the beginning of the fulfillment of the promise. It is the real symbol, the expression and the reality, of God's saving, self-bestowing love at work in the world. It is the bringing to visibility and to an initial accomplishment of the self-bestowing love that has always been present to every aspect of the universe and its creatures.

Resurrection as Ontological Transformation

I have been proposing that the resurrection can be seen as a completely free act of God that, through God's eternal choice, comes from within creation as its deepest meaning. It is not separate from the act of self-bestowal in creation. It is the culmination of the one divine act of self-bestowal that finds its ultimate expression in Christ. It is also the culmination in our history of the self-transcendence of creation into God. It is the sacrament of the salvation of the whole world.

With this in mind, I turn now to the fundamental issue of the objectivity of the resurrection. It is all too easy to maintain a noninterventionist theology of resurrection in a reductivist model, where the resurrection is understood simply in terms of the subjective experience of the disciples. But such a reductivist theology not only fails to represent the Christian tradition adequately, it also fails to provide a basis for the eschatological transformation of creation. It has little to offer suffering creation.

In the next chapter, I will take up Athanasius's theology of redemption through incarnation. In this theology, something ontological happens through Christ's life, death, and resurrection: "For he became human that we might become divine." God takes flesh, and flesh is adopted and deified.[6] Rahner takes up this theology of deification and applies it to the whole creation. He asks why the theology of the resurrection, when compared with its New Testament origins, has suffered such an "astonishing process of shrinkage" in the theology of the West.[7] He thinks that a central reason for this shrinkage was the adoption by the West of a purely juridical notion of redemption: Jesus, because of his full divinity and full humanity, is able to make proper satisfaction for human sin. In this kind of theology, the focus is on the cross but not on the resurrection.

In the East, by contrast, the resurrection has played a central role in the theology of salvation. Salvation occurs because God takes humanity and the whole creation to God's self in the incarnation. The incarnation culminates in the death and resurrection of Christ, and these events promise final fulfillment. The resurrection transforms humanity and creation from within. This theology of resurrection is concerned with ontological change rather than with legal relation. Because God embraces creaturely life in the incarnation, and above all in its culmination in resurrection, creaturely life is changed forever. Human beings and in some way the whole of creation are taken up into God. The resurrection of Christ is the beginning of this adoption and divinizing transformation of all things.

In this ontological model of the redemption, God takes creaturely reality as God's own in the incarnation, and this culminates in the resurrection of the crucified.[8] In the life and death of Jesus, a piece of this world, part of creaturely reality, is handed over fully in freedom into God in complete obedience and love, and in the resurrection this creaturely reality is fully taken up into God. In the creaturely humanity of the risen Jesus, God irrevocably adopts creaturely reality as God's own reality, divinizing and transfiguring the creature. What occurs in Jesus, as part of the physical, biological, and human world, is *ontologically* and not simply juridically the "beginning of the glorification and divinization of the whole of reality."[9] Because of the unity of the one world that springs from the Creator, this is an event for the whole creation. It is "the beginning of the transformation of the world as an ontologically interconnected occurrence."[10]

In raising the crucified, God divinizes and transfigures the creaturely humanity of Jesus, and this is an event for the whole of creation. The resurrection of Jesus is an objective change in the world of creatures: it is "the beginning of the transformation of the world as an ontologically interconnected occurrence."[11] In this event, Rahner insists, the final destiny of the universe is decided. All things, the whole evolving world of creaturely reality, will be transfigured in Christ. This transfiguration is not only promised in Christ's resurrection, but already begun: the risen Christ is the "pledge and beginning of the perfect fulfillment of the world." Jesus, risen from the dead, is the "representative of the new cosmos." As the risen one, Christ has a new relationship to the whole creation. He is freed from "the limiting individuality of the unglorified body" and is able to be present to creation precisely as the risen one and as the power of resurrection life.[12] The Parousia of Jesus, his final glorious return, will be the disclosure of this new relation to creation that is attained by his resurrection.

The created humanity of Jesus, taken up into God in the resurrection, is forever that which unites the created universe and God. Jesus is always and everywhere the way to God: "This created human nature is the indispensable and permanent gateway through which everything created must pass if it is to find the perfection of its eternal validity before God." Jesus is always "the gate and the door, the Alpha and the Omega."[13] In this theological vision, the created humanity of Jesus has eternal significance not only for the eternal life of human beings in God, but also for the final transformation of the whole of creation.

The resurrection of Christ is understood not only as a unique and radical transformation of the crucified one, but also as the beginning of the transformation of all things in God. It is not the revival of a corpse to live again in the old way but the "eschatological victory of God's grace in the world."[14] Rahner insists that our future participation in resurrection life will be a completely unforeseeable and unimaginable transfiguration of our spiritual, bodily, social selves. He sees continuing identity in resurrection life as provided not by the molecules that make up our bodies before death, which in this life are always subject to metabolic processes, but by the free, spiritual subject that can be called the soul. This means that finding a corpse in a grave could not be taken as evidence that there is no resurrection.[15]

Christ in his risen, bodily reality is the hidden presence that gives meaning and direction to the universe. The transfiguration of the world has begun in the risen Christ and is "ripening and developing" to the point where it will become manifest in the final fulfillment of all things.[16] Clearly, this is not a theology with a purely psychological or interior understanding of the resurrection and its effects. It has no interest in a reductivist view of the resurrection. It makes the very large claim that the resurrection is the central event in the history of the universe, that it is the irreversible expression of God's saving love in our world, and that it has already begun transforming the whole of creation from within. But as I have been attempting to show, this large claim is made about a divine action that springs from the God who is always at work from within creation, rather than being seen as some kind of intervention from without. It is seen as the radical transformation, unpredictable fulfillment, and the real meaning and goal of God's work of creation, rather than as the kind of miracle that overturns the natural world and its laws.

Resurrection Expressed in Creation through Secondary Causes

brings in the issue of suffering?

The proposal being advanced here is that a response to the issue of suffering built into creation requires a theology of divine action that is both eschatological and noninterventionist. I have discussed three lines of thought that support a noninterventionist theology of resurrection as an unpredictable act of God that springs from within creation and that gives creation its meaning: the resurrection as the center of God's *one* differentiated act of self-bestowal, evolutionary Christology, and resurrection as the sacrament of God's universal saving love. Then I have argued for an objective and powerful theology of resurrection as an ontological event, the beginning of the divinizing transformation of all things. Taken together, these arguments begin to make plausible the claim that the resurrection can be seen as an objective, transformative, but noninterventionist act of God.

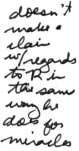

To take this proposal a little further, it will be necessary to consider whether the resurrection is interventionist in the sense of bypassing, overturning, or changing the laws of nature. Does the resurrection involve God as primary cause acting without the mediation of secondary causes? Or is the resurrection the great act of God in our history that takes effect in the created order through created causes? Any response to this question needs to be tentative. My own response will be not only tentative but partial, considering only what I take to be the three fundamental ways in which the resurrection affects creation: in the experience of the Christian community today, in the appearances to the first disciples, and in the eschatological transformation of all things. I will argue that in each of these cases, it is possible to think of the divine act of resurrection as being communicated to, and affecting, creatures through secondary causes.

What I will not address directly is the great act by which God raises up and transforms Christ crucified. This is not something to which we have direct access. Although it is often pictured in Christian art, it is not described in the New Testament. This transcendent act of God is hidden from our sight, and we know it only through its effects on the Christian community. What we do have are the proclamations of the resurrection, the stories of the appearances of the risen Christ, and the empty-tomb stories. I will not discuss the empty tomb but will limit my discussion to the three effects of resurrection mentioned in the previous paragraph. I will propose that these effects can be understood as God acting through secondary causes.

Experience of the Risen Christ in the Christian Community Today

The essence of the church is to be the visible sign and agent of the resurrection at work in the world. Of course, the Christian community is often a poor witness. But its mission is to be the visibility of the resurrection, the vital sacrament in the world of the risen one. This is true above all of the church gathered for Eucharist. In every Eucharist, the Spirit is invoked over the gifts of creation, bread and wine, and over the gathered community that they be made into Christ. To participate in the Word and Eucharist in the Christian assembly is not only to be caught up in the memorial of Jesus' life, death, and resurrection, but also to encounter the risen Christ in the present.

This encounter is at the center of Easter faith. In his exploration of the structure of resurrection belief, Peter Carnely points out that Christians who base their lives on the gospel and commit themselves to belief in the resurrection do so not only because they see it as reasonable, and not only because they put their trust in the first witnesses to the risen Christ. They also commit themselves on the basis of experiences of the Spirit now.[17] In the light of what is proclaimed in the Christian community, they can recognize the Spirit they encounter as the Spirit of Jesus. Carnely sees this experience of the Spirit as a kind of "empirical" basis for Easter faith. The Easter proclamation of the church sheds light on the contemporary experience of the Spirit. The Easter stories of the church and the experience of the Spirit illuminate each other.

Christians of today encounter the risen Christ not only in the Word of God proclaimed in the Christian community, and not only through participation in the Eucharist, but also in words, persons, and events in the world. In the light of the Word of God, they meet the risen one in the experience of grace that occurs in the midst of life. The eucharistic experience of Christ is interlinked with the mysticism of everyday life. One who encounters Christ in the Eucharist can recognize the presence of this same Christ in experiences of the natural world, in the encounter with the human other, and in solitude. Eucharistic experience is meant to awaken, deepen, and bring to full expression the experience of the risen Christ in daily life.[18]

is the eucharist brought about by 2ndary causes?

When we experience Christ in hearing the Word proclaimed or in our participation in the Eucharist, human words and actions have become mediations of grace to us. Christ is present to us in and through the secondary causes that make up the eucharistic event. It is a mediated, sacramental experience of the risen Christ. The same is true when something in daily life, whether it be a moment of shared humanity, of terrible grief, or of wonder, opens out into an experience of grace. Experiences of grace are mediated by sacraments and by sacramental encounters with persons, events, and the world of nature. When we reflect on them or speak about them, we can express them only in words and images that come from everyday life. Experiences of the risen Christ, both those that occur through word and sacrament in the assembly of the church and those that occur in the mysticism of daily life, arise in encounters with fellow creatures in the world. They occur only through secondary causes and always have a sacramental structure.

but if the priest brings about the consecration & therefore the eucharist, doesn't he stand in persona christi?

The Easter Appearances

Clearly, the Easter appearances of Jesus to the first disciples had a distinctive character. Many of the disciples who encountered Jesus beyond death had walked with him in Galilee and accompanied him to Jerusalem. Their experience was distinct because they had known him in life and death and now knew him as the risen one. It was distinct from later Christian experience in a second way, in that the appearances, along with the outpouring of the Holy Spirit, had a church-founding character. For these reasons, the witness of the first disciples is irreplaceable. All later Christian life depends upon their experience and their testimony. But were these experiences of the risen Christ miraculous interventions in the sense that they broke the laws of nature? Or did they take place in and through the laws of nature, and thus in and through secondary causes? It is important in this context to remember the point made in the previous chapter, that the expression *laws of nature* refers not only to our existing scientific theories and laws, but also to those aspects of the natural world that are not yet well mapped by our scientific theories and laws.

Historically, it seems clear that there is no evidence that can tell us exactly what kind of experience was involved in the appearances of the risen Christ to the first disciples. The Gospels certainly indicate both continuity and radical transformation between the experience of Jesus in his lifetime and the encounters with the risen Christ, but they do not determine for us the nature of the appearances. Theologically, however, there is reason to think the appearances were not the same as everyday experience of other persons in our lives or the experience the disciples had of Jesus during his own lifetime. As Rahner insists, the experience of the risen Christ is not to be thought of as one among other encounters, but as an experience that is sui generis:

> Such a resurrection, into a human existence finalized and bringing history to fulfillment, is essentially an object of knowledge of an absolutely unique kind. It is essentially other than the return of a dead man to his previous biological life, to space and time which form the dimensions of history unfulfilled. Hence it is not in any way an ordinary object of experience, which could be subsumed under the common condition and possibilities of experience.[19]

Rahner suggests that the best analogy for understanding the appearances may be the experience Christians of today have of Christ in the Spirit, rather than the model of imaginative visions or that of everyday sense experience.[20] Rahner gave over many of his essays to articulating the nature of the experience of God, as transcendental experiences that occur in and through the experience of creaturely realities in the world. I have discussed this in chapter 4 and in detail elsewhere, and here simply note that this experience is an experience of grace in which God really does act, but which we experience in a truly human and creaturely way.[21]

What I am suggesting, then, is that the resurrection appearances may have the structure of an experience of grace that occurs in and through the experience of created realities, where the disciples recognize the one they encounter as the same Jesus who had walked with them in Galilee but who is now radically transformed as the power of new creation. The encounters with the risen Christ may have been mediated by the assembly of disciples, the Word of God, the breaking of the bread, the natural world, the love of another human being, or the experience of prayer. What matters is that they were experienced as unique revelations of the crucified Jesus, risen from the dead as the power of new life from God. It is possible, then, to understand these experiences as occurring in a nonintervention-ist way by means of secondary causality. At the same time, they can be understood as church-founding encounters with Jesus, in which the risen one reveals himself as alive beyond death with the fullness of bodily life, transformed in God and embodying resurrection life.

The Eschatological Transformation of Creation

The third issue to be addressed at this stage concerns the ontological change that the resurrection promises and initiates. If the resurrection is the beginning of the transformation of the whole creation in Christ, how does this involve the laws of nature? Are existing laws of nature over-turned, or do new laws of nature appear? Again, it is helpful to note that "laws of nature" include not only what science has already mapped, but also aspects of the natural world that are not yet well understood. We need not see God's act of resurrection as overturning natural laws or as introducing new ones, since God has been creatively involved with every aspect of the universe from the beginning, precisely as the one who would raise Jesus from the dead and bring all creation to its consummation.

The resurrection, and the final participation of creation in it, had always been the very meaning of creation. The resurrection is that for which the processes and regularities of the natural world exist. The God of resurrection is the God of creation. God is present in the Spirit to every creature in the long history of the universe as the God of self-bestowing resurrection love. God creates a universe that is capable of being trans-formed from within. As Robert John Russell says, God creates a universe that is transformable by resurrection:

> Our starting point, based on the bodily resurrection of Jesus, is that the New Creation is not a replacement of the old creation, or a second and separate creation *ex nihilo*. Instead, God will transform God's creation, the universe, into the New Creation *ex vetere*, to use Polkinghorne's phrase. It follows that God must have created the universe *such that it is transformable*, that is, that it can be transformed by God's action. In particular, God must have created it precisely with those conditions and characteristics which it needs as preconditions in order to be transformable by God's new act. Moreover, if it is to be transformed

and not replaced, God must have created it with precisely those conditions and characteristics which will be part of the New Creation.[22]

Because God creates a universe capable of being transformed in new creation, there is no need to understand this transformation as an intervention that overturns or bypasses natural laws. And I do not think it needs to be seen as introducing new laws of nature. Rather, it can be seen as the instantiation of potentialities that God had placed in the natural world from the beginning, potentialities that have always been directed toward resurrection and new creation.

In this chapter, I have several times pointed back to the previous chapter, where I took up William Stoeger's distinction between two meanings of "the laws of nature": on the one hand, the phrase refers to the laws contained in our scientific theories, which are only a partial description of reality; on the other, it can refer to something far wider—the relationships, processes, and causal connections of the natural world itself, much of which escapes our scientific theories. All of the relationships found in this second, wider meaning of the laws of nature are secondary causes. This makes it possible to think that the final eschatological transformation of creation, begun in the resurrection, may occur through secondary causes that exist in the natural world but are not mapped, or not mapped well, by our scientific theories.

The impact of the resurrection on the universe may be through a new, and to us unforeseeable, instantiation of potentialities of nature that are already built into God's creation from the beginning. This view fits well with Rahner's idea that the eschatological consummation of the universe will take place as the act of God, but as an eschatological act of God that works in and through the self-transcendence of creation itself. This will be the final culmination of God's one act of self-bestowal that involves creation, the Christ-event, and the final fulfillment of all things. The God who is at work in every aspect of creation, enabling it to exist and to act, is the God who is the absolute future of the whole creation. In God's eschatological act, God will embrace the whole of creation in self-bestowing love, bringing every part of it to its proper fulfillment. But as Rahner insists, this self-bestowing love is already at work as "the most immanent element in every creature."[23]

The Divine Act of Resurrection   105

I have argued for a theology of resurrection that makes strong objective claims about Christ's resurrection and its liberating eschatological consequences. At the same time, I have proposed that the resurrection can be understood in noninterventionist terms as the central expression in our history of God's one act that embraces creation and redemption, an act that consistently finds expression through secondary causes. The physicist Paul Davies is a learned and helpful contributor to discussions between science and theology. Many years ago, I heard someone ask him, "What do you think about Christianity?" His response was to say that Christianity is based on the miracle of the resurrection, and as a scientist, he did not hold for exceptions to the laws of nature. My own theological response, framed inwardly at the time and made more explicit here, is that the resurrection is not best thought of as simply a miracle that overturns the laws of nature. It is far, far more than this. It is the event that gives meaning and direction to the whole universe and to all of its laws. It does not come from without but from within, from the presence of the creative, saving God who enables creation not only to emerge and unfold, but also to come to its final fulfillment.

7

God's Redeeming Act: Deifying Transformation

In the second chapter of this book, I discussed the life, death, and resurrection of Jesus as fundamental to a Christian view of divine action. Now I will return to the Christ-event to focus directly on the divine act of redemption. My proposal is to build upon Athanasius's incarnational theology in a contemporary theology that I will call "deifying transformation." In the next chapter, I will explore how this theology of redemption can be understood in relation to evolution, the scapegoat mechanism, and the Christian doctrine of original sin.

While biblical words like *redemption* and *salvation* can be used to bring out distinct aspects of the Christ-event, I will use them interchangeably to refer to *all* that God does for us in Christ. In this usage, while forgiveness of human sin is a central dimension of human redemption, it is not all of redemption. Redemption involves not only human beings but the whole creation (Rom 8:23). It involves not only forgiveness, but also healing, reconciliation, liberation from death, participation in resurrection life, new creation, transformation in Christ, and communion in the life of the Trinity.

It is important to acknowledge that for many people today, the theology of redemption is something of a scandal. On the basis, perhaps, of half-remembered sermons or a general impression of what Christians believe, they associate redemption with a vengeful and violent god who demands appeasement. In this context, it is not surprising that theologians have found the need to rethink the theology of redemption, and it seems that we are at the beginning of a much-needed renewal in this most fundamental area of Christian theology.[1]

The New Testament uses a wide variety of images for what God does for us in Christ. Pauline scholar Joseph Fitzmyer points out that Paul uses ten different images drawn from biblical tradition and from Jewish and Hellenistic life: justification, salvation, reconciliation, expiation, redemption, freedom, sanctification, transformation, new creation, and glorification.[2] Each of these is taken from a specific context and has its own resonances. The variety is necessary because no one image or concept is sufficient to express the overwhelming action of God in Jesus. In a recent book, Peter Schmiechen points to a helpful distinction between images and theories of redemption.[3] Images can exist alongside each other, with each providing a partial insight into the Christ-event, without necessarily forming a coherent whole. A theory, by contrast, attempts to provide a coherent account of Jesus' life, death, and resurrection that carries meaning for the Christian community and for the world. Theories are often based upon one particular image or concept, such as in a theory of sacrifice or of atonement.

Twenty-first-century Christians are in need of a theory of redemption that can offer a viable alternative to traditional theories such as those that have been built around sacrifice, satisfaction, and substitutionary atonement. It is important to acknowledge that these theories have carried genuine meaning for Christians in other eras. And, of course, to propose an alternative to a *theory* built around an image like sacrifice does not mean rejecting the biblical *image* of sacrifice. The image can still have meaning within an alternative theory. A first critical test of any such theory is what it communicates of God: Is it faithful to the God proclaimed in Jesus' words and deeds, the God of boundless compassion and self-giving love? Or does it misrepresent the God of Jesus as the source of terrible violence, as needing to be appeased, or as demanding punishment for sin in blood?

A second critical test, in our ecological age, is to ask whether the theory is large enough to embrace all of creation. An ecological theology of redemption would take seriously and build upon the range of New Testament texts that speak of the creation and reconciliation of all things in Christ (John 1:1-14; 1 Cor 8:6; Rom 8:18-25; Eph 1:9-10, 20-23; Col 1:15-20; Heb 1:2-3; 2 Pet 3:13; Rev 5:13-14; 21:1-5; 22:13). A theology of redemption that can respond to the suffering of creation will need to embrace animals and the whole biological world.

A theology of redemption for today will be one that that communicates the meaning of the Christ-event in a way that is faithful to the central Christian tradition and is coherent and life-giving for believers in the twenty-first century. It will refuse to locate violence in God but will reveal redemption as the act of the God proclaimed in the words and deeds of Jesus. It will include the biological world as well as the world of matter. I will work toward such a theology in two steps. First, I will discuss a classical theology of redemption and deification through incarnation, in a rereading of Athanasius. Then I will build on this in a sketch of a theology of redemption for today, understood as deifying transformation.

Redemption and Deification through Incarnation: Athanasius

As bishop of the great city of Alexandria, Athanasius (c. 296–373) lived a life dominated by commitment to what he saw as the integrity of Christian faith, in the midst of the tumultuous politics of the empire, the ugly schism in his local church with a group called the Melitians, and his fierce controversy with the Arians. Of his forty-six years as bishop, he spent seventeen years in exile. Because of his engagement in the conflict with Arian thought, he was constantly defending Nicaea's teaching that it is truly God who embraces creation in the Word made flesh. I will highlight three aspects of Athanasius's incarnational theology: the God–creation relationship, Christ's death and resurrection, and deification.

The God–Creation Relationship

For Athanasius, the created world has a goodness, beauty, and harmony that come from the continual presence and creative action of divine Wisdom. Athanasius uses Wisdom and Image as alternative ways of speaking of the eternal Word, or Son of God. The universe of creatures does not have, in itself, a reason for its own existence. It exists only because divine Wisdom enables it to exist. Alvyn Pettersen, a recent commentator on Athanasius, says that Athanasius sees the created world as "both very fragile and most wonderful."[4] Athanasius's approach to creation is sacramental, because he sees it as bearing the imprint of God's own Wisdom.[5]

Athanasius thinks divine Wisdom is revealed to us in several ways: Wisdom comes to us in creation, in the depths of the human soul, in the biblical word, and above all, in the bodily humanity of Jesus. In the following text, for example, we find Athanasius expressing three of these manifestations of Wisdom: those in the created universe, our experience as human beings, and the flesh of Jesus. He writes: "[God] has placed in each and every creature and in the totality of creation a certain imprint (*typon*) and reflection of the Image of Wisdom. . . . We become recipients of the Creator-Wisdom, and through her we are enabled to know her Father. . . . [God] has made the true Wisdom herself take flesh and become a mortal human being and endure the death of the cross, so that henceforth all those that put their faith in him may be saved."[6]

Because God desires to make God's self known in an unambiguous way, Wisdom is revealed not only in the diversity of creation, including our human depths, but also in an unparalleled way in the flesh of Jesus. There is always an inner link between creation and incarnation in Athanasius's theology. The same Wisdom/Word of God is involved in both. Pettersen writes, "Athanasius's stress upon Christ as the Wisdom of God and upon creatures as witnessing to the Agent of their creation encourages one to see a strong continuity and not discontinuity between God's work as Creator and Redeemer. . . . It invokes in one the memory that salvation is to include this world."[7] All things are created in the Word of God, and the redeeming work of this same Word involves the whole creation.

Athanasius's view of the relationship between God and creation finds expression in his double foundational theological work, *Against the Greeks–On the Incarnation*. He points to a God who is "beyond all being" and beyond all human conception. God is the generous source of all created being.[8] Creatures, in contrast, exist ex nihilo, not only in terms of their origin, but at every moment of their existence. They derive from nonbeing and tend toward disintegration and nothingness. The universe of creatures exists only because, in the divine generosity, God continually enables creatures to exist by the Word:

So seeing that all created nature according to its own definition is in a state of flux and dissolution, therefore to prevent this happening and the universe dissolving back into nothing, after making everything by his eternal Word and bringing creation into existence, he did not abandon it to be carried away and to suffer through its own nature, lest it run the risk of returning to nothing. But being good, he governs and establishes the whole world through his Word who is himself God, in order that creation, illuminated by the leadership, providence, and ordering of the Word, may be able to remain firm, since it shares in the Word who is truly from the Father and is aided by him to exist, and lest it suffered what would happen, I mean a relapse into non-existence, if it were not protected by the Word.[9]

Clearly, the Word is the agent not only of *original* creation, but of what today would be called *continuous* creation. While Athanasius sees every creature in the universe as held in being by the Word of God, his more direct focus is on the human creature. The God who is good and generous and who "envies nothing its existence" and "makes everything through his Word, our Lord Jesus Christ," then does something even more wonderful for human beings:

And among these creatures, of all those on earth he has special pity for the human race, and seeing that by the definition of its own existence it would be unable to persist forever, he gave it an added grace, not simply creating humans like all irrational animals on the Earth, but making them in his own image and giving them also a share in the power of his own Word, so that having as it were shadows of the Word and being made rational, they might be able to remain in felicity and live the true life in paradise, which is truly that of the saints.[10]

In creating human beings, God gives them a special grace, a participation in the image of the Word, so that unlike other creatures, they will not die but live in God. They share in the eternal life of the Word. Human beings are creatures of both nature and grace. By nature we are mortal, but grace constitutes us in the image of the Word and gives us eternal life.[11] But sin has damaged the image of God in us and made us subject to death. Eternal life is lost because human beings have sinned and are fallen from original grace. Sin is a destructive inversion of the proper

kenosis: self-emptying

human structure of being. Instead of being ordered to God, humans from their origin have become turned in on self and on creatures that become idols.

While Athanasius sees the human as constituted in a structure of ascent to life before God, he sees sin as a descent, a fall. He thinks of God's redeeming action toward us in Christ as a gracious kenotic descent. Khaled Anatolios points out that the incarnation that culminates in Christ's death and resurrection is a divine descent that "accompanies, supplants, and reverses human fallenness, even while reasserting the divine glory that was manifest in the act of creation."[12] Sin destroys the structure of creation, and God responds with a new creation. Athanasius insists that both creation and new creation are the work of the same eternal Word: "We must first speak about the creation of the universe and its creator, God, so that in this way one may consider as fitting that its renewal was effected by the Word who created it at the beginning. For it will appear in no way contradictory if the Father worked its salvation through the same one by whom he created it."[13]

There is a structural interrelationship between Athanasius's view of the God–creation relationship and his theology of incarnation. The whole of Athanasius's theology is essentially a vision of salvation in Christ and, structurally, this vision is based upon his conception of the relationship between God and creation. This is because at the center of Athanasius's debate with Arians is the question of whether the Word is part of creation or truly divine. Does the eternal Word belong to the world of creatures or to God? While the Arians appeared to locate the Word on the side of creation, Athanasius defends the divinity of the Word and locates the Word in God. The whole discussion is about the place of the Word in the God–world relationship. For Athanasius, the Word belongs with God and, precisely because of this, can really become incarnate in the world and thus transform the world in God. God and creation meet in Christ the Word. The saving act of incarnation is precisely about the union of God and the created universe in Jesus Christ.

As Anatolios puts it, the relation between God and creation is the *architectonic center* of Athanasius's theological vision.[14] The whole structure of his thought is built upon this relationship. This understanding of God and creation is directly christological. And his Christology is a

Christology of God and the whole creation: "His account of the relation between God and creation is thus ultimately a Christology conceived in the most universal terms."[15] Athanasius's understanding of redemption in Christ is cast in terms of the divine action by which God heals, liberates, and transforms creation through the incarnation of the Word.

The Central Place of Christ's Death and Resurrection

It would be quite wrong to think that Athanasius's incarnational theology is centered on the birth of the Savior. His focus is far more on the death and resurrection of Christ. For Athanasius, it is not a matter of choosing between an emphasis on incarnation and an emphasis on death and resurrection, as it is for some contemporary theologians. In his view, the incarnation of the Word involves taking on and overcoming death. The death and resurrection of Christ are what overcomes the death that holds sway as the result of human sin. In the view of Athanasius, the defeat of death and corruption is at the center of the saving work of Christ. This event of salvation occurs by the Word taking bodily humanity, the body that is damaged by sin and doomed to death, in order to renew in humanity the image of the Word and bring it to resurrection life:

> So the Word of God came in his own person, in order that, as he is the image of the Father, he might be able to restore the human who is the image. In any other way it could not have been done, without the destruction of death and corruption. So he was justified in taking a mortal body, in order that in it death could be destroyed and human beings might be again renewed in the image. For this, then, none other than the image of the Father was required.[16]

While Athanasius recognizes that we might have been saved from sin simply by a decree of God, he thinks this would have returned us to an original state from which we might easily fall again. In Christ, something radically new occurs: the divine goodness transforms our humanity from within, securing our future in God.[17] We are saved by the Word entering into bodiliness, that has been deformed by sin and become subject to death, so that death is defeated from within and we are bound securely to the life of God.

In Athanasius's view, sin confronted God with a dilemma. While God's goodness continues to want our salvation and life, God's truthfulness cannot simply ignore the original divine decree that stated that "death and corruption" would be the consequences of sin.[18] Athanasius asks, "What is God, in God's goodness, to do?"[19] On the one hand, God cannot go back on God's word, which says death and corruption are the result of sin. On the other hand, once God had made human beings partakers of the divine image, it would be unworthy of the divine goodness to leave them to corruption and death. The dilemma is resolved by the incarnation of the Word. Incorruptibility is restored through the resurrection of Christ.

For Athanasius, it is clear that sin and death need to be transformed. This transformation occurs in the incarnation, above all in the death and resurrection of Jesus. Athanasius uses sacrificial language for the death of Christ, influenced by the New Testament and also, it seems, by the Eucharist. Jesus, the Word of God, "intercedes" for us, "offering" his own body as a "sacrifice" and a "ransom" for human sin, thus liberating humanity from its descent into death.[20] In the death and resurrection of the Word made flesh, Athanasius sees humanity as attaining ultimate security and stability in communion with the living God.

The radically ontological nature of this transformation is made clear by the way Athanasius speaks of creatures being made "proper" to God or "appropriated to God" in Christ. In his Trinitarian theology, he uses the word *idios*, meaning "belonging to" or "proper to," in order to show that the Son belongs to the very being of the Father. He then uses the same kind of language to speak of the ontological transformation of humanity that occurs in Christ. Through the enfleshed Word, we are made proper to God or appropriated to God, so that we belong to God in the most radical way.[21] We are adopted into God's life and are changed at the deepest level of our being. *incarnatio changes us*

Deification in Christ

Particularly in his later writings, Athanasius uses the word *deification* to speak of this ontological transformation. The first time this word appears in a Christian sense is the well-known exchange formula in *On the Incarnation* 54: "For he became human that we might become divine."[22]

Athanasius is clearly building on Irenaeus: "He became what we are in order to make us what he is in himself."[23] Athanasius goes on to use the language of deification freely in his *Orations against the Arians*. In his fine study of deification, Norman Russell points out that in all of the thirty instances where Athanasius speaks of Christian deification, he uses only the verb *theopoieō* and the noun he coins, *theopoiēsis*.[24]

In the Christian tradition, deification never means that we become divine in the sense of possessing the divine nature. It means that, by God's grace, the Spirit of God dwells in us, and we become adopted children of God (Rom 8:14-17). Through this indwelling Spirit, we participate in divine life, so that the Scripture can speak of us as "participants of the divine nature" (2 Pet 1:4). We are taken into the life of the Trinity. This is understood as a real transformation in God, a real participation in God by grace. It is not understood as a loss of our humanity, but the fulfillment of our humanity. We are understood as creatures who are radically oriented to God and who become most truly ourselves, most fully human, in love with God.

Athanasius gives priority to an ontological rather than to an ethical notion of deification. In an ethical approach, closeness to God is thought of as occurring through living a Christian life, and deification is thought of as a process. But what Athanasius emphasizes is the radical change that occurs in reality when the Word is made flesh. The incarnation brings about a change in the very being (the ontology) of creation. He sees a profound transformation already at work in the world in the Word made flesh. Through the flesh assumed by the Logos, God communicates divine life to all flesh in principle. It is then transmitted in practice to human individuals in the life of the Spirit. Athanasius sees this as working out in Christian life through faith and the sacraments of the church.

In the once-for-all ontological transformation that occurs in the incarnation, the body of Jesus is the instrument (*organon*) for the salvation of all. The flesh of Jesus is the *organon* of salvation, although flesh (*sarx*) in Athanasius stands for the whole human nature, soul as well as body.[25] It is precisely Athanasius's emphasis on the flesh that can, I believe, find new meaning today in a theology of the redemption of all flesh in the incarnation of divine Wisdom. Athanasius opposes the Arian view that the Word of God is deified. He insists that the Word is the source of deification and is not subject to deification. He points out that even in the past, long before the birth of the Savior, the Word of God was the source of deification. It is through the eternal Word that Moses and others were long ago adopted and deified as children of God.[26]

But Athanasius does see a very important deification at work in the incarnation. It is deification not of the eternal Word but of the bodily humanity of Jesus. And it is this deification of the created flesh of Christ that is fundamental to our salvation: "The Word was not diminished in receiving a body, that he should seek to receive a grace, but rather he deified that which he put on, and moreover bestowed it freely on the human race."[27] The Word of God takes on fallen flesh, and as a result, we share in his deified flesh. The body of Christ was prepared "that in him we might be capable of being renewed and deified."[28] For Athanasius, there is solidarity in the flesh: both the body of Christ and our fleshly humanity are deified. The Logos assumes a created human body "that having renewed it as its creator, he might deify it in himself, and thus bring us all into the kingdom of heaven in his likeness."[29] Later Athanasius writes, "For if the works of the Word's divinity had not taken place through the body, humanity would not have been deified; and again, if the properties of the flesh had not been ascribed to the Word, humans would not have been delivered completely from them."[30]

Anatolios comments, "Our whole salvation and deification are rooted in our human condition's being 'ascribed' to the Word, for that is what essentially constitutes our being 'Worded.'"[31] As I have said earlier in this chapter, this deification is not about us becoming anything but fully human, in the way that is faithful to God's intention. As Thomas Weinandy puts it, "Deification is not then the changing of our human nature into something other than it is, that is, into another kind of being." Rather, "deification for Athanasius is the making of humankind into what it was meant to be from the very beginning."[32] It makes us into the image of the Word and takes us into the divine life of the Trinity, and thus enables us to be the human beings that God wants us to be. And this whole process occurs only through the action of the Holy Spirit in us.

In his *First Letter to Serapion*, Athanasius focuses his attention on the Holy Spirit. Having argued vigorously for the divinity of the Word, he now argues in a similar way for the divinity of the Spirit. Since it is by the Spirit that we become "partakers of the divine nature" (2 Pet 1:4), the Spirit who divinizes us must be divine.[33] In the context of articulating his theology of the Spirit, Athanasius speaks of creation being deified in the Spirit through the Logos. He writes of the Holy Spirit:

> In him [the Holy Spirit], then, the Logos glorifies creation, and deifying it and adopting it brings it to the Father. That which unites creation to the Logos cannot itself belong to the created order. And that which adopts creation cannot be foreign to the Son. . . . The Spirit does not belong to the created order, but is proper to the Godhead of the Father, in whom the Logos also deifies created things. And he in whom creation is deified cannot himself be outside the divinity of the Father.[34]

This text is remarkable not only because it is an early defense of the full divinity of the Holy Spirit, but also because it speaks of the creation being deified and adopted. The Holy Spirit unites creation to the Word. The adoption and deification of creation are the work of the Word and the Spirit together, and both are equally divine. It may be that, when Athanasius speaks of creation in this text, humanity is still at the forefront of his mind. But there is at the very least openness to a more universal development of thought, to the idea that in some way the whole creation is adopted and deified in Christ. This is confirmed in another text, where we find Athanasius speaking quite explicitly, with Romans 8, of creation itself being delivered from the bondage of corruption into the glorious freedom of the children of God:

> The truth that refutes them is that he is called "firstborn among many brothers" (Rom 8:29) because of the kinship of the flesh, and "firstborn from the dead" (Col 1:18) because the resurrection of the dead comes from him and after him, and "firstborn of all creation" (Col 1:15) because of the Father's love for humanity, on account of which he not only gave consistence to all things in the Word but brought it about that the creation itself, of which the apostle says that it "awaits the revelation of the children of God," will at a certain point be delivered "from the bondage of corruption into the glorious freedom of the children of God" (Rom 8:19, 21).[35]

Athanasius sees creation as destined to share with human beings in the final transformation of all things. Creation springs from divine Trinitarian life and will find its fulfillment in God. In responding to the Arians, he asks how God can be Creator of a world of creatures if God is not first Father of the Word. If the divine essence is not fruitful but barren, if it is a light that does not bring forth light, if it is a fountain that does not flow, how can it suddenly become fruitful in the creation?[36] Thomas Weinandy points out that this is a new and very insightful question.[37] Athanasius is proposing that the dynamism of the divine life, in which the Word is eternally begotten and the Spirit eternally proceeds, is the necessary foundation for the creation of a universe of creatures. If God is a mere monad, if there is no dynamism and no distinction in God, how could such a God even conceive of creating diverse creatures?[38] The abundant fruitfulness of the divine life is the necessary prerequisite for God's free decision to create a world of creatures. The universe of creatures springs from the dynamism of divine Trinitarian life and will find its fulfillment in this divine life.

Exploring a Theology of Redemption as Deifying Transformation

There is a great difference between the issues that pressed in upon Athanasius in the fourth century and those that challenge twenty-first-century theology. While Athanasius needed to defend the divinity of the Word against his Arian opponents, a twenty-first-century theology finds itself confronted by a human-induced crisis of the community of life on earth and, among other things, the need to develop an ecological theology. There are differences in theological assumptions, particularly with regard to the cause of human death. Athanasius assumed a reading of Genesis in which human beings were originally preserved from death by the grace of God and then lost this gift by willfully turning from God in sin. Along with many others, I differ from Athanasius in seeing our biological death as part of our participation in the evolutionary community of life on earth, rather than as the result of human sin. It is important to acknowledge, however, that sin distorts our approach to life and death and inflicts death on a massive scale to human beings and to other creatures of our planet. The narrative of the fall continues to offer an account of the tendency to sin that confronts us, from our origin, in the violence of our history, in our social structures, and in the depth of our own beings, something I will take up in the next chapter.

While differences in context and in assumptions need to be taken into account, Athanasius's theology of redemptive deification can provide the basis for a theology of redemption for today that I am calling a theology of deifying transformation. I will sketch out this approach by considering three levels of transformation—that of human beings, the biological world, and the material universe—and then by focusing briefly on the participatory nature of this redemptive transformation.

The Deifying Transformation of Human Beings

Earlier in this chapter, I referred to Fitzmyer's account of the ten different images for the saving work of Christ found in Paul. One of these ten is that of transformation, and Fitzmyer notes that this image was current in the Hellenistic literature in Paul's day, and that Paul had no hesitation in borrowing it and applying it to the Christ-event.[39] The image is viable for today, in part because it can describe God's action in Christ in truly universal terms yet in a way that does not exclude but is open to other images and concepts of redemption.

In Paul's usage, transformation is often connected with the image of light. Paul sees God, through the risen Christ, as shining creative and redeeming light on human beings, which reshapes and transforms them. This is a powerful transformation by which we participate in Christ, who is the only true image of God. He writes in 2 Corinthians, "And all of us, with unveiled faces, seeing the glory of the Lord as though reflected in a mirror, are being *transformed* into the same image from one degree of glory to another; for this comes from the Lord, the Spirit" (2 Cor 3:18; emphasis added). A little later, Paul says of this transformation, "For it is the God who said, 'Let light shine out of darkness,' who has shone in our hearts to give the light of the knowledge of the glory of God in the face of Jesus Christ" (2 Cor 4:6). Fitzmyer sees this as "one of the most sublime" of Paul's descriptions of the Christ-event.[40]

In Philippians, Paul speaks of the future transformation of our lowly bodies by the risen Christ: "He will *transform* the body of our humiliation that it may be conformed to the body of his glory, by the power that enables him to make all things subject to himself" (Phil 3:21; emphasis added). The transformation, which is already at work in us in the Spirit, will bear fruit in that great and unimaginable transformation of resurrection life. In his exhortation to the Romans, Paul calls them to be transformed by the renewing of their minds in Christ: "Do not be conformed to this world, but be *transformed* by the renewing of your minds, so that you may discern what is the will of God" (Rom 12:2; emphasis added). In an aside on these texts, Fitzmyer points to the interconnection between this Pauline notion of transformation in Christ and the later patristic theology of deification: "From this image Gk patristic writers derived the later idea of *theōsis*, or *theopoiēsis*, the gradual 'divinization' of the Christian—their practical equivalent of justification."[41]

If deifying transformation is to be thought of as an adequate theology of redemption, it will need to be open to and to include the insights offered in the Pauline doctrine of justification, the idea that in Christ, we are radically forgiven, freed, and made right before God as a sheer act of grace. It will involve all that is meant by the concepts of justification and sanctification. The transforming act of God is not something we earn or accomplish, but something we receive by trusting faith. It is a transformation that radically changes our lives, so that we become the dwelling place of the Spirit:

> But you are not in the flesh; you are in the Spirit, since the Spirit of God dwells in you. Anyone who does not have the Spirit of Christ does not belong to him. But if Christ is in you, though the body is dead because of sin, the Spirit is life because of righteousness. If the Spirit of him who raised Jesus from the dead dwells in you, he who raised Christ from the dead will give life to your mortal bodies also through his Spirit that dwells in you. (Rom 8:9-11)

In this transformation in Christ, we are justified by grace, and the Spirit dwells in us, and this Spirit is a promise of our participation in that further transformation of the whole of bodily existence in resurrection life. In Pauline theology, the experience we have now of the Spirit is the down payment and guarantee (2 Cor 1:22; 5:5; Eph 1:13-15) and the first fruits of God's harvest (Rom 8:23). In a wonderful text, Paul spells out the meaning of the transformation that God works for us even now: "For all who are led by the Spirit of God are children of God. For you did not receive a spirit of slavery to fall back into fear, but you have received a spirit of adoption. When we cry, 'Abba! Father!' it is that very Spirit bearing witness to our spirit that we are children of God, and if children, then heirs, heirs of God and joint heirs with Christ" (Rom 8:14-17).

In the transforming act of God in Christ, we are already made into God's beloved children by the Holy Spirit. Because of this Spirit, we can, with Jesus, address God in trusting family language as *Abba*. What the later church will call a Trinitarian structure to the transformation is already at work in us: in and through the Christ-event, we are transformed by the power of the Spirit and are made adopted children of God, sisters and brothers to Jesus, addressing God with him as *Abba*. We are brought into a radically new relationship to the triune God, and in this God to the rest of creation. In the language of John's Gospel, we are born again from above by the Spirit and thus already have eternal life (John 3:3-8). In the language of the Second Letter of Peter, we become "participants of the divine nature" (2 Pet 1:4).

In my view, this concept of deifying transformation is to be understood in relation to the other New Testament images and concepts for the Christ-event. It does not replace them but sees them from the perspective of a radically transforming act of God in Christ. This act of God involves many dimensions, including the forgiveness of sin, being made right before God by the free gift of God's grace, the indwelling of the Holy Spirit, the call to discipleship that involves living in the new way of the kingdom of God, practical commitment to the liberation of the poor and to the good of the community of life on earth, communion in the life of the Trinitarian God, and the beginning and promise of resurrection life.

The Deifying Transformation of the Material Universe

The Bible begins with a celebration of God's creation of the universe and its creatures and finding them all to be good. It then unfolds the great drama of sin and redemption. It concludes in Revelation with wonderful images of a creation that is transformed and renewed by the act of God. The biblical account is not one of God saving human beings by taking them out of this world, but of God bringing healing and new creation to them in the context of a healed and renewed creation. I have already referred to the series of texts that tell of the transformation of "all things" in the universe by the Christ-event (John 1:1-14; Rom 8:18-25; 1 Cor 8:6; Eph 1:9-10, 20-23; Col 1:15-20; Heb 1:2-3; 2 Peter 3:13; Rev 5:13-14; 21:1-5; 22:13). Tom Wright sums up the early Christian view of this transformation when he says, "They believed that God was going to do for the whole cosmos what he had done for Jesus at Easter."[42]

Athanasius sees the incarnation as an event that has a radically transforming effect in the whole creation. His idea of redemptive incarnation is a theory of redemption cast in the most universal terms—those of creation and God. It is not limited to a focus on human sin, although it certainly embraces liberation from sin. It unites creation and incarnation in a theology of Wisdom/Word: it is through the Wisdom of God that living creatures flourish on earth in all their diverse forms, from bacteria to whales and human beings. It is this same divine Wisdom who becomes flesh, with a limited, specific body and the particular face of Jesus, embracing bodily existence and death in love, in an act that is radically forgiving, and that transforms death into life, bringing salvation to human beings and to creation itself. The relationship between God and creation is the *architectonic center* of this theology of salvation in Christ.

The theology of the Eastern Christian church keeps alive this idea that we are redeemed and deified with the rest of creation, even when creation is not the center of theological attention. Orthodox theologian Vladimir Lossky, for example, says, "Divine love always pursues the same end: the deification of men, and by them, of the whole universe."[43] Dumitru Staniloae sees the material universe, like humankind, as "destined for transfiguration, through the power of the risen body of Christ."[44] Paul Evdokimov writes that the second coming of Christ, the Parousia, "coincides with the transformation of nature and it will be visible not within history but beyond it."[45] Boris Bobrinskoy speaks of the importance of "a deification that is both personal and cosmic."[46] Hope for the universe is not foreign to the Western tradition and is enshrined in the teaching of the Second Vatican Council and in the *Catechism of the Catholic Church.*[47] The council affirms the final consummation and transformation of the universe and points out how little we know of them: "We do not know the moment of the consummation of the earth and of humanity, nor the way the universe will be transformed."[48]

In the previous chapter, I noted how Karl Rahner insists on the fundamental Christian insight that the resurrection is not only the promise but also the beginning of the divine act by which the whole universe is transformed and deified. Even though the resurrection of Christ is only the beginning of this universal deification, it is also final in the sense that it expresses God's unchangeable commitment to bring the whole creation to its fulfillment. So Rahner says that what has occurred in Jesus, as part of the physical, biological, and human world, is ontologically "the embryonically final beginning of the glorification and divinization of the whole of reality."[49] The resurrection of the crucified Jesus is the beginning of the deification of the world itself. It is "the beginning of the transformation of the world as an ontologically interconnected occurrence."[50] In this event, the final destiny of the universe is decided. All things, the evolving world of creaturely reality, will be transfigured in Christ. God's self-giving to creation in the incarnation reaches its culmination in the resurrection, and this is the beginning of a transformation of the whole world of matter. In this final transfiguration, it will become evident that the risen Christ has already been at work in the material universe and now brings it to its completion in God.

Neil Darragh points out that the flesh embraced by God involves matter and physical processes: "To say that God became flesh is not only to say that God became human, but to say also that God became an Earth creature, that God became a sentient being, that God became a living being (in common with all other living beings), that God became a complex Earth unit of minerals and fluids, that God became an item in the carbon and nitrogen cycles."[51] In Jesus of Nazareth, God becomes a vital part of all the interconnected systems and physical processes of our planet, part of the evolutionary history of life on Earth, part of the story of the expanding and evolving universe. God embraces all this in order to bring it to its completion. In the eyes of Christians, something radically new has happened in the universe of which we are part—something that is a promise and the beginning of a liberating and healing transformation of all things in new creation.

The Deifying Transformation of the Biological World

God enters into "flesh" in Jesus of Nazareth, that flesh might be transformed and deified. But what does this mean for animals and other living creatures? While many in the Christian tradition have supported the biblical idea that "all things" are transformed in Christ, there has been comparatively little positive discussion of the way this might have its effect on animals. In this section, and more fully in the chapter that follows, I will suggest that we can see this "all things" as including every wallaby, dog, and dolphin. They are created through the eternal Wisdom of God and participate in some real way in redemption and reconciliation through Wisdom made flesh in Christ.

A foundation for this claim can be found in a number of texts mentioned already in this chapter, including Rom 8:18-25 and Col 1:15-20. In the theological approach proposed here, the solidarity of the flesh in the doctrine of the incarnation, and its culmination in resurrection, is not limited to the human community. Flesh can be understood as involving the whole 3.7-billion-year evolutionary history of life on our planet, with all its predation, death, and extinctions, as well as its diversity, cooperation, interdependence, and abundance. Flesh involves all the interconnected ecological relationships that make up life on our planet. The Christ-event is saving not only for human beings, but also in some real way for other creatures, including dogs and horses and eagles. We "wait for a new heavens and new earth, where righteousness is at home" (2 Pet 3:13) and where all God's creation finds its fulfillment.

Danish theologian Niels Gregersen argues that, in Christ, God enters into biological life in a radical or deep incarnation, and that the cross of Christ reveals God's identification with creation in all its complexity, struggle, and pain:

> In this context, the incarnation of God in Christ can be understood as a radical or "deep" incarnation, that is, an incarnation into the very tissue of biological existence, and system of nature. Understood this way, the death of Christ becomes an icon of God's redemptive co-suffering with all sentient life as well as with the victims of social competition. God bears the cost of evolution, the price involved in the hardship of natural selection.[52]

In this vision, the Word becomes flesh in solidarity with all flesh, and this includes not only humanity but also the whole of biological life. The cross of Christ represents not only God's identification with suffering humanity and God's will to bring forgiveness and healing to human beings, but also God's identification with suffering creation and God's promise of new creation that will bring healing and fulfillment to all things. The meaning of the incarnation, of becoming flesh, is not restricted to humanity, but involves all the networks of interconnected organisms, the whole of biological life. Speaking about the self-emptying love of God revealed in the life, death, and resurrection of Jesus, John Haught writes:

> An evolutionary theology, I would suggest, may picture God's descent as entering into the deepest layers of the evolutionary process, embracing and suffering along with the *entire* cosmic story, not just the recent human chapters. Through the liberating power of the Spirit, God's compassion extends across the totality of time and space, enfolding and finally healing not only human suffering, but also all the epochs of evolutionary travail that preceded, and were indispensable to, our own emergence.[53]

The whole story of the universe and of life on Earth is embraced by God's providential and redeeming love, so that "the whole of nature in some way participates in the promise of resurrection as well."[54] There are, of course, further questions to ask about this. If animals are saved in Christ, what does it mean? How does this happen? In my view, these questions need to be addressed in the context of eschatology. In chapter 9, I will attempt a partial answer to them in a discussion of God's final, eschatological act of salvation. In this chapter, I am simply attempting a sketch of a theology of redemption as deifying transformation that involves human beings, the material universe, and other living creatures. The proposal being made is that God can be understood as redemptively involved with every aspect of the evolutionary history of life on Earth, and as the faithful companion of the lives and deaths of individual creatures.

The struggle and creativity of creation and the lives of individual creatures can be seen as paschal, as being taken up in Christ. Resurrection is revealed as the meaning of the whole creation. God is understood as acting in and through the processes of the natural world, suffering with suffering creation, promising the fullness of life, and faithfully enabling creation to reach its promised fulfillment. In the Word made flesh, God embraces the whole labor of life on Earth, with all its evolutionary processes, including death, predation, and extinction, in an event that is both a radical identification in love and an unbreakable promise.

A Participatory Theology of Redemption

As the final part of this sketch of a theology of redemption as deifying transformation, it is essential to note again that while redemption is to be understood as the great liberating act of God, it is also an act in which human beings participate. There is no competition between God's action and ours. The character of divine action is such that it enables participation. In chapter 2, I agreed with Marcus Borg and others that the kingdom of God proclaimed by Jesus is a participatory kingdom. The coming kingdom is radically the act of God, but it involves our human actions. Jesus calls us to a kingdom way of being, living, and acting.

We are called to radical conversion, to following Jesus in right action in the light of the coming kingdom, in what is sometimes called the *orthopraxis* of the kingdom. Liberation theologian Gustavo Gutierrez has shown us that our attempts at authentic human and political liberation can be seen as partial anticipations of God's eschatological saving act.[55] Central to this gospel way of life is the preferential option for the poor, the hungry, the sick, the stranger, and the oppressed. Our commitments, our loves, our sufferings, are all taken up by God and have eternal meaning in God's redeeming, healing, and deifying act.

There is also a sense in which the rest of creation is called in its own way to participate in God's act of deifying transformation, insofar as God acts only in ways that respect the autonomy and proper independence of each creature and each process. God's final fulfillment will involve the kind of participation that is appropriate to the character of each creature. Divine action both in creation and redemption has the character of participation, because God works with, in, and through creaturely processes and entities, always respecting each process and each entity in its own integrity. This is a theme I will take up again in chapter 9, when considering God's eschatological act.

In this chapter, I have proposed that the ancient theology of deifying transformation can be a helpful and coherent way of understanding redemption for the twenty-first century. It offers a viable alternative to other theories of redemption, such as those of satisfaction, substitutionary atonement, and sacrifice. It has the great advantage of bringing into focus God's overwhelming and unthinkable generosity. And it proposes that God's redeeming act involves not only human beings, but also the universe itself and the whole world of biological life. In the next two chapters, I will take this theology of redemption further, first exploring how God's saving act liberates us from our tendency to scapegoat others and make them into enemies, and then taking up the final, eschatological salvation of our universe and its creatures.

8

God's Redeeming Act: Evolution, Original Sin, and the Lamb of God

In this chapter, I will explore the theology of redemption further, asking how it is related to human evolutionary history and to the Christian doctrine of original sin. Original sin has fallen out of favor with some Christians, but I am convinced that we need to retrieve it and bring it alive for the twenty-first century. It is deeply interconnected with salvation in Christ and can be fully seen only from the perspective of his life, death, and resurrection. It tells us something painfully true about our humanity that we need to know and acknowledge—something we ignore only at great peril. I will begin with a brief discussion of the human tendency to scapegoat others, and then explore what evolutionary science might suggest about the origins of this tendency. With this context in mind, I will outline a theology of original grace and original sin, and a view of redemptive transformation in Christ as the end of scapegoating and the beginning of new creation.

The Scapegoat Mechanism

violence against others is part of orig. sin

While I do not want to suggest that the human tendency to violence against others is the whole of original sin, I do want to propose that it is a central aspect of it. When we reflect on recent human history, we look back through years of extreme violence, through hundreds of local conflicts, the killings of noncombatants, the rapes, the maiming of children,

129

and the torture, to the Second World War with its unforgettable horrors, which include the firebombing of great cities and their helpless civilian populations, nuclear destruction of Hiroshima and Nagasaki, and the unthinkable violence of the Shoah. It is hard to avoid the conclusion that the human race has an endless capacity to make other people into a common enemy and to unleash violence against them.

The same pattern appears in daily life when we build intimacy with others or bond together by making someone else a victim of our gossip or our put-downs. We create a form of community by making another a scapegoat or an enemy. This mechanism is evident in the populist tactic of politicians who seek to ingratiate themselves with voters by attacking "outsiders" such as asylum seekers, or the prisoners who fill our jails. The pattern of scapegoating is at work when adults connect to each other and build relationships by talking about or ridiculing another in a way that excludes and damages that other person. It is obvious in the playground when children exclude or gang up on a vulnerable child. It is evident in all forms of bullying.

Because I am convinced that this pattern of "us and them" is deeply involved in both original sin and our salvation in Christ, I find important resources for a renewed theology of redemption in René Girard's analysis of violence in terms of the "scapegoat mechanism"[1] and in the work of theologians influenced by him, including Raymund Schwager, James Alison, and Sebastian Moore.[2] Girard sees violence as grounded in the rivalry that flows from our imitation (*mimesis*) of others. We want what we see others wanting. What we desire is largely determined by what others desire. We want as they want. In my view this in itself is not a bad but a good thing. A child's desires are largely learned from parents. Learning the desire that comes from following models is in itself good. It is a necessary part of learning to live and to love. Ultimately, it involves the desire for God.

Girard points to the way this pattern of imitation leads to conflicting desires and to the way violence can erupt from a conflict of desires. The violence is often contained when, instead of rivals killing each other, they unite against a common enemy: "Suddenly the opposition of everyone against everyone else is replaced by the opposition of all against one. Where previously there had been a chaotic ensemble of particular conflicts, there is now the simplicity of a single conflict: the entire community on one side, and on the other, the victim."[3]

It is not my intention to engage critically with Girard's extensive work in anthropology and comparative religion. I want simply to take up his ~scapegoating in light of evolution~ idea of the scapegoat mechanism as a central theme in a renewed theology of original sin and salvation and to explore this in relation to our evolutionary inheritance. Not long before his death, Raymund Schwager explored these ideas, locating the origin of the scapegoat mechanism at the beginning of human evolutionary history and seeing it in relation to the doctrine of original sin. He proposed that original sin can be understood, at least in part, in the exclusion of others and the tendency to violence that has become part of our cultural and genetic inheritance. In his view, "sin has become woven into the natural tendencies of human life" through the course of our evolutionary history.[4] I will attempt to develop the connections linking our evolutionary history, scapegoating and the doctrines of original sin and redemptive transformation in Christ.

In this chapter, I will begin by suggesting that the successful evolutionary strategy of cooperation among early humans had as its underside the construction of enemies and victims. Then I will bring this scientific insight into dialogue with the theological claim that early human beings emerged in a world of original grace, but that sin found expression in various ways, including the enduring tendency to make others into scapegoats and enemies. The result is a human condition constituted both by God's free self-offering in grace and by a tendency to sin carried not only in our culture but also in our genes. Finally, I will propose that the life, death, and resurrection of Jesus can be seen as the decisive act of God, by which we not only are confronted with what we do to victims, but also are forgiven, healed and liberated, and brought into the inclusive realm of the new creation.

Evolutionary Science on Human Emergence

The great biologist Ernst Mayr describes the evolution of the human primarily in terms of an increase in the size of the brain. The first instances of *Homo* in the fossil record occur when the brains of australopithecines grew from about 450 cubic centimeters to more than 700 cubic centimeters.

The first recorded species at this new level of brain size are *Homo rudolfensis* and *Homo erectus*. There seems to have been a sudden increase in size in *Homo rudolfensis* and then a slower growth in *Homo erectus* until the brain reached a size of about 800 to 1,000 cubic centimeters. In Neanderthals, the brain grew to about 1,600 cubic centimeters, but relative to body size it was less than that of modern humans, who have an average brain size of about 1,350 cubic centimeters.[5]

The human brain is the most complex thing known to science. An adult brain contains about thirty billion nerve cells (neurons). In the highly developed cerebral cortex of the human, there are about ten billion neurons with something like a million billion connections between them (the synapses).[6] What led to the emergence of the human brain and to this level of complexity? What caused the tripling of the size of the brain over a relatively short four million years?

It used to be thought that the most important elements in the emergence of humans were their two-legged (bipedal) motion and their tool use. More recently, it has become clear that the bipedal *Australopithecus* had an apelike nature. And scientists have discovered that a number of other animals use tools. So while these elements remain fundamental, Mayr proposes that two further interrelated factors are essential contributors to the increase in size of the brain: (1) the movement out from the safety of the trees to the vulnerability of the plains, and (2) the development of speech as the human system of communication.[7] Once small bands of *Homo* no longer depended on the trees for avoiding predators, enhancement of intelligence and increased capacity for communication provided a survival and reproductive advantage. As the brain grew in size, extended parental care was essential, since infants were born with undeveloped brains because of the need to negotiate the birth canal. Parental care involved passing on nongenetic information. Learning and the transfer of cultural information became an intrinsic dimension of human life.

Edward O. Wilson points to the way that genes and culture reciprocally influence one another in human evolution.[8] He speaks of "epigenetic rules," which are hereditary regularities in our brains that bias our cultural evolution in certain ways. Some of these, such as the way we see colors, are traits inherited from our primate past that are tens of millions of years old. Others, such as the neural mechanisms for language, are uniquely human and may go back only several hundred thousand years. Our cultural life is shaped in part by these genetic predispositions. But, Wilson insists, it also works the other way. Culture shapes the genetic inheritance of the human community: "Culture helps to select the mutating and recombining genes that underlie human nature."[9]

What is unique to human evolution, as opposed, for example, to chim- *cultural* panzee or wolf evolution, is that a large part of what shapes it is cultural. *influences* Wilson makes it clear that this understanding of gene-culture coevolu- *evolution* tion does not mean endorsing a rigid genetic determinism. But he sees some genetic tendencies, such as the tendency to territorial expansion and defense, as so powerful that they give rise to cultural universals in human societies. While territoriality is absent from some species, human beings have emerged as a territorial species. This, Wilson points out, does not mean that war is inevitable, but "that war arises from both genes and culture and can best be avoided by a thorough understanding of the manner in which these two modes of heredity interact within different historical contexts."[10]

Studies of primates suggest that intelligence is related to social interaction (the social-intelligence hypothesis). Primates that live in large groups and face the more complex games of "social chess" have the largest cerebral cortex.[11] For early human beings, changes in brain size, language skills, social organization, and means of subsistence were all interrelated. Richard Leakey writes, "The beginnings of the hunting-and-gathering way of life surely increased the complexity of the social chess our ancestors had to master. Skilled players of the game—those equipped with a more acute mental model, a sharper consciousness—would have enjoyed greater social and reproductive success."[12] In this way, natural selection would have raised consciousness to new levels. With early human beings, the capacity to read others that had survival value would have included a growing awareness of how others feel—the capacity for empathy. Emotional intelligence had value in terms of survival and reproduction.[13]

It seems clear that brain development and language gave small groups of early humans an advantage in adapting to new situations insofar as it enabled them to cooperate with each other, forming communities of mutual support and defense. This means, according to Mayr, that not only care for one's offspring, and not only altruism toward *mutual support w/in a community →survival*

relatives (kin selection), but also altruism among members of the same social group was favored by natural selection.[14] There was an evolutionary advantage in helping one another within the group. This tendency toward mutual support and cooperation has been selected for in human evolutionary history.

But this was *not* true of outsiders. The tendency was to close ranks over against the outsider. While care for one another within the group has an evolutionary advantage, the emergence of ethical behavior that extends love, compassion, or help to outsiders is not favored by natural selection. Mayr makes it clear that the genetic tendency that comes from our evolutionary past is toward benevolent behavior with insiders and suspicion and hostility toward outsiders as competitors or enemies. He argues that real ethical behavior thus requires a *transformation* of our evolutionary inheritance, "a redirecting of our inborn cultural tendencies toward a new target: outsiders."[15] He insists that it requires a new cultural factor, such as the preaching of a prophet or the teaching of a great philosopher, to move us to include outsiders within the range of our ethical concern and commitment.

Original Grace and Original Sin in Evolutionary History

Theologians have made connections between original sin and evolution in a number of ways. Some have seen the connection in terms of genetic tendencies that come from our prehuman ancestors.[16] Others think of it in terms of the dissonance between these inherited biological tendencies and human cultural imperatives.[17] Others have seen it in relation to the "fall upward" that comes with human consciousness.[18] I am convinced that we do have tendencies, such as the instinct to advance the possibility of one's own survival, the fight-or-flight mechanism, and the impulse to territoriality, that we inherit from our prehuman ancestors. But as I have argued elsewhere, these are not to be seen as sin or as the fruit of sin.[19] They are simply part of being a bodily, finite, and fallible creature. With Rahner, I see this state of affairs, which is part of the "concupiscence" of the human condition, as morally neutral and as part of God's good creation.[20] In Stephen Duffy's terms, this kind of tendency is not to be seen as "the child of sin" but more as "the companion of finitude."[21]

evolutionary tendencies are morally neutral

But we can rightly speak of real sin at work in our origins—sin understood as the rejection of grace and as the rejection of God. One of the forms that this sin takes, I will suggest, is that of making others into scapegoats and enemies. Before exploring this further, it is important to situate it in the context of a more original grace. I take grace to be God's presence in the Holy Spirit, offering God's self in love to every human person. As I have pointed out in chapter three, in a Christian perspective, shaped by the resurrection of Christ, the whole of human history can be understood in terms of divine self-giving. God gives God's self to us in the Word who has been made flesh and in the Spirit poured out. This divine self-bestowal governs the whole action of God in creation, redemption, and final fulfillment. It governs the whole economy of God. While the grace of the Holy Spirit is profoundly interconnected with the Christ-event, grace did not begin to become present in our world only with the Christ-event. The Spirit of God, who is always the Spirit of Jesus Christ, was already present with the prophets of Israel and already at work in the lives of indigenous Australians forty thousand years ago. *humans were created surrounded*

When human beings first emerged in evolutionary history with their *by* capacity for self-reflection and freedom, they emerged into a world of *divine* grace. They emerged in a world where God was already present to them *love* at the very center of their existence in self-offering love. By God's free decision, love surrounded and held them. Not a love that was forced on them, but a love that was quietly present to them as an offer that they might freely accept or reject. They were constituted as creatures constantly invited into freedom. To accept this grace, to say yes to love, is to live in God, to be saved. Of course, it was always possible to freely reject this offer in sin. Through God's free action, God gave God's self to human beings in self-offering love from the very beginning. To be human, then, is to stand always before the offer of boundless love.

This theology of original grace, articulated with clarity by Karl Rahner throughout his career, is widely accepted by many theologians.[22] A theology of God's saving grace as offered to all human beings has become the official teaching of the Catholic Church since the Second Vatican Council.[23] Can more be said about the invitation offered in this original grace? We can find the shape and content of this invitation articulated in the gospels. When Jesus is asked to spell out what he sees as the first command of the Torah, he replies, "The first is, 'Hear, O Israel: the Lord our God, the Lord is one; you shall love the Lord your God with all your heart, with all your soul, and with all your mind, and with all your strength.' The second is this, 'You shall love your neighbor as yourself.' There is no other commandment greater than these" (Mark 12:29-31). But then who is the neighbor? Where are the boundaries? When Jesus is asked this question in Luke's version of this incident, he replies with the parable of the Good Samaritan (Luke 10:29-37). This parable shatters all human attempts to restrict the neighbor to kin, to those of our own clan, to those of our own faith. The neighbor includes the other. In Jesus' most radical articulation of this, we are told simply, "Love your enemies, do good to those who hate you, bless those who curse you, pray for those who abuse you" (Luke 6:27-28; Matt 5:44).

all humans are part of our community

According to Jesus, the proper response to the grace of God is love of God with one's whole heart and love for one's neighbor as one's self. This makes fully explicit what was already implicitly contained in the invitation of grace for the first human beings. The invitation of grace, including original grace, is an invitation to love God with one's whole self and to love the other, without boundaries. And these two loves are distinct but inseparably united: "Those who say, 'I love God,' and hate their brothers or sisters, are liars; for those who do not love a brother or sister whom they have seen, cannot love God whom they have not seen" (1 John 4:20).[24]

If original grace was structured as an invitation and address to human freedom, if it was God's self-offering in love, then it invited a human response. The response that was invited, I am proposing, was love of God with one's whole self and love of the other as oneself. And this love of the other was not simply love of one's kin or one's group or tribe. The love required by the boundless grace of God is a love that does not know boundaries. It is a love of the enemy. When this theological datum is brought into relationship with what science has to tell us about our human origins, it can form the basis for a theology of original sin and redemption that can have vital meaning in a world in which there is so much violence.

response to God's love is to love God & others

The proposal is that early human beings evolved as creatures of self-reflection and freedom, with the capacity for wonder and for pondering the ungraspable mystery at the heart of things. They had endlessly questing minds and unquenchable hearts searching for love that knows no limits.

God's grace was freely given. God was with them from the beginning as self-offering love. This love constantly invited them into a love of God with their whole hearts and a love of the other that is not bounded. Early human beings had to learn to adapt and survive in a dangerous world. From very early in their history, they emerged as creatures whose great advantage in evolutionary terms was their capacity for language and for forming community in small groups. The development of the brain was interrelated with the development of language and of social life. In this context, bands of early humans adapted, survived, reproduced, and flourished. They had to deal with tensions and rivalry within the group, and they did this, at times, by diverting the aggressive potential of the group toward a victim or the enemy, in the scapegoat mechanism.[25] This proved to be a successful evolutionary strategy.

Insofar as forming strong links within a group was achieved by means of polarizing over against others as victims or as enemies, the invitation of original grace was at least partially rejected over and over again. It is the rejection of God that constitutes the sin of our origins. And this rejection found expression, among other ways, in the scapegoat mechanism. The tendency to sin is carried not only in culture but in our genetic inheritance. The tendency to bond together for mutual support (in itself undoubtedly a great good in our evolutionary history) and the tendency to create community *by means* of the mechanism of rejecting or attacking others as victims or enemies are both part of our human inheritance. Precisely that which makes us most human, and which has been at the center of our evolutionary adaptation, is our interpersonal life. This has been achieved, in part, by making others into scapegoats or enemies. This means that not only cooperation and community, but also exclusion and aggression toward the outsider, have been selected for in human biological history. A tendency to sin and violence has become part of human genetic and cultural inheritance.

But this tendency can be freely resisted. We also remain constituted as people of grace, as creatures to whom God offers God's self in interpersonal love. And this offer constantly invites us into a compassion that knows no boundaries. This invitation breaks through in human history, in the work of the Spirit revealed in prophets, artists, saints, and great leaders, and in the grace-filled generosity of many people in ordinary circumstances. For the Christian community, it finds its radical expression in Jesus of Nazareth, in his word and deeds, his death and resurrection. This community sees Jesus as the sinless one in whom the sin of our origins is definitively overcome by a divine act of boundless mercy and forgiveness.

The End of Scapegoating and the Beginning of New Creation

In a world where humans have learned to survive and flourish in a competitive environment by building social relations, and often in the process diverting the aggressive potential of their group outward against a victim or a common enemy, Jesus appears, sent by the God he called *Abba,* and empowered by the Spirit, to bring healing and liberation. He proclaims a realm of God, in which violence and sin are overcome, and which embodies a limitless divine compassion. He brings good news for the poor, the captives, the blind, and the oppressed. He heals the crippled and ill, and liberates those afflicted by mental illness. He calls disciples to follow him, women and men together in a new inclusive family that represents the coming reign of God. He shares meals with outcasts and public sinners, announcing God's priority for the poor and marginalized, enacting divine forgiveness and anticipating the inclusive joy of the kingdom. Consistently, he takes the side of the poor and the victims, and claims this as the place of God.

Jesus' commitment leads to his death. He dies at the hands of the Romans in a form of execution that was designed to be brutal and public and so to instill horror. Jesus dies in fidelity to the way he lived. As Marcus Borg puts it, he died because of his passion:

> But Jesus was not simply an unfortunate victim of a domination system's brutality. He was a protagonist filled with passion. His passion, his message, was about the kingdom of God. He spoke to peasants as a voice of religious protest against the central economic and political institutions of his day. He attracted a following, took his movement to Jerusalem at the season of Passover, and there challenged authorities with public acts and public debates. All of this was his passion, what he was passionate about—God and the kingdom of God, God and God's passion for justice.[26]

Good Friday, Borg says, is "the collision between the passion of Jesus and the domination system of his time."[27] It is worth remembering that this same system in its different forms killed many others, including John the Baptist, Paul, Peter, and James. Borg sees Jesus' death as the almost inevitable result of the way he lived. But, rightly in my view, he rejects any idea of a divine necessity for the way Jesus died. After the resurrection and the experience of God's saving and forgiving love, Jesus' disciples could look back and see God as providentially at work in his death, bringing life and healing. In this context, they could sometimes speak of Jesus' death as foreordained by God (Luke 24:26-27; 1 Pet 1:18-20). But these texts should not be taken as if God wanted or required the sinful act of crucifying Jesus. Rather, they are a biblical way of affirming that God can transform a radically evil deed and make it the vehicle for grace, healing, and abundant life.

[margin note: crucifixion was not necessary, but shows God's power]

Raymund Schwager insists, "The Cross, according to the clear witness of the kingdom-message, was in no way necessary."[28] Jesus came preaching a kingdom that involved radical conversion. He called for a faith that could move mountains, and a willingness to lose one's life in order to gain it through God in a new way. Jesus was inviting his hearers into the dynamism of God's kingdom, which would subvert the whole history of sin and heal the sickness of human nature. Schwager is right in his argument that Jesus' proclamation of the kingdom was a genuine offer of salvation from God. What Jesus wanted, and what God wanted, first of all, was that Jesus' kingdom proclamation would be met by a response of genuine conversion, which by God's grace would have been part of the inauguration of the kingdom, and the beginning of the end of violence.

Because death is part of what needs to be transformed in God, Jesus' mission would always have involved his death and the transformation of death by God in resurrection life. But God did not want Jesus to be rejected, humiliated, and brutally executed by the Romans. Conversion was the proper response to Jesus' proclamation of the reign of God. It represented God's way of salvation and grace. The call to conversion was rejected, and Jesus himself was cast out and killed with extreme violence. Jesus did not strike back but allowed himself to be hit by the collective violence of his enemies, giving his life in fidelity to God and in nonviolent love for others, including those who persecuted him. Jesus died as a scapegoat.

[margin note: Jesus' death was necessary, his crucifixion was not]

Girard points out that even the disciples of Jesus, like Peter, as distinct from some of the women, were caught up in the "mimetic contagion" that occurs when a crowd turns against a victim.[29] What finally makes this story of mob violence so different, according to Girard, is the knowledge of Jesus' disciples, and those who ponder this story throughout history, that Jesus was innocent. The knowledge of his radical innocence has the capacity, over time, to unmask and subvert the whole scapegoat mechanism.[30]

Jesus' complete innocence destroys the scapegoat mechanism

But Jesus is not only innocent but also the victim who forgives. This forgiving victim invites and challenges us to embrace a new way of life of mutual forgiveness that puts an end to scapegoating. Sebastian Moore points out how Christ crucified and risen transforms the lives of those who follow him: Jesus, who challenged all scapegoating, is made the scapegoat on the cross; the risen one does not remain simply a victim but becomes one whose beauty attracts us. We are drawn to the side of victims by the risen Christ. He meets us by the lake: "There is Jesus, on the side of the excluded, inviting us across to that side! And so he shines before us as God's alluring alternative to the way we live."[31]

Theologically, what happens in the cross is an act of God that brings healing and liberation to our world. Jesus came proclaiming the nearness of God's kingdom, but he and the kingdom message were rejected with a violent backlash. As Schwager notes, this reaction did not stop God from bringing life to the world, and it did not throw Jesus off his course:

> He used this very massive and violent backlash to live out the ultimate consequences of his own message. He gave himself non-violently for those he sought to win though they collectively expelled him. The only means still at his disposal was that in dying he entrusted his case to the heavenly Father and Judge in whom he had placed his hope from the beginning. The Father did not, in spite of Jesus' experience of abandonment, leave him to his fate, but awakened him to new life and elevated him to his right hand. Together they sent that Spirit who continued the work begun on earth and who at the same time retroactively clarified that Jesus' entire work of salvation, indeed the whole creation, had begun in the power of the Spirit.[32]

God does not directly will the violent and evil act of crucifixion, but takes it up, transforming it in the power of the Spirit to be the means of salvation for the whole creation. Jesus, who gave himself in love, in a profound Yes to God, is raised up by God as the principle of resurrection life for all. In Jesus' death and resurrection, "God uncovers and overcomes the whole subliminal, violent and repressed past of humanity."[33] Through God's act in Jesus' life, death, and resurrection, "The law of revenge became the law of redeeming love. The curse was repaid with a blessing. The conspiracy of hatred was replaced with an outpouring of love."[34]

James Alison suggests that in this new way of being, as opposed to working ourselves into a moral stupor trying to forgive others, the priority is to understand ourselves as *undergoing* being forgiven. It is because we undergo being forgiven that we can forgive. Because we are continually approached by our victim who forgives us, we can live redemptively as part of the new creation: "We are people who are constantly undergoing 'I AM'—that is to say, God—coming towards us as one who is offering forgiveness as our victim."[35] Redemptive living, undergoing forgiveness from our victim, means living in solidarity with victims, outsiders, and enemies and challenging the scapegoat mechanism wherever it operates in our society and in the life of the church. Forgiving and being forgiven involve reestablishing, repairing, deepening, and expanding our relationships with God and with the others in our lives.

It is important to see all of this, with Athanasius, as a partial description of the objective act of God by which God unites God's self with creation in order to heal, transform, and deify it. As Rahner says, in the risen Christ, part of the physical, biological, and human world is ontologically and not simply juridically the "beginning of the glorification and divinization of the whole of reality."[36] God's overturning of the scapegoat mechanism is one fundamental dimension of the ontological act of salvation that Athanasius and Rahner articulate. Such an ontological transformation involves a transformation of all our relationships—with the triune God, with other human beings, and with other creatures. The liberation from violence, from all our scapegoating, is integral to the objective, transforming act of God that takes place in the Christ-event, the consequences of which will not be fully seen until the whole creation is transfigured and finds its fulfillment in God.

Jesus, the ultimate scapegoat, the Lamb of God, is the end of all scapegoating and the beginning of a radically inclusive new creation. Something has occurred in principle that is to be lived out by those who follow the way of Jesus in the power of the Holy Spirit. Salvation in Christ is communal. It forms us into an inclusive community. Through the sending of the Holy Spirit, Jesus' disciples are formed and sent as a community of salvation. As a tendency to sin is built into communal life by way of our cultural and genetic inheritance, so nonviolent liberating love is to be lived out in the community of those born again of the Spirit (John 3:1-10). In this sense, the church is the sacrament of salvation in the world, a community witnessing to new creation and to divine nonviolent love in and for the world.

9

Final Fulfillment: The Deifying Transformation of Creation

In chapter 7, I proposed that a theory of redemption for the twenty-first century can be found in the concept of deifying transformation. God becomes a creature of flesh and blood that creatures might become divine through participation in the life of God. In this theology of redemption, salvation is understood as coming from God's action in the whole Christ-event. Salvation from God finds expression in Jesus as God-with-us, in his person, in all that makes up his life, death, and resurrection.

For human beings, redemption in Christ involves forgiveness of sin and the gift of the Spirit that makes us sons and daughters of God, transforms us in Christ, restores and renews in us the image of God, and is the promise and the beginning of our participation in resurrection life, in the communion of the Trinity. Ultimately, our final salvation as human beings is about communion, our communion in the dynamic life of the triune God, with other human persons in the communion of saints, and our communion with the whole of God's creation.

What does final fulfillment mean for the rest of creation? This is the issue I will explore further here. The focus will be on the way in which the wider creation can be thought to share in resurrection life. I will start from the assumption of Christian faith in the bodily and personal resurrection of humans and will ask how the rest of creation might be thought of as participating with humans in resurrection life. The guiding thought in this exploration is that, in the incarnation, God has embraced not just humanity, and not just the whole world of flesh, but the whole universe and all its dynamic history, and that this embrace constitutes an unbreakable promise. As Walter Kasper has put it: "God has accepted the whole world finally in Jesus Christ, and God is faithful, so the world and history will not simply vanish into nothingness, rather God will be its 'all in all' at the end (1 Cor 15:28)."[1]

I will begin with what I take to be fundamental in this kind of discussion: an acknowledgment of what we do not know of God's future. Then, with this in place, I will take up the promise of hope for creation found in the New Testament, particularly in Paul's Letter to the Romans, and in patristic theology, exemplified in Maximus the Confessor. This will lead to an exploration of insights from Karl Rahner's theology of hope for the material universe. Then, in the final section, I will take up hope for the animals, arguing that they too will share in their own way in the final transformation and deification of all things.

We Hope for What We Do Not See: God as Absolute Future

At the end of the passage from Romans that I will discuss in the next section, Paul writes, "For in hope we were saved. Now hope that is seen is not hope. For who hopes for what is seen? But if we hope for what we do not see, we wait for it with patience" (Rom 8:24-25). The resurrection of the body and the renewed creation are not realities we can see or even imagine, because what we see is the empirical reality that surrounds us, and what we can imagine is based upon what we already experience. According to Paul, God's transforming act in resurrection involves a radical change in bodily existence. What is sown in the grave as perishable, dishonored, weak, and physical will be raised as "imperishable," "in glory," "in power," and as a "spiritual body" (1 Cor 15:44). As a risen body is beyond the grasp of our minds, so a universe transfigured in Christ is beyond imagining. We hope for what we do not see.

A Christian theologian is called to be critically aware of the limits of theological concepts and words about the future. She is called to an abiding awareness of what we do not know, and to a careful respect for the limits of language in speaking about what is ultimately unspeakable. There are serious theological reasons for this. These reasons were articulated by Karl Rahner in a well-known article in the mid-twentieth century.[2] In his work, two fundamental principles can be found to guide the interpretation of eschatological statements. The first is that *the future of our world in God remains radically hidden to us*. The Scriptures insist that God has not revealed the day when the end will come (Mark 13:32), and it is not simply the timing of the end that is hidden. The future has been announced and promised in Christ and his resurrection, but it is announced and promised precisely as hidden mystery. God is hidden mystery not in the sense of something puzzling that might be solved, but in the sense of a wonderful abundance of life and love that is always infinitely more than our concepts, images, or words. The future is nothing else than the coming toward us of this incomprehensible God. Rahner insists that it is God who is our absolute future. The revelation of God's promise in Christ does not mean that what was unknown is now made known, clear, and manageable. It is rather "the dawn and the approach of mystery as such."[3] Because the future is the coming of God, it always escapes our comprehension. It is always a mistake, then, to interpret biblical images in literal terms as something like an "eyewitness" account of what is to come.[4]

The second principle is that *the future will be the fulfillment of the salvation in Christ that is already given to us*. It will be the fulfillment of what we experience in God's self-communication in Christ and in the grace of the Holy Spirit. Our knowledge of God's future is based upon what can be derived from our experience of Jesus and the Spirit, and from what we can see as the promised fulfillment of this experience we already have. We do not have supplementary knowledge of the eschatological future over and above what we have in the theology of Christ and of grace, but we can transpose these to their fulfillment. This means that all genuine theological knowledge of the future is an inner moment of the eschatological present, the promise and the hope of the experience of Christ and the Spirit we have now.

For the Christian, who views the future as God's self-bestowal, the future is truly unknown and uncontrollable, and this is something that leaves a great deal of room for freedom, for hope, and for trust.[5] Of course, we are inescapably tied to our imaginations, and images have their proper place in expressing religious ideas. But it is fundamental not to mistake the image for the reality. The image might be the great wedding feast, or Paul's angelic trumpet, or Matthew's sheep and goats. But the reality that the images point to is based upon the experience we have of the grace of Christ already at work in us and drawing us into a future in God.

The absolute future is nothing else than the fulfillment of God's self-bestowal. This is the consummation of the divine action of creation and redemption, a fulfillment promised and initiated in the life, death, and resurrection of Jesus. Christianity proclaims that the becoming of the universe will end not in emptiness but in the divine self-bestowal. Moreover, this absolute future is already at work within history. It is already the divine creative power at work in all things, the Creator Spirit immanent in every aspect of creation, bringing the universe to its fulfillment. The future of God has already found irreversible expression in Jesus. His resurrection is both the promise and the beginning of the absolute future, which is the transformation of human beings and the whole of the universe. This absolute future, which is God who gives God's self to creatures, not only comes toward us as the future of our world, but also is "the sustaining ground of the dynamism towards the future."[6] This is the God who is the absolute mystery of love from which creation comes and to which it is directed.

Hope for the Whole Creation in the New Testament: Romans 8:18-25

For some Christians, the concept of salvation is centered on the individual human person, and at times simply on the individual human soul. The biblical notion, by contrast, is of resurrection of the body, the coming of the reign of God, communion with others in the life of God, and the transformation of the whole creation. In the Bible, human beings are understood in relationship with each other and in relation to the wider creation. The biblical narrative begins with God creating all the diverse creatures of our universe and declaring them to be good. After the terrible destruction caused by human sin, God makes a solemn covenant not only with Noah and his family, but with every living creature, and declares that the sign of this covenant with every creature of flesh will be the rainbow (Gen 9:16). The Bible concludes with a vision of a new heaven and new earth, a transformed world, a place where God dwells with God's people, a place of healing and life, where the leaves of the tree of life, growing alongside the river of life, are for "the healing of nations" (Rev 22:2).

Biblical hope is for a forgiven and renewed humanity within a transformed creation. It finds expression in the famous image of the peaceable animals, where the wolf lives with the lamb, the lion eats straw like an ox, children play safely near snakes, and God proclaims, "They will not hurt or destroy on all my holy mountain; for the earth will be full of the knowledge of the LORD as the waters cover the sea" (Isa 11:6-9). This promise occurs in a series of prophetic texts (Isa 43:19-21; 55:12-13; Ezek 34:25-31; Hos 2:18; Zech 8:12; Mic 4:4) and in the divine commitment to create "new heavens and a new earth" (Isa 65:17; 66:22).

The New Testament sees the resurrection of Jesus as involving the whole creation. Jesus risen from the dead is the Wisdom and Word of God, the one in whom all things are created and sustained (John 1:1-14; 1 Cor 8:6; Heb 1:2-3). He is the one in whom all things are to be redeemed, recapitulated, and reconciled (Rom 8:18-25; Eph 1:9-10, 20-23; Col 1:15-20). The risen Christ is the beginning of the new creation, the promised new heavens and new earth (2 Pet 3:13; Rev 21:1-5; 22:13). In this new creation, every creature of earth, sky, and sea will sing praise to the Lamb, who has redeemed the whole creation (Rev 5:13-14). Each of these texts contributes an important element to an overall understanding of the divine promise in relation to the whole creation. I will take up just one of them, Paul's reflection on suffering and the promise of God in chapter 8 of Romans:

> I consider that the sufferings of this present time are not worth comparing with the glory about to be revealed to us. For the creation waits with eager longing for the revealing of the children of God; for the creation was subjected to futility, not of its own will but by the will of the one who subjected it, in hope that the creation itself will be set free from its bondage to decay and will obtain the freedom of the glory of the children of God. We know that the whole creation has been groaning in labor pains until now; and not only the creation, but we ourselves, who have the first fruits of the Spirit, groan inwardly while we wait for our adoption, the redemption of our bodies. For in hope we were saved. Now hope that is seen is not hope. For who hopes for what is seen? But if we hope for what we do not see, we wait for it with patience. (Rom 8:18-25)

In exploring this text, I will gather up insights from three specialist New Testament scholars. The Pauline authority Joseph Fitzmyer points out that in this text, Paul is clearly thinking of redemption (*apolytrōsis*) in Christ as applying not only to human beings but also to the whole creation: "It is no longer considered from an anthropological point of view; it is now recast in cosmic terms. Human bodies that are said to await such redemption (8:23) are merely part of the entire material creation, which is itself groaning in travail until such redemption occurs. For the Christ-event is expected to affect not only human beings, but all material or physical creation as well."[7]

Creation is held in bondage to decay and death, and in this, it shares the lot of humanity, but it also shares with humanity the hope of redemption. The word Paul uses for decay (*phthora*), Fitzmyer tells us, "denotes not only perishability and putrefaction, but also powerlessness, lack of beauty, vitality, and strength that characterizes creation's present condition."[8] The freedom of creation from this bondage will occur in and with the glorification of the sons and daughters of God. Fitzmyer points out that Paul is here talking about the fulfillment of the biblical promise of "new heavens and a new earth" found in Isa 65:17 and 66:22.[9]

Australian Pauline scholar Brendan Byrne sees this passage from Romans as one of "the most singular and evocative" texts in the whole of Paul's work.[10] What is distinctive, he says, is the way in which it includes the whole of nonhuman creation within the sweep of salvation alongside human beings. Byrne carefully analyzes the meaning of the word *creation* (*ktisis*) as Paul uses it here. He establishes that "it refers to the entire non-human world which the biblical creation stories present as the essential context for human life."[11] Byrne goes on to show that Paul presupposes a Jewish tradition that sees nonhuman creation as intimately bound up with the fate of human beings. This tradition goes back to the creation story of Genesis (Gen 3:17-19). Creation and humanity are understood as sharing a "common fate" in the prophetic literature of the Bible, particularly in the texts I have mentioned earlier in this section.[12] Paul builds on this "common fate" tradition, proclaiming that nonhuman creation will share with human beings in the final restoration of all things in Christ, which will involve a cosmic renewal. Paul's point is that the sufferings of the present are a small price to pay for the coming glory. As Byrne notes, Paul does not minimize the suffering of the present, but sets it in a wider framework, one that looks beyond the present to "the full realization of God's design for human beings and their world."[13]

N. T. Wright, the Bishop of Durham, says of this same text, "The greatest Pauline picture of the future world is Romans 8:19-25."[14] Wright has no doubt that the transformation of the whole creation in Christ is fundamental to Paul's vision.[15] He writes:

> Creation as we know it bears witness to God's power and glory (Romans 1:19-20), but also to the present state of futility to which it has become enslaved. But this slavery, like all slaveries in the Bible, is then given its Exodus, its moment of release, when God does for the whole cosmos what he did for Jesus at Easter. This is the vision that is so big, so dazzling, that many even devout readers of Paul have blinked, rubbed their eyes, and ignored it, hurrying on to the more "personal" application in the following paragraph.[16]

But, Wright insists, this is where Paul's whole argument of the justice of God comes to one of its great climaxes. Wright sees Romans 8 as the deepest New Testament answer to the "problem of evil," to the question of God's justice. Paul is declaring that "the renewal of creation, the birth of the new world from the labouring womb of the old, will demonstrate that God is in the right."[17] I mentioned in the last chapter that Wright, in a more recent book on biblical hope, says of Paul and the other first Christians that "they believed that God was going to do for the whole cosmos what He has done for Jesus at Easter."[18]

Paul's image of creation groaning in giving birth to new creation can find new meaning in a new context, as is evidenced in Christopher Southgate's recent important theological work on the suffering of creation.[19] It may be that the context of Paul's thought was the apocalyptic expectation of cosmic turmoil that would precede the final victory of God.[20] But Paul's reflection also seems shaped by what he saw in the natural world around him. His image functions anew in the context of an understanding of the world shaped by evolutionary biology, a world of fertility, generativity, and wonderful creativity, but also of struggle and suffering and death. The metaphor of birthing is at the origin of the word *nature*. In the world of nature as understood in evolutionary terms, suffering and death seem to be the shadow side of prolific creativity.[21]

Earth has given birth to bacteria, trilobites, dinosaurs, mammals, and human persons, with their immensely complex brains. It has been a labor that has brought forth staggeringly diverse and complex forms of life, but in a process that has been very costly. In the Pauline vision, it has not yet reached its completion and fulfillment. It will not be fulfilled until it shares with human beings in God's final redemption and transformation of all things. Creation groans still as something even more radically new is being born. With the information we have today, I imagine that Paul would see God at work in this whole process of the evolution of our universe over the past 13.7 billion years and the evolution of life on Earth over the past 3.7 billion years. Paul sees God in Christ as promising a future not just for human beings but for the whole laboring creation, when God will bring it all to redemption and fulfillment.

Hope for the Universe in Patristic Tradition: Maximus the Confessor

In the Eastern patristic tradition, creation and redemption are held together. For Irenaeus, they form one story of what God has done for us through the Word and in the Spirit. The whole history of creation is taken up and recapitulated in Christ. The visible universe is destined to be restored and to share in glorification and deification with the human community saved by Christ. As I have pointed out in chapter 7, deification does not mean that we creatures possess the divine essence, but that God has created us so that our true fulfillment is to be found in our graced participation in God. We will become fully ourselves by participating in the divine life of the Trinity as God's beloved adopted children. In this same chapter, I referred to the way Athanasius could speak of creation as being deified in the Spirit through the Word of God. He writes of the Holy Spirit, "In him, then, the Logos glorifies creation, and deifying it and adopting it brings it to the Father."[22] Athanasius sees nonhuman creation as participating in some way with human beings in glory, deification, and adoption. We may hope that the rest of creation will reach fulfillment in God, not in the personal way that is appropriate to humans, but in ways appropriate to each creature.

This theology has been the common heritage of the Eastern Christian tradition and much of the Western, although it has seldom received sustained theological attention. It finds influential expression in the thought of Maximus the Confessor (580–662). Maximus has a cosmic theology of the incarnation and of redemption in Christ. The incarnate Word of God restores the unity of the whole creation and brings it to God. He sees God originally as having called human beings to be the bond of union in all the divisions and the different aspects of cosmic reality. The human was meant to be a "microcosm" (a little universe), mediating and uniting the extremes of the cosmos, drawing the created order into harmony within itself and into union with God.[23] Because of the fall, human beings have failed in this function. In the incarnation, God unites and recapitulates all things in the Word made flesh. The Word of God brings reconciliation to humanity and the whole universe.

Maximus sees God as creating the universe of creatures with the incarnation in mind. The incarnation is "the end for whose sake all things exist."[24] All things are created in the eternal Word. Maximus plays on the relationship in Greek between the *Logos*, the eternal Word of God, and the *logoi*. The *logoi* are the fundamental meanings of individual creatures in their diversity. The *logoi* represent the distinct ways that different created entities participate in the *Logos* of God. All are brought into unity and right relationship in Christ, the *Logos* made flesh: "By his own initiative, he joins together the natural ruptures in all of the natural universe, and brings to fulfilment the universal meanings (*logoi*) of individual things, by which the unification of the divided is realized. He reveals and carries out the great will of God his Father, 'summing up all things in himself, things in heaven and things on earth' (Eph. 1:10), since all were created in him."[25]

Jesus Christ, the *Logos* of God, unites in himself the *logoi*, the fundamental meanings of each created being, and brings all to unity and healing. In the Word made flesh, all the ancient polarizations of creation are overcome. Christ unites human beings with himself, so that we bear his image and share his role with regard to the rest of creation: "With us and through us he encompasses the whole creation through its intermediaries and the extremities through their own parts."[26] This seems to give human beings an important role in the healing and reconciliation of the wider creation.

For Maximus, and for the wider Eastern tradition, the transfiguration of Christ is an important symbol of the transformation of creation in Christ. Not only Jesus, but his garments, are transfigured, and these garments become a symbol of the wider creation sharing in Christ's transfiguration. Human beings, who are renewed in Christ, participate in his transfiguration and participate with him in the transformation and healing of the whole cosmos.

The Deification of the Universe: Karl Rahner

In the opening chapter, I described some of the characteristics of the universe discovered by the science of the last hundred years. Cosmologists tell us that the observable universe is made up of something like a hundred billion galaxies. It is expanding and evolving. We can trace its history back to the first second of its existence, about 13.7 billion years ago, when it was extremely small, dense, and hot. As the galaxies move away from one another, the rate of expansion seems to be increasing.

There are two scientific scenarios for the future of the universe. Either it will stop expanding at some point in the future and then begin to collapse back into an extremely small, dense, and hot state, or it will continue to expand and cool forever. The present view of many cosmologists is that the universe is destined to expand forever, becoming less energetic and incapable of supporting life. Clearly, all carbon-based life is destined for extinction. In about 5 billion years, our Sun will become a red giant, engulfing the orbit of Earth and Mars, and eventually become a white dwarf star. In 40 billion to 50 billion years, star formation will have ended in our galaxy and in others.[27]

This is a bleak scenario of the future. Where does it leave Christian hope? How can the predictions that science makes about the future be reconciled with the promise of new creation? In previous chapters, I have discussed the resurrection as the promise of new creation and pointed to Rahner's conviction that the resurrection of the crucified Jesus is the beginning of the deification of the world itself. Rahner insists that what has occurred in Jesus, as part of the physical, biological, and human world, is ontologically "the embryonically final beginning of the glorification and divinization of the *whole* reality."[28] This is not to be confused with any form of pantheism but is an appeal to the ancient Greek and Latin patristic idea that we participate by God's grace in Trinitarian life. The word *ontological* suggests that this deification has occurred in principle in Christ, that something began in the Christ-event that is already at work in the whole of reality. The future of our world has begun in him, and this future is our participation, along with the rest of creation, in the life of God. This transforming, deifying participation in God will be the real fulfillment of our humanity and the appropriate fulfillment of the rest of creation. Rahner, in line with much of the biblical and Christian tradition, sees our human fulfillment, our deification, as profoundly linked to that of the rest of creation.

I will explore this idea of the final deification of the material universe against the background of the scientific picture of endless dissipation. This will involve a consideration of the mysterious nature of matter itself, its radical transformation in new creation, and the real continuity between the universe that we are part of today and God's new creation.

The Deification of Matter

In the biblical and patristic traditions, the material universe was seen as God's good creation and destined to share with human beings in God's final fulfillment when Christ comes again. Often, the focus was on the human. But the human being was seen as necessarily bodily and as interconnected with the rest of the created world. Final fulfillment of human beings was understood as involving a new relationship with the triune God, with the human community, and with the wider creation. This tradition is a precious resource for contemporary theology. In the light of more recent understanding of the history of the universe and of life on our planet, and confronted by twenty-first-century ecological issues, the theological meaning of nonhuman creation and its future in God needs to be raised today in a less anthropocentric way.

In exploring this issue, it is worth noting that we do not know much about matter. William Stoeger has pointed out that there is a common tendency to think of the spiritual as mysterious and of matter as more or less straightforward and easy to understand. Common sense suggests that the world of matter is easily grasped. But in this case, common sense misleads us. We certainly know a great deal about the physical laws that govern the universe. But the more we know about general relativity, particle physics, quantum mechanics, the origins of matter in the early universe, and the nucleosynthesis of elements in stars, the more counterintuitive and mysterious matter becomes. And we are far from understanding the relationship between the ever-changing matter that makes up our bodies and our personal and interpersonal "I." The mysterious nature of matter, as well as all that we mean by spirit, suggests that we might well be open to a future for matter and spirit that exceeds anything we can imagine at present.

Karl Rahner insists that matter really does matter to God. God created a universe of creatures as an act of self-bestowing love, always intending to embrace the material world in the incarnation and to bring it to its fulfillment in Christ. Some Christians have seen the material world as a kind of stage for the drama of salvation—a stage that will have no further use in eternal life. Rahner insists, by contrast, that matter is not something to be cast aside as a transitory part of the journey of the spirit. It has been carried from the beginning by God's self-bestowing love. We know that our universe began from a tiny, dense, and extremely hot state and has been expanding ever since, allowing galaxies to form, stars to ignite, and planets like Earth to form. This whole process, and every aspect of it, has been carried by the triune God, present in love to every part of it. Every emergent aspect of the universe is sustained by the Source of All, created in the Word and empowered by the Holy Spirit.

Rahner speaks of this self-bestowal in love as "the most immanent element in every creature." Therefore, he can say, "It is not mere pious lyricism when Dante regards even the sun and the other planets as being moved by that love which is God himself as he who bestows himself."[29] This means that the innermost principle of the movement of the galaxies and their stars, the innermost principle of the expanding and evolving universe, is God present in self-bestowing love.

Because of God's creation of a material universe in self-giving love, because of the incarnation, and because of the resurrection, God and matter go together. As Creator, God has been intimately engaged with the material universe at every point. God has become flesh and become matter in the incarnation. In the risen Christ, part of the material universe is already taken into God as pledge and beginning of the fulfillment of material creation in God. Speaking of the deification of the material universe is claiming that the universe will reach its own proper fulfillment in being taken up in God's self-giving love. This is to be distinguished from the interpersonal fulfillment offered to human beings. It is the fulfillment of matter precisely as matter. While it is distinguished from the deifying interpersonal fulfillment of human beings, it is profoundly connected with it.

This means, Rahner says, that Christians are, or perhaps ought to be, "the most sublime of materialists."[30] We cannot think of our fulfillment without thinking of the fulfillment of the material universe, and we cannot conceive of the risen Christ except as existing forever in the state of incarnation. This means that "as materialists we are more crassly materialist than those who call themselves so."[31] We recognize that matter will last forever and be glorified forever.

Radical Transformation

Rahner couples his claim that matter has an eternal destiny with the insistence that matter will undergo a radical transformation, "the depths of which we can only sense with fear and trembling in that process which we experience as our death."[32] If, as Rahner claims, the only way we can get a sense of the radical nature of the final transformation is by analogy with our own deaths, clearly this new creation is not simply an outcome of the ongoing evolution of the universe or of human progress as the sciences understand and model it.[33]

This is an important insight. It can be taken further in relationship to the death of Christ. The real basis for understanding the radical nature of the transformation of the universe is the transformation that occurs in the crucified Jesus, just as the reality of the continuity between Jesus who was crucified and the risen Christ indicates the continuity between this universe and new creation. Both radical transformation and real continuity need to be stressed. I will take up the continuity between creation and new creation in the next section, but need to say a word about it now. The whole argument of this book has stressed that God's act of creation, incarnation, and final fulfillment is one differentiated act. God creates a world to bring it to fulfillment. And God acts in the world in and through creation itself, in ways partially revealed and modeled in the sciences, and in ways transcending them. All of this suggests that new creation comes from God's acting in deep communion with creation rather than coming upon it from outside.

At the same time, God's act will transform creation in bringing it to its fulfillment in the life of the Trinity. New creation transcends and transfigures the old. As Paul Evdokimov points out, the day of the coming of Christ cannot be numbered with other days: "The hand of God seizes the closed circle of empirical time and lifts it to a higher horizon, a different dimension. This 'day' closes historical time but does not itself belong to time. It cannot be found on our calendars and for this reason we cannot predict it."[34] Time, space, and matter will reach their fulfillment and find their future in the boundless life of God. We have no information from the Scriptures or any other source about the nature of this deification of our universe—only the promise given in Christ and his resurrection of a future in God.

Jürgen Moltmann has been strong in his insistence that only a radical act of God can bring healing and redemption to the whole creation. We will not be redeemed by evolutionary processes. Salvation can come only from a universal transformation of this present world, of the kind described in Revelation, where God says, "See, I am making all things new" (21:5). This means, according to Moltmann, that "everything created, everything that was here, is here, and will be here" is to be made new. The new, eternal creation is to be the new creation of this world that we know.[35] Richard Bauckham has also vigorously criticized the importing of Enlightenment optimism and views of historical and evolutionary progress into eschatology.[36] Moltmann and Bauckham are right when they claim that final salvation cannot come from more of the same, but only from a radical act of God that transforms the whole creation. But as will become clear in the next section, I see this radical act of God as the completion of the divine self-bestowal of God at work in creation from the beginning, and as the full realization of God's intentions for creation. What brings creation to its God-intended completeness will be an act of God from within creation, rather than an action from without.

New creation depends upon a transforming act of God, as radical as the act by which God raised Jesus from the dead. This theological insight can shed some light on the problem I have described concerning the difference between biblical hope and the current scientific picture of the future of the universe as expanding endlessly, becoming cold and lifeless. The problem is based in part on an assumption that the universe can be thought of as evolving seamlessly toward new creation. If the theological idea of God's final transformation of creation is presumed to coincide with the far distant future of the universe, there is obviously a problem reconciling theological eschatology and scientific predictions. But I do not think there are theological reasons to make this assumption. Theologically, we have a promise that the universe will be transformed and find its culmination in God. Theology has no information about when or how this will be. The theological claim is not that the universe will evolve into a perfect state at the end and that this will then coincide with the divine act that makes all things new. If God's act is a radical one, if the best analogy for this kind of transformation is what happens in death—above all, the death of Christ—then the divine act of making the whole universe new does not depend on the universe gradually evolving toward perfection.

It is fundamental to remember that the resurrection of the crucified one did not depend on any obvious movement toward completion or perfection in the life and ministry of Jesus. Jesus' mission was interrupted by what seemed catastrophic. The resurrection was the transformation of a brutal execution and a disastrous end to Jesus' ministry into unpredictable new life. The resurrection was a radical overturning of the rejection and savage violence and apparent failure of Jesus' mission. Yet at a deeper level, Christians have come to see that God's act of raising Jesus up was also in fact in profound *continuity* with Jesus' life lived in love and with his death as the most radical expression of this love.

Real Continuity

While I agree with Moltmann and Bauckham about the radical transformation involved in new creation, I want to affirm more strongly than they do the continuity between this creation we experience and God's new act. God is creatively at work in this creation we experience, God gives God's self in love to this creation, and it is this creation that will be transfigured in God's eschatological act that brings creation to fulfillment. There is a deep continuity between creation and new creation. This continuity is grounded ultimately in God's fidelity to what God has created.

There is radical continuity, as well, because God acts in and through the universe of creatures, in the divine act that encompasses not only creation and redemption, but also the completion of God's work. This continuity between creation and new creation is expressed in Rahner's notion of self-transcendence. He holds that God gives to creatures themselves the capacity for the new. Because of God's creative and redeeming presence to creatures, they can become something they were not. When matter comes to life on earth, when life becomes self-conscious and personal, this occurs through God enabling creation to transcend itself and become something new. Above all, when one of us in the human and creaturely community, Jesus of Nazareth, is so radically open to God, so one with God, that we rightly see him as God-with-us, then we can say that in this person, creation transcends itself into God.

According to Rahner, God will continue to work through the self-transcendence of creation when God brings all to fulfillment.[37] All that constitutes our cosmic, social, and personal history—the emergence of the universe, the evolution of life on earth, and our human history—will be taken up and find fulfillment in the life of God. On the one hand, the coming reign of God will not be simply the outcome of the evolution of cosmic history, and it will not be simply the result of the history that is planned and accomplished by humans. On the other hand, it will not simply come upon creation as an act of God from outside. It will be the deed of God, but this deed of God is to be understood as the *self*-transcendence of the natural world and its history, both cosmic and personal.

In cosmic terms, this suggests that the coming of God will fulfill rather than overturn the laws and processes at work in the history of our universe and the evolution of life on Earth. In chapter 6, I referred to an important insight from Robert John Russell: he argues that the new creation is not to be seen as a replacement of the old, or as a new creation ex nihilo. Rather, God must have created the universe "such that it is transformable."[38] God created a universe with precisely those characteristics that are needed as preconditions for God's act of new creation. These conditions and characteristics of the present creation are created in such a way that they can be transformed in new creation. It seems to me that what Russell is describing here is an important part of what Rahner means when he speaks of God's action occurring in and through the self-transcendence of our cosmic and evolutionary history.

This view of the continuity between creation and self-transcendence in new creation is a matter of great importance for our human actions. It gives them ultimate importance. They will have a place in God's future. Rahner points out that there is a dialectical tension between two statements, both of which are true: on the one hand, human history will endure, and on the other hand, it will be radically transformed. The tension between them is fundamental, because it "maintains in us an openness to the future while still according a radical importance to the present." Our own history and our own acts contribute to God's future. History is not left behind but "passes into the definitive consummation of God."[39]

Our own efforts, our ecological commitments, our struggles for justice, our work for peace, our acts of love, our failures, our own moments of quiet prayer, and our sufferings all have final meaning. Human history and our own personal story matter to God. The Word of God has entered into history for our salvation. History is embraced by God in the Christ-event. In the resurrection, part of our history—the created humanity of Jesus—is already taken into God. We are assured that all of our history has eternal meaning in God. This means that our stories have final significance, as taken up into God and transformed in Christ.

Hope for the Animals

In Revelation 5, the angels, with the four living creatures who represent creation and with the elders, all sing a hymn of praise to the Lamb who has been slain. Then all living things join in:

> Then I heard every creature in heaven and on earth and under the earth and in
> the sea, and all that is in them, singing,
> > "To the one seated on the throne and to the Lamb
> > be blessing and honor and glory and might
> > forever and ever!" (Rev 5:13)

In this vision, every creature of the natural world joins the great chorus praising the Lamb. The text brings out the universal nature of creaturely participation in this hymn: "the doxology has four terms, 'heaven,' 'earth,' 'under the earth,' 'sea,' indicating that all nature—heaven, hell (Heb. *sheol*), earth and the sea . . . joins in the praise."[40] All creatures in all four realms of sky, ground, underground, and sea unite in a song of praise, celebrating redemption in the Lamb who was slaughtered. All are imagined as participating in the joy of the new creation.

How are we to understand this text? While the postbiblical tradition has found ways to affirm that new creation in Christ involves hope not only for human beings but for the universe itself, it has not often dealt explicitly with hope for other animals. Implicitly, of course, Paul's words about suffering creation can be taken as involving the living, biological world. Can we make a more explicit claim? I propose that we can. As always, such a claim needs to be prefaced by acknowledging how little information we have about the nature of the life of the new creation. We know very little, but what we do know is the nature of God revealed to us in Jesus and the promise given to our world in his resurrection. This, I will propose, allows us to say some important things about hope for the other animals. I will attempt to do this in five steps, working from what I have already discussed in this book to more tentative suggestions.

1. Individual animals are known and loved by God. In the Gospel of Matthew, we find Jesus, as a way of calling his disciples to radical trust in God's providence, pointing to God's care for each single sparrow: "Yet not one of them will fall to the ground apart from your Father" (Matt 10:29). The Wisdom of Solomon tells us that God creates each creature only out of love. Animals, birds, and insects exist because God loves them. They are called forth and held in existence by divine love (Wis 11:24-26). The God of Jesus is a God of radical compassion, a compassion that has no boundaries. Such a God can be thought of as knowing each creature's experience, delighting in each, suffering with each, and embracing each in love. The biblical God is a God of tenderness and compassion for all creatures. Another resource for a theology of God's feeling for animals is reflection on our own capacity as human beings to relate to other animals. At our best, we have the capacity for feeling with them, of feeling empathy with their pain and joy in their well-being and vitality. This, surely, can give us a glimpse into the Creator's feeling for living things. We are right to think that our human experience of compassion for other creatures is but the palest reflection of the divine knowing and loving of animals.

2. The Creator Spirit is interiorly present to each creature, enabling it to exist and to act. What confers existence on each animal is the presence of God in the Spirit. As Aquinas taught, creation is a relationship by which God is interiorly present to each creature, enabling it to exist and to act. Aquinas says that nothing is more interior to an entity than its existence, and this means that God's presence and creative action are what is most interior to all things.[41] God is closer to each creature than it is to itself. In the language of the Bible, the Spirit breathes life into all things of flesh. They have life only because of the Breath of God: "If he should take back his spirit to himself, and gather to himself his breath, all flesh would perish together, and all mortals return to dust" (Job 34:14-15). Psalm 104, the great celebration of God's creation, sings of the heavens, the earth, the living creatures of the land and sky, and the sea with all its life-forms small and great, and sees them all as held in being by God's Spirit:

When you take away their breath, they die
   and return to their dust.
When you send forth your spirit, they are created;
   and you renew the face of the ground. (Ps 104:29-30)

The Spirit is creatively present to every creature, dwelling in each, surrounding it with love, holding it in a community of creation, and accompanying it in its life and in its death.

3. Animals participate in some way in redemption in Christ. When Revelation envisions all living creatures "in heaven and on earth and under the earth and in the sea" singing praise to the one sitting on the throne and the Lamb who had been slain, it is clear that all these creatures are thought of as sharing in some way in the redemption brought about by the crucified and risen Christ. When Paul speaks of the groaning of creation and sees it as awaiting its participation in our redemption, it seems clear that the suffering creation he has in mind includes nonhuman biological life. When Colossians and Ephesians insist that "all things" in the cosmos are recapitulated (Eph 1:10) and reconciled (Col 1:20) in Christ, it would seem that "all things" would include not only the material creation, the cosmic powers, and human beings, but also other animals.

While the Christian tradition has not often reflected carefully on the redemption of animals, a theology of incarnation, such as is found in the great patristic theologians like Athanasius, is a theology cast in the widest possible terms—those of God and the whole creation. God embraces and takes to God's self the whole creation in the incarnation. In a particular way, God embraces flesh, not just human flesh, but all the flesh that is so intimately connected with it. In taking flesh in Jesus of Nazareth, God becomes part of the history of biological evolution of life on earth, with the whole web of life and all that supports it. We human beings are in deep solidarity with other animals because of our common ancestry and genetic history. All of this is what God embraces in the incarnation. This kind of reflection can suggest that God's redemptive act in the incarnation may be seen as taking the whole world of flesh into the divine life, in the new creation and the deification of all things in Christ. But the question remains: What does it mean to speak of other animals participating with us in the new creation?

4. Each animal abides forever in the living memory of God. In Luke's version of the saying about the sparrow, Jesus states that not one sparrow is "forgotten before God" (Luke 12:6). It is held eternally in the divine memory. This concept of the divine memory provides the basis for an approach to the final redemption of other living creatures. The biblical and liturgical concept of memory offers an important resource. In the liturgy of the church, we remember the wonderful things God has done in creation and redemption. When we celebrate the Eucharist in memory (*anamnēsis*) of Jesus, we are dealing with a remembrance that not only brings to mind the past, but also acts powerfully in the present and anticipates an eschatological future. This experience of living memory may provide a pale analogy for God's redemptive memory. What is being suggested here is that God can be thought of not only as present with each creature in the Spirit, loving it and conferring on it existence and the capacity to act, but also as inscribing it eternally in the living memory and experience of divine Trinitarian life.

According to the Bible, while we human creatures are called to remember God, what is primary is God's remembrance of us and of the rest of creation. God remembers God's covenant with us forever (Ps 105:8). Human beings pray that God will hold them in the divine memory (Job 7:7; 10:9; 14:13; Ps 78:39). Humans exist because God remembers them and holds them in provident care (Ps 8:4). Alexander Schmemann writes of this biblical concept of memory:

> Memory refers to the attentiveness of God to his creation, the power of divine providential love through which God "holds" the world and *gives it life*, so that life itself can be termed abiding in the memory of God, and death the falling out of this memory. In other words, memory, like everything else in God, is *real*, it is that life that he grants, that God "*remembers*"; it *is* the eternal overcoming of the "nothing" out of which God called us into "his wonderful light."[42]

In this view, the divine memory is what enables creatures to be and to interact. The divine memory is powerfully and wonderfully creative. To be held in the divine memory is to be continually created "ex nihilo," to be enabled to exist, to find food and water, and to reproduce. The divine memory creates. It makes things live. It enables a diverse world of creatures to evolve on our planet. In response to God's creative remembrance, humans are the creatures who particularly are called to remember God. This is the human gift and responsibility: the human person is one who "comprehends the world as God's world, receives it from God and raises it up to God."[43] In response to God, who keeps the whole of creation in mind and brings it to life, human beings are called to remember the Creator and thus enter more fully into the life bestowed on them. The human remembrance of God is "the reception of this life-creating gift, the constant *acquisition* of and increase in life."[44]

Based on the faithful love of God revealed in Christ, it can be said that God will not forget any creature that God loves and creates. Each is inscribed eternally in the divine life. The sparrow that falls to the ground is not abandoned but is gathered up and brought to redemptive new life in Christ, in whom "creation itself will be set free from its bondage to decay" (Rom 8:21). The sparrow that falls to the ground is among the "all things" that are reconciled (Col 1:20), recapitulated (Eph 1:10), and made new (Rev 21:5) in the risen Christ. The shared life of God can be thought of as involving the holding and treasuring of every creature of every time in the living present of the Trinity. In the communion of saints, we can be thought of as coming to share the divine delight in each creature. The communion of saints would, then, open up as the communion of all creation. The capacity we already have to treasure all that makes up the history of life offers a hint of what might be possible to God. Again, our memory, even our liturgical remembering, can only be a poor analogy for the divine capacity to hold all things and make them live in the eternal memory of the triune God.

In the incarnational theology being suggested here, each sparrow is known and loved by God, participates in redemption in Christ, and is eternally held and treasured in the life of the Trinity. The creatures that spring from the abundance of divine Communion find redemption in being taken up eternally into this divine Communion in a way we cannot fully articulate. John Haught speaks of the whole of creation as being redeemed by being taken up into the enduring divine experience of the world. He says that everything in creation, "all the suffering and tragedy as well as the emergence of new life and intense beauty," is being *saved* by "being taken eternally into God's feeling for the world."[45] Individual creatures abide permanently within the everlasting compassion of God.

In this proposal, individual creatures are taken up into the living experience of the Trinity and are celebrated, respected, and honored in the divine Communion and in the communion of saints. I have already pointed out that we know very little about the *how* of our risen life in Christ, and we know less about that of other creatures. We hope for what is beyond our capacity to imagine because our hope is in the God who remains always incomprehensible mystery. We hope for what we do not see (Rom 8:24) and cannot imagine, the transformation of the whole creation in Christ. What we know is the promise of God given in the resurrection of the Word made flesh. We can hope that, in our participation in the communion of saints, we will also participate in God's delight in other animals within the abundance of creation that reaches its fulfillment in God. In particular, we may hope that the relationship we have with particular creatures, such as a beloved dog, does not end with death but is taken into eternal life.

5. *There is reason to hope that animals participate in resurrection life in Christ.* I have been proposing that each animal is known and loved by God, is the dwelling place of the Creator Spirit, participates in redemption in Christ, and abides forever in the living memory of God. Can more be said? I think it can. It can be said that animals will reach their redemptive fulfillment in Christ. They will not only be remembered and treasured, but be remembered in such a way as to be called into new life. As I have said, we do not have an imaginative picture of the new creation. Any imaginative picture we can form based on our present experience will quickly prove inadequate. But this is true, as well, for the resurrection of human beings. We can imagine the resuscitation of a corpse, but we cannot imagine the radical transformation of resurrection. The fact that resurrection life is beyond imagination does not mean it is not real. Our imaginations are of limited use and do not function well in dealing with God, who is the absolute future and the power of new life. Of course, they are also inadequate for dealing with quantum physics and with cosmology. What is real can be beyond our imaginations and our concepts.

The basis for hope is not our imagination but the God revealed in Jesus. As I pointed out in chapter 9, we need a negative theology of the future. We need to know what we do not know. What we have is hope based on our experience of God with us in Jesus and in the Spirit. As Elizabeth Johnson has said, our hope is not based upon information about the future but on "the character of God" revealed in the Christ-event.[46] What I am proposing is that we can think that, based on the character of God revealed in the Christ-event, individual animals and birds will participate in some way in risen life. They will find their fulfillment in God. The God of resurrection life is a God who brings individual creatures in their own distinctiveness *in some way* into the eternal dynamic life of the divine communion.

In Revelation, the one sitting on the throne says, "See, I am making all things new" (Rev 21:5). I am proposing that this "all things" includes other animals. It is clear that God will respect the particular nature that is specific to each creature. What is appropriate fulfillment for a human being may not be appropriate to a crab, a mosquito, or a bacterium. It is important to remember that great theologians such as Thomas Aquinas and Bonaventure saw the diversity of creatures as expressing the boundless abundance of the divine goodness. There is every reason to hope that the diverse range of creatures that spring from the abundance of the divine communion will find redemption in being taken up eternally into this communion in ways that are appropriate to each. Because God relates to each creature on its own terms, final fulfillment will fit the nature of each creature. With this in mind, I think it can be said that individual creatures will find their proper redemption in the divine communion in a way that we cannot fully imagine or articulate.

10

Prayers of Intercession

If God is not an interventionist God, as this book has argued, is there any reason to ask God for things? What is the point of intercessory prayer? It is clear that Christian biblical, liturgical, and spiritual tradition strongly supports this form of prayer. According to the New Testament, Jesus himself insists that his followers approach God with their needs. In Matthew's Sermon on the Mount, for example, Jesus says:

> Ask, and it will be given you; search, and you will find; knock, and the door will be opened for you. For everyone who asks receives, and everyone who searches finds, and for everyone who knocks, the door will be opened. Is there anyone among you who, if your child asks for bread, will give a stone? Or if the child asks for a fish, will give a snake? If you then, who are evil, know how to give good gifts to your children, how much more will your Father in heaven give good things to those who ask him! (Matt 7:7-11)

Jesus proclaims a God who is ever willing to respond to the needs of God's children. If a human being will come to the aid of a friend who asks for help, if a parent will give a hungry child the food for which the child asks, how much more responsive will be God's care for those who ask. The God of Jesus, the one who can be addressed as *Abba*, is a God who cares about our well-being and our ordinary human needs and wants us to express them directly in trusting prayer.

For those who seek to follow the way of Jesus, there can be no doubt about such a clear Gospel invitation. But the question for many people today is how this kind of prayer makes sense in the context of a world that is shaped by natural forces, many of which are well explained by science. All of us have been influenced by a scientific worldview, which appears to leave little room for God answering our prayers. We are left asking ourselves: Are we praying that God will act in a way that is outside of or overturns the laws of nature?

This book has proposed that God can be understood as working consistently in and through the natural world, both the laws of nature that we already understand and those that are still to be articulated. God certainly acts in special and specific ways, but I have argued that in these special divine acts, too, God acts consistently through created causes. It has been further proposed that God works creatively with finite limitations in God's love and respect for the integrity of creatures and creaturely processes. I see no opposition between intercessory prayer and this idea of a God who acts consistently through creaturely causes, because I believe that God can and does respond to our prayers through such secondary causes and that in this prayer God invites our further participation in the praxis of the kingdom. Intercessory prayer is fundamental to Christian life and remains very much so for those committed to a view of a God who acts in and through the created world. I will suggest four reasons why intercessory prayer remains a matter of great importance for those who hold this view: (1) God wants our participation, (2) we need to share what matters to us with the Beloved, (3) through intercession, we can be led to entrust ourselves to God, and (4) at the heart of intercessory prayer is the desire for God.

God Wants Our Participation

The God described in these pages is a God who acts powerfully, who does things, but who does them through the mediation of creaturely causes that have their own integrity. This is not a God who does nothing. In this view, God really can and does respond to our prayers, but does so through secondary causes. This is a God who does things for us, who does things that are personal. In this view, however, God accepts and works with the limits involved in respecting creaturely processes. This means, then, that if I pray for something that would involve God overturning the laws of nature, then God may respond in a way that is for my good but also respects the integrity of the laws of nature.

The God revealed in Jesus is a God who wants our participation. John Dominic Crossan and N. T. Wright are two eminent biblical scholars who disagree on some important issues. But, greatly to their credit, they have been prepared to enter into a creative and public dialogue with each other.[1] One of the areas where they differ is on their view of the kind of eschatology at work in the kingdom preaching of Jesus and in the proclamation of the resurrection. Crossan puts little emphasis on the future. He sees Jesus proclaiming a kingdom of justice, love, mercy, and peace that challenges us to be involved in the here and now. We are invited to collaborate and participate in the new world of God's reign. Wright insists, rightly in my view, on the element of future promise in Jesus' words and deeds. But he states that he and Crossan are as one on the idea that the kingdom proclaimed by Jesus is a participatory kingdom. He tells us that he loves Crossan's language of "collaborative eschatology."[2] The two scholars agree that the message of the New Testament is that we are called to participate in the new creation proclaimed and inaugurated in the resurrection of Jesus. The God of Jesus is a God who wants our active participation in the cause of the kingdom of love, justice, and peace.

This is consistent with the argument being made throughout this book that God does not act as one cause among others in the world, but acts as Creator—not just another secondary cause—in and through the mediation of creaturely causes. These creaturely causes include the laws of nature, but they also include free human beings and their words and actions. They also include our prayers of intercession. Of course, it is true that if we pray for something that is good for our world, such as for a peaceful resolution of the conflict between Israel and Palestinians in the Middle East, God already knows this is needed. And we can be sure that if we are deeply pained by this conflict, God is pained infinitely more. If we long for peace, God longs for it with a divine longing.

In our prayer, it is not that we are telling God something that God does not know. It is more that we are participating with God in the divine feeling for the Jewish and Palestinian communities, in the divine longing for a just peace between them, and in the divine action for peace. This divine action finds expression in many ways: in neighbors who reach out to each other across ethnic and religious lines, in political leaders who take initiatives aimed at just peace, in religious leaders and others who witness to peace in the public arena, and in all those ordinary people around the world who commit themselves to act for peace. When we pray for peace in this way, we are drawn into the participatory kingdom of Jesus. We participate with him in the coming reign of God, the kingdom of love, of justice, and of peace.

In Jesus of Nazareth, God has committed God's self to us and has done this forever. God will never be a God without a world. God will never be God without us. God is forever God-with-us. God has entered into a partnership with us. Of course, this is, from one important perspective, a radically unequal partnership. Who are we, as finite and sinful creatures, to think of ourselves as partners with the incomprehensible mystery of God? But God, in the divine freedom, has decided otherwise. As Athanasius and others have taught us, God became a human creature that we might become divine, in the sense of participating in divine life by grace. We are made partners with God. By God's sheer grace, we are part of God's work of new creation. God wants us to participate in God's action in our world, by our own words, actions, and prayers of intercession.

To pray in this way is to be open to what the Spirit is already doing in our world. And it is to be open to what God longs for and wants to do through ourselves and others. It sensitizes us to the deeper reality at work in the persons in our lives, in the concrete situations we encounter, and in the events of our world. It expresses and leads us further into a gospel way of life that gives priority to the poor and is committed to peacemaking and care for the global community of life on our planet. It enables us to say yes to the invitation to be involved in and cooperate with the prompting of grace in a wholehearted and committed way, both as individuals and as communities.

Sharing What Matters with the Beloved

In our relationships with friends and with partners in marriage, it is fundamental to share what really matters to us. When something is troubling us or bringing us a great deal of joy, and we hold it in and do not share it with our friend, we are closing off the possibility of intimacy in this area of life. If this happens regularly, we know that it damages relationships. We are not bringing our real selves to the friendship, but choosing to stay at a distance. In contrast, when we do communicate what we are feeling, no matter how ordinary it seems, and know that we are received by the other, then there is the possibility of deepening intimacy and of building the relationship.

Those involved in the ministry of spiritual direction report that this pattern operates in a similar way for a person in his or her relationship to God. A woman suffering great grief over the death of her friend tells her spiritual director that she is finding difficulty in prayer. God seems not to be there for her. She is restless and unengaged. The spiritual director asks what she feels about her friend's death, and she finally says that she is angry—angry with life and angry with God. The spiritual director's response is to suggest she might tell God directly about this anger. A man is anxious about the possibility of a new position in his workplace. He reports that he cannot concentrate in his prayer. He spends the whole time in distraction. Sometimes he asks God's help in getting the position he seeks, but this ends up in him thinking about and working through all the possible scenarios at work. The spiritual director's response is to suggest he get in touch with his anxiety and bring this to his meeting with God in prayer, simply naming how he feels to God and waiting on God's response.

William Barry points out that when we speak of God's "response" to our prayer, this does not mean that we expect to hear the voice of God, as though God were a human being with a voice speaking in the same room.[3] God's response is not of this kind. It occurs in different ways for different people, through the mediation of their own persons. One person may have an inner imaginary conversation with God or with Jesus. Barry gives the example of a man struggling with an addiction who asks Jesus to remove it. He hears the response "I can't. But we can overcome it together."[4] For another person, a phrase from scripture may come to mind and feel like an answer to prayer. For others, a response may come later in an "aha" experience that shows a way forward. God communicates with us through the mediation of our own imaginations, memories, and thoughts.

Slowly, perhaps with the help of some spiritual direction, we can learn to discern what is of God.

The experiences of spiritual directors can tell us that, very often, what leads to deeper intimacy with God is bringing the real experience of our lives to the Beloved. This is also true in our liturgical and everyday experience of prayer of intercession. We come to God as we are, with our everyday needs, hopes, and anxieties. Some of these may involve our concern about great issues of our time, such as in my own country, Australia, justice for indigenous people or the drought that is damaging much of the country. We rightly pray in the Eucharist for such things. To bring a drought to God in the intercessory prayer of the Eucharist is not necessarily to be asking God to intervene to overturn the natural world. It may be more to bring our own deep concerns about our land to God, and to ask that we might participate with God, working through created causes, in caring for this land.

We might pray for the healing of a friend who is diagnosed with cancer. When we do this, we are not necessarily asking God to act in an interventionist way. We may be bringing a person we love to our God and bringing what really matters to us in this moment to God. Our prayer for healing might be that God would work through created causes to bring healing, and these created causes could include the skill of a surgeon, excellent nursing care, and the love of family and friends. I believe there are circumstances where both love and prayer contribute to healing. Perhaps these act as secondary causes, tapping into potentialities within the natural order that are not yet well modeled or explained by science but that one day may be much better understood.

In our individual prayers of intercession, we can bring our own most ordinary and modest needs to God. We ask for help in completing an assignment, in dealing with a difficult person, in mending a relationship, in dealing with a busy day. We pray for peace as we approach a situation we fear. We pray for a good outcome as we await a medical diagnosis for ourselves or for someone we love. We ask for our "daily bread." We thus bring the everyday, the ordinary things of our lives, to God. When we do this, we are drawn sometimes into a new way of seeing that for which we pray, as William Barry points out:

God does not need information; so our petitions are not to let him know that, for example, Aunt Jane is dying. Something else is involved. It is a question of trusting that God wants to know my feelings about Aunt Jane's illness and about Aunt Jane herself. I may not want my favorite Aunt to die. If I think about it at all, I will also not want Aunt Jane to suffer and drag on a miserable life for my sake. What do I want for Aunt Jane? As I talk to God about her and about my feelings for her, I may come to realize that I want for Aunt Jane what I would want for myself under the same circumstances, to die peacefully if she must die now, to know deep within herself that God loves her and is with her, to know that I care deeply about her.[5]

When we bring our real concerns to God and are prepared to wait on God's response, we can be brought to a new understanding of what we really want. We slowly come to a sense of how God feels about our concerns. In the process, we can be "weaned from expecting magical solutions." Our intercessory prayer can have more the flavor of "communing with God" about one's friends or about suffering brothers and sisters throughout the world.[6] It can lead us once more to act in a way that is more consistent with God's boundless compassion that we meet in our prayer. What really matters is to pray as we are, as Brian Gallagher insists: "God loves real people, as we are, warts, carbuncles and all. Relationship thrives on reality and openness. Some of the best advice about prayer I've ever heard is 'to pray as you are, not as you're not.' Just be yourself. . . . Pray as the kind of person you are—talkative, quiet, informal. . . . Pray in the mood you're in—miserable, excited, hurting. . . . Pray with what's on your mind right now."[7]

Entrusting Ourselves to God

Karl Rahner is a strong defender of intercessory prayer. In agreement with what has been said in the previous section, he holds that what is fundamental in this form of prayer is that we come to God simply as we are. We place ourselves before God with our ordinary needs, anxieties, and hopes. We do not need to be already transformed, already in perfect conformity to God's will. We simply bring what is in us to God, coming before God in our everyday neediness. Along with this readiness to bring the everyday to

God, Rahner sees genuine Christian prayer of intercession as possessing a second fundamental characteristic: when we bring our mundane needs to God, we entrust ourselves to God. Rahner says, "One cannot come to God in prayer without giving him oneself, one's whole existence, in trusting submission and love, and in acceptance of the incomprehensible God who is beyond our understanding not only in his essence but also in his free relationship to us and must be accepted as such."[8]

Authentic prayer of petition unites ordinary human needs, the stuff of our lives, with an attitude of entrusting ourselves and our needs to a God whom we do not control or manipulate, but who remains for us incomprehensible mystery. Ultimately, Christian prayer is modeled on the prayer of Jesus, who prays, "Abba, Father, for you all things are possible; remove this cup from me; yet, not what I want, but what you want" (Mark 14:36). Intercessory prayer is profoundly human because, like the prayer of Jesus, it springs from real human need. It is profoundly divine because, again like the prayer of Jesus, it takes us to the place of surrender to God.[9]

Entrusting of ourselves to God does not mean that our earthly need is simply brushed aside. It still has its own integrity and importance. In fact, we may be led in prayer to an even deeper commitment to this issue or person for whom we pray. But we also find new freedom in entrusting it to God. What we are concerned about ceases to be absolute, because it is given into God's love, the only real absolute of our lives.

Rahner has published several books of prayers. One of his prayers is addressed to "God of my Daily Routine." He prays, "If every day is 'everyday,' then every day is *Your* day, and every hour is the hour of Your grace."[10] In intercessory prayer, our everyday becomes recognized as God's day. What is true of prayer of intercession is true of Christian life in general. We are called by the gospel to place our whole being into the hands of God as confidently as a child takes the hand of her mother or father: "The profoundest secret of the Christian life and of Christian prayer is to become a child in relations with God—a child whose quiet confidence and silent submission do not fail in moments of trial when God appears to have turned from us."[11] The more our prayer becomes a prayer of radical trust, the more it imitates the prayer of Jesus, the more truly human it becomes. And insofar as this happens, our everyday becomes the place of God, and we seek and find God in all things.

Herbert McCabe has said something similar to Rahner. He sees all prayer as finally a prayer of abandonment, "even when it is that excellent prayer when we are most concerned about what we desperately need and want."[12] Our prayer of intercession is a participation in Christ's prayer. The prayer that is Jesus' life finds its ultimate expression in the self-giving love of the cross, and this prayer is answered in the resurrection.[13] All Christian prayer is a participation, in the Spirit, in Christ's death and resurrection. Even when a prayer of petition concerns something very specific and concrete that arises directly out of our own neediness, like doing well in an interview, insofar as it is truly prayer, it is always a participation in Christ's prayer. Because we are transformed in the Spirit, because the Spirit of God dwells in us, our prayer of intercession is not simply the prayer of a creature to the Creator, but always the prayer of a daughter or son, always a participation in Christ. When we pray it is always the work of the Holy Spirit in us: "Likewise the Spirit helps us in our weakness; for we do not know how to pray as we ought, but that very Spirit intercedes with sighs too deep for words. And God, who searches the heart, knows what is the mind of the Spirit, because the Spirit intercedes for the saints according to the will of God" (Rom 8:26-27).

In our prayer of intercession, the Spirit of God groans within us, praying for what we cannot even articulate. We pray with Christ Jesus to the one he called *Abba*. We are drawn into his prayer, and we become the locus of the divine relationships, the divine dialogue between Jesus and his *Abba*. When we come to prayer of intercession, it is always the work of grace, the gift of the Spirit. Our daily and personal needs and hopes, along with our great longings for our planetary community, are brought to this divine Trinitarian dialogue, transformed, and taken up, so that they participate in the divine longing and the divine action of self-bestowing love at work in all things.

Prayer as Desire for God

In 412, Augustine wrote a famous letter on prayer, "To Proba." A widow from a wealthy and powerful Roman family, Anicia Faltonia Proba had fled from Rome during the invasion of the city by Alaric and the Goths. She gathered a group of women and sailed to Carthage, where she established a community of Christian women. Augustine's letter was a response to her request for help with prayer. Proba was disturbed about what she should ask for in prayer. She took seriously Paul's words from Rom 8:26 that "we do not know how to pray as we ought." She feared that, if she prayed for other than what she ought, this might do more harm than good. For what ought she to pray?

Augustine sums up his response with this deceptively simple advice: "Pray for a happy life."[14] He sees it as appropriate to pray for all that leads to true happiness. This might include such things as marriage, celibacy, children, health, and even honors, power, and possessions, if these are sought for the sake of the genuine good of others. We are right to pray for life and for health of mind and body. We ought to pray not only for ourselves and for our families and friends, but also for enemies, as the Gospels command us. All of this and much more Augustine sees as included in praying for an authentically happy life.

But the test of what leads to true happiness is to see all these things in relationship to the one thing that is our ultimate happiness—our life in God: "Therefore all things which are the objects of useful and becoming desire are unquestionably to be viewed with reference to that one life which is lived with God and is derived from him."[15] Only one thing is our happiness, the one thing proclaimed by the psalmist: "One thing I ask of the Lord, that will I seek, to dwell in the house of the Lord all the days of my life" (Ps 26:4). For this great gift we are urged to "pray without ceasing" (1 Thess 5:7).

Augustine recognizes that there are special times in a day or week when we pray using words, but he sees these particular prayer times as reflecting a deeper ongoing prayer. This deeper prayer is the uninterrupted desire for God: "Multiplied words are one thing, long-continued warmth of desire is another." In most cases, he says, prayer "consists more in groaning than in speaking, in tears rather than in words." This longing desire for God is the truest and most important form of prayer. Words are certainly helpful to us, enabling us to consider and reflect on what we ask, but they are not a means by which "we expect that God is to be either informed or moved to compliance."[16]

One of the things that prayer of intercession does is make us more open to receive what God wants to give. Our prayers stir up in us the desire by which we might receive the grace that God wants to bestow on us. Augustine proposes that all our prayers of intercession for ourselves, our friends, or even our enemies should be modeled on the prayer taught by Jesus. They can be tested against his prayer. They are genuine insofar as they reflect such words as "Hallowed be your name," "Your kingdom come," and "Give us today our daily bread."

All the different things we pray for are ultimately directed to the one thing that will make for true happiness. Our prayer is a longing and a thirsting for the fountain of life. However, we do not yet see clearly the fulfillment of our hope. The God we long for is beyond our grasp in this life. We long for the peace beyond all understanding (Phil 4:7). We long for the God beyond all our concepts and words. We hope for what we do not see (Rom 8:25). We know that all our images of our future life in God are inadequate. Augustine speaks of a "learned ignorance" about what is hoped for, a not-knowing that is taught by the Spirit of God, who intercedes for us with sighs too deep for words (Rom 8:26).[17]

Clearly, Augustine values prayer for everyday things, but also clearly, he sees that prayer for these daily goods, in their concreteness and specificity, exists within an ongoing prayer that is a profound longing, an unquenchable desire of our being for the living God. All the particular things we ask of God have their own proper legitimacy, but they are ordered to that "one thing" for which we thirst.

At the beginning of this chapter, I referred to Jesus' parable in the Gospel of Matthew about the parent who responds to the needs of a child. It concludes with the words "How much more will your Father in heaven give *good things* to those who ask him!" (Matt 7:11; emphasis added). In the Lukan version of this same parable, Jesus concludes with the words "How much more will the heavenly Father give *the Holy Spirit* to those who ask him!" (Luke 11:13; emphasis added). It seems that for Luke, the one thing that unites and includes all that we pray for, in all our specific prayers of intercession, is the gift of the Spirit, given to the disciples at Pentecost. This Holy Spirit is the gift of God's self, the source of life, joy, strength, and mission for the disciples.

While the Christian tradition affirms the central importance of asking God for the specific and everyday things we need, it also affirms that ultimately there is "one thing" we need to ask for: the grace of being drawn more deeply into the love of God. Of course, to ask for this gift is risky. We risk being drawn into boundless love. There is much in us that resists such love. But we can come to know our own resistance, and we can pray for freedom, knowing that the Spirit of God not only prays in us but also frees us to receive the gift offered to us.

Conclusion

In my experience, whenever someone speaks on the issue of divine action, it provokes questions about the meaning and value of intercessory prayer. It seems that many people have serious questions about this practice. There is a widespread sense that intercessory prayer is out of step with a scientific worldview, that it no longer rings true. Part of the problem, I believe, is that many people have understood God's action in one of two ways: (1) God is an interventionist God who acts in ways that overturn or bypass the laws of nature (in which case intercessory prayer certainly makes sense), or (2) God is a noninterventionist God who creates the universe but allows it to take its own course (in which case intercessory prayer does not seem to make sense).

Neither of these positions is proposed in this book. I have argued for a view of God as achieving the divine purposes by acting consistently as Creator in a noninterventionist way through created causes, through the laws of nature we understand, and through the natural world that our laws do not yet describe, acting always and everywhere, in and through every aspect of creation. This divine action enables the universe and all its creatures to exist, to act, and to emerge into the new, and it involves God working creatively with limitations that spring from God's loving respect for created causes, both human and nonhuman. God meets us personally in the life of grace and acts providentially for our good. This is a description of a God who can and does answer prayers.

There is every reason to bring our prayers to God. I have described four of these reasons in this chapter: God wants our participation, we share what really matters with the Beloved, we are led to entrust ourselves radically to God, and our prayer for specific needs involves and leads to prayer for the one thing that grounds and unites them all, the love of God. The view of divine action proposed here supports prayer of intercession in all these ways. It is not advocating prayer that asks God to overturn natural laws, but when people do pray in this way, there is reason to think God hears and responds in ways that are appropriate and loving. My argument, however, has been that asking God to overturn nature is *not* necessarily what we are doing in intercessory prayer. We can think of our prayer as bringing our needs to a God who, in creation and redemption, is always bestowing God's self upon us and upon all creation in richer and fuller ways. We are asking that we might be ever more open to this gift and to whatever it may mean for us and for the wider creation. We are drawn into the divine compassionate love for the creatures of our planet and to the praxis of the kingdom, committed anew to the work of justice and peace and to the integrity of God's creation.

In intercessory prayer, we bring our concerns, hopes, fears, and joys to a God who cares for us as a parent cares for his or her child, a God who acts for our good in and through created causes. This view of divine action fully supports prayer for healing of someone we love, for strength to do a task, for peace in our world, and for all the things that matter to us. We bring what matters to the Beloved, and we entrust ourselves to our God, who acts for our good in and through the natural world, who waits upon and respects the integrity of natural processes and human freedom, who draws us to participate in God's saving action in the world, and who promises to bring all to redemptive fulfillment in Christ.

Notes

Preface

1. Christopher Southgate, *The Groaning of Creation: God, Evolution and the Problem of Evil* (Louisville: Westminster John Knox, 2008).

2. Nancey Murphy, Robert John Russell, and William R. Stoeger, eds., *Physics and Cosmology: Scientific Perspectives on the Problem of Natural Evil* (Vatican: Vatican Observatory; Berkeley, Calif.: Center for Theology and the Natural Sciences, 2007).

Chapter 1: Characteristics of the Universe Revealed by the Sciences

1. See William R. Stoeger, "Divine Action in a Broken World," in *Science and Religion . . . and Culture in the Jesuit Tradition: Perspectives from East Asia*, ed. Jose Mario C. Francisco and Roman Miguel G. de Jesus (Adelaide: ATF, 2006), 7–22; "Key Developments in Physics Challenging Philosophy and Theology," in *Religion and Science: History, Method, Dialogue*, ed. W. Mark Richardson and Wesley J. Wildman (New York: Routledge, 1996), 183–200; "Contemporary Cosmology and Its Implications for the Contemporary Science–Religion Dialogue," in *Physics, Philosophy and Theology: A Common Quest for Understanding*, ed. Robert John Russell, William R. Stoeger, and George Coyne (Vatican City State: Vatican Observatory, 1988), 219–47.

2. Ian Barbour, *When Science Meets Religion: Enemies, Strangers or Partners?* (London: SCM, 2000); Arthur Peacocke, *Theology for a Scientific Age: Being and Becoming—Natural, Divine and Human* (Minneapolis: Fortress Press, 1993); John Polkinghorne, *Belief in God in an Age of Science* (New Haven: Yale University

Press, 1998); Robert John Russell, *Cosmology, Evolution, and Christian Hope: Theology and Science in Mutual Interaction* (Kitchener, Ont.: Pandora, 2006); Nancey Murphy and George F. R. Ellis, *On the Moral Nature of the Universe: Theology, Cosmology and Ethics* (Minneapolis: Fortress Press, 1996); John F. Haught, *God after Darwin: A Theology of Evolution* (Boulder, Colo.: Westview, 2000); Philip Clayton, *Adventures in the Spirit: God, World, Divine Action* (Minneapolis: Fortress Press, 2008); Christopher Southgate, *The Groaning of Creation: God, Evolution, and the Problem of Evil* (Louisville: Westminster John Knox, 2008).

3. Peacocke, *Theology for a Scientific Age*, 38.

4. William R. Stoeger, "The Mind-Brain Problem, the Laws of Nature, and Constitutive Relationships," in *Neuroscience and the Person: Scientific Perspectives on Divine Action*, ed. Robert John Russell, Nancey Murphy, Theo C. Meyering, and Michael Arbib (Vatican City State: Vatican Observatory, 1999), 136–37.

5. Ibid., 139.

6. William R. Stoeger, "Describing God's Action in the World in Light of Scientific Knowledge of Reality," in *Cosmos and Chaos: Scientific Perspectives on Divine Action*, ed. Robert John Russell, Nancey Murphy, and Arthur R. Peacocke (Vatican City State: Vatican Observatory; Berkeley, Calif.: Center for Theology and the Natural Sciences, 1995, 1997), 242–43.

7. Stephen Jay Gould, *Wonderful Life* (New York: Norton, 1989).

8. Ibid., 51.

9. Simon Conway Morris, *Life's Solution: Inevitable Humans in a Lonely Universe* (Cambridge: Cambridge University Press, 2003).

10. Ibid., 196.

11. See Nicola S. Clayton and Nathan J. Emery, "Canny Corvids and Political Primates: A Case for Convergent Evolution in Intelligence," in *The Deep Structure of Biology*, ed. Simon Conway Morris (West Conshohocken, Pa.: Templeton Foundation, 2008), 128–42.

12. William R. Stoeger, "The Immanent Directionality of the Evolutionary Process, and Its Relationship to Theology," in *Evolutionary and Molecular Biology: Scientific Perspectives on Divine Action*, ed. Robert J. Russell, William R. Stoeger, S.J., and Francisco J. Ayala (Vatican City State: Vatican Observatory; Berkeley, Calif.: Center for Theology and the Natural Sciences, 1998), 184.

13. See John D. Barrow and Frank Tipler, *The Anthropic Cosmological Principle* (Oxford: Oxford University Press, 1986); John D. Barrow, *The Constants of Nature: From Alpha to Omega* (London: Jonathan Cape, 2002).

14. See, for example, Robert John Russell, *Cosmology: From Alpha to Omega* (Minneapolis: Fortress Press, 2005); and the articles in Ted Peters, Robert John Russell, and Michael Welker, eds., *Resurrection: Theological and Scientific*

Assessments (Grand Rapids: Eerdmans, 2002); George F. R. Ellis, ed., *Eschatology from a Cosmic Perspective* (Philadelphia: Templeton Foundation, 2002); John Polkinghorne and Michael Welker, eds., *The End of the World and the Ends of God: Science and Theology on Eschatology* (Harrisburg, Pa.: Trinity, 2000).

15. For recent examples, see Joseph Zycinski, *God and Evolution: Fundamental Questions of Christian Evolutionism* (Washington, D.C.: Catholic University of American Press, 2006); Ted Peters and Marty Hewlett, *Evolution from Creation to New Creation: Conflict, Conversation, and Convergence* (Nashville: Abingdon, 2003); Arthur Peacocke, *The Palace of Glory: God's World and Science* (Adelaide, Australia: ATF, 2005); and Haught, *God after Darwin*; and among many others, my earlier works: *Jesus and the Cosmos* (Mahwah, N.J.: Paulist, 1991); and *The God of Evolution: A Trinitarian Theology* (Mahwah, N.J.: Paulist, 1999).

16. Ursula Goodenough, *The Sacred Depths of Nature* (Oxford: Oxford University Press, 1998), 143–51.

17. Holmes Rolston III, *Science and Religion: A Critical Survey* (New York: Random House, 1987), 134.

18. Southgate, *The Groaning of Creation*, 9.

19. Ibid., 9–10.

20. Rolston, *Science and Religion*, 288.

21. Southgate, *The Groaning of Creation*, 8–9.

Chapter 2: Divine Action in the Christ-Event

1. For Mark, 1:15; 4:11; 4:26; 9:1, 47; 10:14; 12:34; 14:25; 15:43. For the other material common to Matthew and Luke (Q), Luke 6:20 and Matt 5:3; Luke 7:28 and Matt 11:11; Luke 10:9 and Matt 10:7; Luke 11:20 and Matt 12:28; Luke 13:18, 20 and Matt 13:31, 33; Luke 13:28 and Matt 8:11; Luke 16:16 and Matt 11:12. For special Matthew, 3:2; 4:17; 5:19-20; 19:24; 21:31; 21:43. For special Luke, 4:43; 9:2, 11, 60, 62; 14:15; 16:16; 17:20; 19:11; 22:16, 18. For John, 3:3, 5.

2. See Norman Perrin, *Jesus and the Language of the Kingdom: Symbol and Metaphor in New Testament Interpretation* (London: SCM, 1976).

3. N. T. Wright, *Jesus and the Victory of God* (Minneapolis: Fortress Press, 1996), 198–243.

4. Amos N. Wilder, *Early Christian Rhetoric: The Language of the Gospel* (Cambridge, Mass.: Harvard University Press, 1964), 72.

5. Gunther Bornkamm, *Jesus of Nazareth* (London: Hodder & Stoughton, 1960, 1973), 69.

6. John Dominic Crossan, *In Parables: The Challenge of the Historical Jesus* (New York: Harper & Row, 1973), 22.

7. John P. Meier, *A Marginal Jew: Rethinking the Historical Jesus*, vol. 2, *Mentor, Message, and Miracles* (New York: Doubleday, 1994), 1041–47.

8. Ibid., 453.

9. Edward Schillebeeckx, *Christ: The Christian Experience in the Modern World* (London: SCM, 1980), 791.

10. Ibid.

11. Edward Schillebeeckx, *Jesus: An Experiment in Christology* (New York: Seabury, 1979), 152–54.

12. James D. G. Dunn, *Jesus Remembered* (Grand Rapids: Eedrmans, 2003), 599–606.

13. Ibid., 604.

14. Ibid., 603.

15. Wright, *Jesus and the Victory of God*, 431.

16. Ibid., 433.

17. John Dominic Crossan, *The Historical Jesus: The Life of a Mediterranean Jewish Peasant* (San Francisco: HarperSanFrancisco, 1991), 344.

18. E. P. Sanders, *The Historical Figure of Jesus* (London: Penguin, 1993), 235–36.

19. On the circles around Jesus, see John P. Meier, *A Marginal Jew: Rethinking the Historical Jesus*, vol. 3, *Companions and Competitors* (New York: Doubleday, 2001), 19–124.

20. Elisabeth Schüssler Fiorenza, *In Memory of Her: A Feminist Theological Reconstruction of Christian Origins* (London: SCM, 1983), 135–36. She speaks of a "discipleship of equals" to describe what she sees as the inclusivity of the movement around Jesus (140–51).

21. See Gerhard Lohfink, *Jesus and Community* (Philadelphia: Fortress Press, 1984), 44–56.

22. Marcus Borg, *Jesus: Uncovering the Life, Teachings, and Relevance of a Religious Revolutionary* (San Francisco: HarperSanFrancisco, 2006), 253–60. John Dominic Crossan and N. T. Wright both agree with Borg about participatory eschatology. In their published dialogue about the resurrection, they disagree about important issues but are as one on the notion of what they call "collaborative eschatology." Robert B. Steward, ed., *The Resurrection of Jesus: John Dominic Crossan and N. T. Wright in Dialogue* (Minneapolis: Fortress Press, 2006), 26–47.

23. Borg, *Jesus*, 260.

24. Ben F. Meyer, *The Aims of Jesus* (London: SCM, 1979), 242.

25. Joel B. Green, "Crucifixion," in *The Cambridge Companion to Jesus*, ed. Marcus Bockmuehl (Cambridge: Cambridge University Press, 2001), 98.

26. Dunn, *Jesus Remembered*, 796–818. He does not support the claim that Jesus drew on the suffering servant of Isaiah 53. In this, he differs from N. T.

Wright, who sees Isaiah 40–55 as thematic for Jesus' kingdom announcement and holds that "Jesus came to see himself as the focal point of God's restoration and fulfillment of Israel" and that "he believed that he was to be the means in his life, and particularly in his death, of the radical defeat of evil." Wright, *Jesus and the Victory of God*, 603. Borg, by contrast, holds that while Jesus may well have known that his journey to Jerusalem could end in his death, he did not see his death as central to his purpose. Marcus Borg, "Why Was Jesus Killed?" in *The Meaning of Jesus: Two Visions*, by Marcus J. Borg and N. T. Wright (London: SPCK, 1999), 82.

27. Dunn, *Jesus Remembered*, 818–24.

28. Schillebeeckx, *Christ*, 729–30.

29. Herbert McCabe, *God Matters* (London: Mowbray, 1987), 93.

30. Herbert McCabe, *God Still Matters* (London: Continuum, 2002), 96.

31. McCabe, *God Matters*, 99–100.

32. Those who propose that God suffers with us include Jürgen Moltmann, *The Cross of Christ as the Foundation and Criticism of Christian Theology* (New York: Harper & Row, 1974); Paul Fiddes, *The Creative Suffering of God* (Oxford: Clarendon, 1978). For criticisms of this position, see Thomas Weinandy, *Does God Suffer?* (Edinburgh: T&T Clark, 2000); Brian Davies, *The Reality of God and the Problem of Evil* (London: Continuum, 2006); and Herbert McCabe, *God Matters*, 39–51. My own position is closer to that of Walter Kasper, discussed later in this section, and Elizabeth Johnson, *She Who Is: The Mystery of God in Feminist Theological Discourse* (New York: Crossroad, 1992), 265–72.

33. Walter Kasper, *The God of Jesus Christ* (London: SCM, 1983), 194.

34. Ibid.

35. Ibid., 195.

36. Ibid.

37. Rowan Williams, *On Christian Theology* (Malden, Mass.: Blackwell, 2000), 234.

Chapter 3: Creation as Divine Self-Bestowal

1. Niels Henrik Gregersen, "Laws of Physics, Principles of Self-Organization, and Natural Capacities: On Explaining a Self-Organizing World," in *Creation: Law and Probability*, ed. Fraser Watts (Aldershot: Ashgate, 2008), 97.

2. Ibid., 98.

3. Ibid.

4. Stuart Kauffman, *Reinventing the Sacred: A New View of Science, Reason and Religion* (Philadelphia: Basic Books, 2008). While Kauffman sees the creativity of

the universe as "God enough" for us (pp. 100, 283), I see it as the created effect of the transcendent Creator.

5. Karl Rahner, *Foundations of Christian Faith: An Introduction to the Idea of Christianity* (New York: Seabury, 1978), 197.

6. Karl Rahner, "Resurrection: D. Theology," *Encyclopedia of Theology: A Concise Sacramentum Mundi*, ed. Karl Rahner (London: Burns & Oates, 1975), 1442; Karl Rahner, "Christology in the Setting of Modern Man's Understanding of Himself and of His World," in *Theological Investigations* (New York: Seabury, 1974), 11:219.

7. Karl Rahner, "The Specific Character of the Christian Concept of God," in *Theological Investigations* (New York: Crossroad, 1988), 21:185–95.

8. Elsewhere, Rahner notes, "God himself through his own being precisely *is* this difference." "Christology in the Setting of Modern Man's Understanding," 224.

9. Rahner, "The Specific Character of the Christian Concept of God," 191.

10. Aristotelian philosophy sees reality as constituted by the two complementary principles, matter and form. While matter is the underlying reality or potentiality, form is that which actualizes matter, determining the nature of an entity. This theory of matter and form (*hylomorphism*) played an important role in scholastic philosophy and theology. As well as the inner causes of an entity, the material and formal causes, there are also the external efficient cause, which causes it to exist, and the final cause, the purpose for which something is made. An exemplary cause is a model or pattern for doing something.

11. See Rahner, *Foundations,* 120–23. In some works, Rahner calls this *quasi*-formal causality, with the *quasi* indicating the uniqueness of this kind of formal causality, in which both divine transcendence and creaturely integrity are fully maintained. See Rahner, "Natural Science and Christian Faith," in *Theological Investigations* (New York: Crossroad, 1988), 21:35–36.

12. What is true of grace is always valid "in an analogous way for the relationship between God's absolute being and being which originates from him." Karl Rahner, "Natural Science and Christian Faith," 36.

13. Rahner, "Christology in the Setting of Modern Man's Understanding," 225.

14. Karl Rahner, "Immanent and Transcendent Consummation of the World," in *Theological Investigations* (London: Darton, Longman & Todd, 1973), 10:281.

15. Karl Rahner, *Hominisation: The Evolutionary Origin of Man as a Theological Problem* (London: Burns & Oates, 1965), 98–101; "Christology within an Evolutionary View of the World," in *Theological Investigations* (Baltimore: Helicon, 1966), 5:157–92; *Foundations,* 178–203.

16. Rahner, "Natural Science and Christian Faith," 37.

17. I discuss this in some detail in *Breath of Life: A Theology of the Creator Spirit* (Maryknoll, N.Y.: Orbis, 2004).

18. Rahner, *Foundations*, 193.

19. Rahner, "Christology in the Setting of Modern Man's Understanding," 223–26.

20. Brian Davies, *The Reality of God and the Problem of Evil* (New York: Continuum, 2006), 233.

21. See, for example, Rahner, *Foundations*, 78–79.

22. Ibid., 79.

23. Ibid.

24. Herbert McCabe, *God Matters* (London: Mowbray, 1987), 13.

25. Herbert McCabe, *God Still Matters* (London: Continuum, 2002), 11–12.

26. See Elizabeth Johnson, "Does God Play Dice? Divine Providence and Chance," *Theological Studies* 57 (1996): 17.

27. Jacques Monod, *Chance and Necessity* (London: Collins, 1972).

28. See Arthur Peacocke, *Theology for a Scientific Age: Being and Becoming—Natural, Divine and Human* (Minneapolis: Fortress Press, 1993), 115–21.

29. D. J. Bartholomew, *God of Chance* (London: SCM, 1984). See also the series of essays in Fraser Watts, ed., *Creation: Law and Probability* (Aldershot: Ashgate, 2008).

30. Bartholomew, *God of Chance*, 97.

31. Peacocke, *Theology for a Scientific Age*, 119.

32. Ibid., 175.

33. Thomas Aquinas *Summa contra gentiles* 3.75.2. Translated by Vernon Bourke in *Summa contra gentiles Book Three: Providence Part 1* (Notre Dame: University of Notre Dame, 1956, 1975), 249.

34. See ibid., 3.72–75.

35. Johnson, "Does God Play Dice?", 15.

36. Ibid., 16; Peacocke, *Theology for a Scientific Age*, 121.

Chapter 4: Special Divine Acts

1. Thomas Aquinas *Summa theologiae* 1.8.1.

2. Maurice Wiles, *God's Action in the World* (London: SCM, 1986), 93.

3. Keith Ward, *Divine Action* (London: Collins, 1990), 74–102, 127.

4. Keith Ward, *God, Chance and Necessity* (Oxford: Oneworld, 1996), 83.

5. Ibid., 93.

6. Robert J. Russell, Nancey C. Murphy, and Chris J. Isham, eds., *Quantum Cosmology and the Laws of Nature: Scientific Perspectives on Divine Action*, 2nd

ed. (Vatican City State: Vatican Observatory; Berkeley, Calif.: Center for Theology and the Natural Sciences, 1996); Robert J. Russell, Nancey C. Murphy, and Arthur Peacocke, eds., *Chaos and Complexity: Scientific Perspectives on Divine Action* (Vatican City State: Vatican Observatory; Berkeley, Calif.: Center for Theology and the Natural Sciences, 1995); Robert J. Russell, William R. Stoeger, and Francisco J. Ayala, eds., *Evolutionary and Molecular Biology: Scientific Perspectives on Divine Action* (Vatican City State: Vatican Observatory; Berkeley, Calif.: Center for Theology and the Natural Sciences, 1998); Robert J. Russell, Nancey C. Murphy, Theo C. Meyering, and Michael A. Arbib, eds., *Neuroscience and the Person: Scientific Perspectives on Divine Action* (Vatican City State: Vatican Observatory; Berkeley, Calif.: Center for Theology and the Natural Sciences, 1999); Robert J. Russell, Philip Clayton, Kirk Wegter-McNelly, and John Polkinghorne, eds., *Quantum Mechanics: Scientific Perspectives on Divine Action* (Vatican City State: Vatican Observatory; Berkeley, Calif.: Center for Theology and the Natural Sciences, 2001).

7. See Robert J. Russell, "Introduction," in Russell et al., eds., *Chaos and Complexity*, 6–13; Russell "Introduction," in Russell et al., eds., *Quantum Mechanics*, ii–iv. Russell has provided a full account of his own view and that of others in three chapters of his recent book *Cosmology: From Alpha to Omega* (Minneapolis: Fortress Press, 2008), 110–225.

8. Murphy sees God as acting in all quantum events, not as the sole determiner of events, but in a mediated action, in the sense that God always acts together with nature at the quantum level. Tracy suggests seeing God as acting in some rather than all quantum events, in order to bring about the effects of God's providence. Russell proposes that God acts in all quantum events until the appearance of life and consciousness, and then God increasingly refrains from determining outcomes, leaving room for top-down causality in conscious creatures, particularly in humans. For a summary of these views, see Russell, "Divine Action and Quantum Mechanics: A Fresh Assessment," in Russell et al., eds., *Quantum Mechanics*, 293–328.

9. Russell, *Cosmology*.

10. Philip Clayton, *Adventures in the Spirit: God, World, Divine Action* (Minneapolis: Fortress Press, 2008).

11. Owen Thomas, in *God's Activity in the World: The Contemporary Problem* (Chico, Calif.: Scholars, 1983), sees the primary causality and the process approaches as two theories of divine action that involve metaphysical positions.

12. On this, see Russell, *Cosmology*, 189–90, 249–72, particularly 252.

13. Russell makes it clear that his own approach to noninterventionist divine action respects the mystery and otherness of God and is not meant as an explanation of how God acts, let alone a description or explanation of a "causal joint." See, for example, *Cosmology*, 126.

14. I have dealt with this in some detail in *Human Experience of God* (New York: Paulist, 1983).

15. Rahner, "Experience of the Holy Spirit," in *Theological Investigations* (New York: Crossroad, 1983), 18:196–97. See also his *Foundations of Christian Faith: An Introduction to the Idea of Christianity* (New York: Crossroad, 1978), 137; "Reflections on the Experience of Grace," in *Theological Investigations* (New York: Seabury, 1974), 3:86–90 ; "The Experience of God Today," in *Theological Investigations* (New York: Seabury, 1974), 11:149–65; "Experience of Self and Experience of God," in *Theological Investigations*, 13:122–32 (New York: Seabury, 1975); "Experience of the Spirit and Existential Commitment," in *Theological Investigations* (New York: Seabury, 1979), 16:24–51.

16. Rahner, *Foundations of Christian Faith*, 88.

17. Ibid., 87.

18. Karl Rahner and Karl-Heinz Weger, *Our Christian Faith* (London: Burns & Oates, 1980), 77.

19. Ibid., 78–79.

20. "The event of God's promise of himself in Jesus makes that deepest promise by God of himself to the world historically accessible and irreversible. It is always and everywhere the fundamental energy and force of the world and its history. It is therefore perfectly possible to understand the event of Jesus without the aid of images of an intervention in the world from outside. In doing without such an image, however, we must let history really be history and clearly realise that this deepest energy and power of the world and its history is God in his sovereign freedom, who, by his free promise of himself, has made himself this deepest energy and force of the world." Ibid., 103–4.

21. See *The Dogmatic Constitution on the Church* of the Second Vatican Council, par. 1 and 48.

22. See, for example, Henri De Lubac, *Catholicism: A Study of the Corporate Destiny of Mankind* (New York: Sheed & Ward, 1950); Edward Schillebeeckx, *Christ the Sacrament of Encounter with God* (New York: Sheed & Ward, 1963); Karl Rahner, *The Church and the Sacraments* (New York: Herder & Herder, 1963).

Chapter 5: Miracles and the Laws of Nature

1. Alan Richardson, *The Miracle-Stories of the Gospels* (London: SCM, 1941), 36.

2. John P. Meier, *A Marginal Jew: Rethinking the Historical Jesus,* vol. 2, *Mentor, Message, and Miracles* (New York: Doubleday, 1994).

3. Ibid., 630.

4. Ibid., 690.

5. Ibid., 831.

6. Ibid., 921.

7. Ibid., 923.

8. *Summa theologiae* 1a.8.1. I am using the Blackfriars edition and translation, *Saint Thomas Aquinas: Summa theologiae* (London: Blackfriars in conjunction with Eyre & Spottiswoode, 1964–80).

9. *De potentia* 3.7.

10. Aquinas, *Summa theologiae,* 1a.22.3.

11. Ibid., 1a.105.6.

12. Michael Behe, *Darwin's Black Box: The Biochemical Challenge to Evolution* (New York: Free Press, 1996).

13. Aquinas *Summa theologiae* 1a.105.6.

14. It is worth noting that this is not necessarily the position of all contemporary followers of Aquinas. W. Norris Clarke, a well-regarded Thomist philosopher, is remarkably sympathetic to "irreducible complexity." See W. Norris Clarke, *The One and the Many: A Contemporary Thomistic Metaphysics* (Notre Dame: University of Notre Dame Press, 2001), 255.

15. Aquinas *Summa theologiae* 1a.104.3.

16. Ibid., 1a.105.7.

17. Ibid., 1a.105.7 ad 1.

18. Ibid., 1a.105.7 ad 2.

19. Ibid., 1a.105.8.

20. Ibid., 1a.105.6.

21. Brian Davies, *The Thought of Thomas Aquinas* (Oxford: Clarendon, 1992), 174.

22. Aquinas *Summa theologiae* 1a.110.4 ad 10.

23. Davies, *The Thought of Thomas Aquinas,* 173.

24. William R. Stoeger, "Contemporary Physics and the Ontological Status of the Laws of Nature," in *Quantum Cosmology and the Laws of Nature: Scientific Perspectives on Divine Action,* ed. Robert J. Russell, Nancey Murphy, and C. J. Isham, 209–234 (Vatican City State: Vatican Observatory; Berkeley, Calif.: Center for Theology and the Natural Sciences, 1993); Stoeger, "The Mind-Brain Problem, the Laws of Nature and Constitutive Relationships," in *Neuroscience and the Person: Scientific Perspectives on Divine Action,* ed. Robert John Russell, Nancey Murphy, Theo C. Meyering, and Michael A. Arbib (Vatican City State: Vatican Observatory; Berkeley, Calif.: Center for Theology and the Natural Sciences, 1999), 129–46; Stoeger, "Epistemological and Ontological Issues Arising from Quantum Theory," in *Quantum Mechanics: Scientific Perspectives on Divine Action,* ed. Robert J. Russell, Philip Clayton, Kirk Wegter-McNelly, and John Polkinghorne (Vatican City

State: Vatican Observatory; Berkeley Calif.: Center for Theology and the Natural Sciences, 2001), 81–98.

25. Stoeger, "Contemporary Physics," 223.

26. Ibid., 224.

27. Ibid., 225.

28. Ibid.

29. Ibid., 221.

30. Ibid., 216.

31. Stoeger, "The Mind-Brain Problem," 130.

32. Ibid., 134–35.

33. Karl Rahner, *Foundations of Christian Faith: An Introduction to the Idea of Christianity* (New York: Seabury, 1978), 258. See also Johann Baptist Metz, "Miracle," in *Encyclopedia of Theology: A Concise Sacramentum Mundi*, ed. Karl Rahner (London: Burns & Oates, 1975), 963.

34. Rahner, *Foundations of Christian Faith*, 261.

35. Ibid., 263.

36. Ibid., 261.

37. Simon Tugwell, ed. and trans., *Albert and Thomas: Selected Writings* (Mahwah, N.J.: Paulist, 1988), 259.

Chapter 6: The Divine Act of Resurrection

1. See, for example, Robert John Russell, "Bodily Resurrection, Eschatology and Scientific Cosmology: The Mutual Interaction of Christian Theology and Science," in *Resurrection: Theological and Scientific Perspectives*, ed. Ted Peters, Robert John Russell, and Michael Welker (Grand Rapids: Eerdmans, 2002), 3–30.

2. In Jesus, we find the "initial beginning and definitive triumph of the movement of the world's self-transcendence into absolute closeness to the mystery of God." Karl Rahner, *Foundations of Christian Faith: An Introduction to the Idea of Christianity* (New York: Seabury, 1978), 181.

3. Ibid., 282–85; See Rahner, "The Theology of the Symbol," in *Theological Investigations* (London: Darton, Longman & Todd, 1974), 4:221–52; Rahner, "Salvation," in *Encyclopedia of Theology*, ed. Karl Rahner (London: Burns & Oates, 1975), 1527.

4. Rahner, *Foundations of Christian Faith*, 284.

5. Ibid., 317.

6. Athanasius *On the Incarnation* 54; *First Letter to Serapion* 1.25.

7. Rahner, "Dogmatic Questions on Easter," in *Theological Investigations* (London: Darton, Longman & Todd, 1974), 4:122.

8. "The redemption was felt to be a real ontological process which began in the incarnation and ends not so much in the forgiveness of sins as in the divinization of the world and first demonstrates its victorious might, not so much in the expiation of sin on the cross as in the resurrection of Christ." Ibid., 4:126.

9. Ibid., 129.

10. Rahner, "Resurrection," in Rahner, *Encyclopedia of Theology*, 1430–42, at 1442.

11. Ibid., 1142.

12. Ibid.

13. Karl Rahner, "The Eternal Significance of the Humanity of Jesus for Our Salvation," in *Theological Investigations* (New York: Seabury, 1974), 3:43.

14. Karl Rahner, "Jesus' Resurrection," in *Theological Investigations* (New York: Crossroad, 1981), 17:22.

15. Karl Rahner, "The Intermediate State," in *Theological Investigations* (New York: Crossroad, 1981), 17:120.

16. Karl Rahner, "The Festival of the Future of the World," in *Theological Investigations* (London: Darton, Longman & Todd), 7:184.

17. Peter Carnely, *The Structure of Resurrection Belief* (Oxford: Clarendon, 1987).

18. Harvey D. Egan, *Karl Rahner: Mystic of Everyday Life* (New York: Crossroad, 1998), 163.

19. Rahner, "Resurrection," 1431.

20. Rahner says, "So far as the nature of this experience is accessible to us, it is to be explained after the manner of our experience of the powerful Spirit of the living Lord rather than in a way which either likens this experience too closely to mystical visions of an imaginative kind in later times, or understands it as an almost physical sense experience." *Foundations of Christian Faith*, 276.

21. Denis Edwards, *Human Experience of God* (New York: Paulist, 1983).

22. See Robert John Russell, *Cosmology: From Alpha to Omega* (Minneapolis: Fortress Press, 2008), 308. See also Russell, "Bodily Resurrection, Eschatology, and Scientific Cosmology," 21. Russell goes further than I do when he sees Easter as "the first instantiation of a new law of nature." He sees this, however, not "as an intervention by God, which breaks the laws of nature, but as an act of God which transforms the regular structure of nature into a new 'paradigm,' that of New Creation." Robert John Russell, *Cosmology, Evolution and Resurrection Hope: Theology and Science in Mutual Interaction* (Kitchener, Ont.: Pandora, 2006), 47–48.

23. Karl Rahner, "Immanent and Transcendent Consummation of the World" *Theological Investigations* 11 (London: Darton, Longman and Todd), 289.

Chapter 7: God's Redeeming Act: Deifying Transformation

1. Recent theologies include Gerald O'Collins, *Jesus Our Redeemer: A Christian Approach to Salvation* (Oxford: Oxford University Press, 2007); Peter Schmiechen, *Saving Power: Theories of Atonement and Forms of the Church* (Grand Rapids: Eerdmans, 2005); Raymund Schwager, *Jesus in the Drama of Salvation* (New York: Crossroad, 1999); idem, *Banished from Eden: Original Sin and Evolutionary Theory in the Drama of Salvation* (London: Gracewing, 2005); Hans Boersma, *Violence, Hospitality, and the Cross: Reappropriating the Atonement Tradition* (Grand Rapids: Baker Academic, 2004); Stephen Finlan, *Problems with Atonement: The Origins of, and Controversy about, the Atonement Doctrine* (Collegeville, Minn.: Liturgical, 2005); S. Mark Heim, *Saved from Sacrifice: A Theology of the Cross* (Grand Rapids: Eerdmans, 2006); Robert J. Daly, "Sacrifice Unveiled or Sacrifice Revisited: Trinitarian and Liturgical Perspectives," *Theological Studies* 64 (2003): 24–42; idem, "Images of God and the Imitation of God: Problems with Atonement," *Theological Studies* 68 (2007): 36–51; Lisa Sowle Cahill, "Quaestio Disputata: The Atonement Paradigm: Does It Still Have Explanatory Value?" *Theological Studies* 68 (June 2007): 418–32.

2. See Joseph A. Fitzmyer, "Pauline Theology," in *The New Jerome Biblical Commentary*, ed. Raymond E. Brown, Joseph A. Fitzmyer, and Roland E. Murphy (London: Chapman, 1968, 1990), 1397–1401

3. Schmiechen, *Saving Power*, 5.

4. Alvyn Pettersen, *Athanasius* (London: Chapman, 1995), 25. For my purposes, I have found helpful the recent works of Khaled Anatolios, *Athanasius: The Coherence of His Thought* (London: Routledge, 1998); and idem, *Athanasius* (London: Routledge, 2004); and Thomas G. Weinandy, *Athanasius: A Theological Introduction* (Aldershot: Ashgate, 2007).

5. Pettersen, *Athanasius*, 35, 46.

6. *Orations against the Arians* 2.78; translation from Anatolios, *Athanasius*, 171–74.

7. Pettersen, *Athanasius*, 51–52.

8. *Against the Greeks* 2.

9. *Against the Greeks* 41. Translation from Robert Thompson, ed. and trans., *Athanasius: Contra Gentes and De Incarnatione* (London: Oxford University Press, 1971), 115.

10. *On the Incarnation* 3 (Thompson, *Athanasius*, 141, modified).

11. Anatolios, *Athanasius*, 42.

12. Ibid., 51.

13. *On the Incarnation* 1 (Thompson, *Athanasius*, 137).

14. Anatolio, *Athanasius*, 39.

15. Ibid., 40.

16. *On the Incarnation* 13 (Thompson, *Athanasius,* 167, modified)

17. Athanasius *Discourses against the Arians* 2.68.

18. Athanasius *On the Incarnation* 3.

19. Ibid., 6.

20. Ibid., 10 (Anatolios, *Athanasius,* 59).

21. See Anatolios, *Athanasius,* 66–74.

22. Thompson, *Athanasius,* 268–69 (modified).

23. Iranaeus *Adversus Haereses* 5, preface. Norman Russell, *The Doctrine of Deification in the Greek Patristic Tradition* (Oxford: Oxford University Press, 2004), 169.

24. Russell, *Doctrine of Deification,* 168. While Athanasius writes of pagan deification some twenty times in his early work, he tends to use it in a Christian sense in the later works.

25. Russell, *Doctrine of Deification,* 186. Athanasius has little to say about the soul of Christ, but as Russell notes, his physical emphasis is a helpful antidote to the intellectualism of Origen, even if it needs the completion that would come with Cyril of Alexandria (188).

26. Athanasius *Orations against the Arians* 1.39.

27. Ibid., 1.42 (Russell, *Doctrine of Deification,* 171).

28. Ibid., 2.47 (Russell *Doctrine of Deification,* 171).

29. Ibid., 2.70 (Russell *Doctrine of Deification,* 172).

30. Ibid., 3.33 (Russell *Doctrine of Deification,* 173).

31. Anatolios, *Athanasius,* 143.

32. Weinandy, *Athanasius,* 99.

33. Athanasius *First Letter to Serapion* 1.25. (Russell, *Doctrine of Deification,* 175).

34. Ibid. (Russell, 175).

35. Athanasius *Orations against the Arians* 2.63.

36. Ibid., 2.2.

37. Weinandy, *Athanasius,* 79.

38. Ibid., 80.

39. Fitzmyer, "Pauline Theology," 1401.

40. Ibid. The Greek word translated as being "transformed" in 2 Cor 3:18 (as in Rom 12:2) is *metamorphoumetha,* while in Phil 3:21, referred to in the section of the text that follows, Paul uses a different word, *metaschēmatisei.*

41. Ibid.

42. Tom Wright, *Surprised by Hope* (London: SPCK, 2007), 104.

43. Vladimir Lossky, *Orthodox Theology: An Introduction* (Crestwood, N.Y.: St. Vladimir's Seminary Press, 1978, 1989), 110.

44. Dumitru Staniloae, *Theology and the Church* (Crestwood, N.Y.: St. Vladimir's Seminary Press, 1970), 211.

45. Paul Evdokimov, *In the World, of the Church: A Paul Evdokimov Reader* (Crestwood, N.Y.: St. Vladimir's Seminary Press, 2001), 26.

46. Boris Bobrinskoy, *The Mystery of the Trinity* (Crestwood, N.Y.: St. Vladimir's Seminary Press, 1999), 5.

47. *Catechism of the Catholic Church* (Homebush, New South Wales: St. Pauls, 1994), pars. 1046–50, pp. 273–74.

48. *The Pastoral Constitution on the Church in the Modern World*, paragraph 39 in *Vatican Council II: Constitutions, Decrees, Declarations*, ed. Austin Flannery (Northport N.Y.: Costello, 1996), 204.

49. Karl Rahner, "Dogmatic Questions on Easter," in *Theological Investigations* (New York: Seabury, 1974), 4:129. See also Karl Rahner, "Resurrection," in *Encyclopedia of Theology: A Concise Sacramentum Mundi*, ed. Karl Rahner (London: Burns & Oats, 1975), 1438–42.

50. Rahner, "Resurrection," 1142.

51. Neil Darragh, *At Home in the Earth* (Auckland: Accent, 2000), 124.

52. Niels Henrik Gregersen, "The Cross of Christ in an Evolutionary World," *Dialog: A Journal of Theology* 40 (2001): 205. I have referred to this quotation from Gregersen and the one from Darragh (n. 51) in an earlier attempt to suggest a theology of deep incarnation in *Ecology at the Heart of Faith* (Maryknoll, N.Y.: Orbis, 2006) and continue to find them particularly suggestive and insightful.

53. John F. Haught, *Christianity and Science: Towards a Theology of Nature* (Maryknoll, N.Y.: Orbis, 2007), 92.

54. Ibid., 93.

55. Gustavo Gutierrez, *A Theology of Liberation* (Maryknoll, N.Y.: Orbis, 1973, 1988), 83–105.

Chapter 8: God's Redeeming Act: Evolution, Original Sin, and the Lamb of God

1. See René Girard, "Violence, Scapegoating and the Cross," in *The Evolution of Evil*, ed. Gaymond Bennett, Martinez J. Hewlett, Ted Peters, and Robert John Russell (Göttingen: Vandenhoeck & Ruprecht, 2008), 334–48; Girard, *Violence and the Sacred* (Baltimore: Johns Hopkins University Press, 1977); Girard, *Things Hidden since the Foundation of the World* (Stanford: Stanford University Press, 1987); Girard, *The Scapegoat* (London: Athlone, 1994); *I See Satan Fall like Lightning* (Maryknoll, N.Y.: Orbis, 2001).

2. See Raymund Schwager, *Jesus in the Drama of Salvation: Towards a Biblical Doctrine of Redemption* (New York: Crossroad, 1999); Schwager, *Must There Be*

Scapegoats? Violence and Redemption in the Bible (New York: Crossroad, 2000); Schwager, *Banished from Eden: Original Sin and Evolutionary Theory in the Drama of Salvation* (Leominster, U.K.: Gracewing, 2006); James Alison, *The Joy of Being Wrong: Original Sin through Easter Eyes* (New York: Crossroad, 1998); Alison, *On Being Liked* (London: Darton, Longman & Todd, 2003); Alison, *Undergoing God: Dispatches from the Scene of a Break-In* (London: Darton, Longman & Todd, 2006); Sebastian Moore, *The Contagion of Jesus: Doing Theology as if It Mattered* (London: Darton, Longman & Todd, 2007). See also the collection edited by Brad Jersak and Michael Hardin, *Stricken by God? Nonviolent Identification and the Victory of Christ* (Grand Rapids: Eerdmans, 2007).

3. Girard, *Things Hidden*, 24.

4. Schwager, *Banished from Eden*, 55.

5. Ernst Mayr, *What Evolution Is* (London: Weidenfeld & Nicolson, 2002), 254–55.

6. Ibid., 251.

7. Ibid., 252.

8. See, for example, Edward O. Wilson, *Consilience: The Unity of Knowledge* (New York: Vintage, 1998), 178–96.

9. Ibid., 179.

10. Ibid., 186. While agreeing with Wilson here, I disagree when he speculates that art, ethics, and religion may be sufficiently explained by empirical science (*Consilience*, 229–90) and when he states, "There is only one class of explanation" (*Consilience*, 291). Wilson has been challenged by theologians including Ted Peters, who accepts the importance of genetic influences from our evolutionary past but rightly rejects the idea that sociobiology can explain, for example, the kingdom message of Jesus simply in terms of the evolution of reciprocal altruism. See Peters, "The Evolution of Evil," in Bennett et al., *The Evolution of Evil*, 1–52. Wilson's position is also challenged by evolutionary biologists such as Francisco Ayala, who celebrates scientific knowledge as a wondrously successful way of knowing and argues that nothing in the world of nature escapes this mode of knowledge, but goes on to say, "Successful as it is, and universally encompassing as its subject is, a scientific view of the world is hopelessly incomplete. There are matters of value and meaning that are outside science's scope." Francisco Ayala, "Darwin's Devolution: Design without Designer," in *Evolutionary and Molecular Biology: Scientific Perspectives on Divine Action*, ed. Robert J. Russell, William Stoeger, and Francisco Ayala (Vatican City State: Vatican Observatory; Berkeley, Calif.: Center for Theology and the Natural Sciences, 1998), 115–16.

11. See the conclusions of Richard Dunbar, reported in Richard Leakey, *The Origin of Humankind* (London: Phoenix, 1994), 149.

12. Leakey, *Origin of Humankind*, 154.

13. Ibid., 153.

14. Mayr, *What Evolution Is*, 257–58.

15. Ibid., 259.

16. Daryl Domning, for example, writes, "We all sin because we have inherited—from the very first living things on earth—a powerful tendency to act selfishly, no matter the cost to others." In "Evolution, Evil and Original Sin," *America* 185 (Nov. 12, 2001): 14–21. See also the book he wrote with Monica Hellwig, *Original Selfishness: Original Sin and Evil in the Light of Evolution* (Aldershot: Ashgate, 2006).

17. See Gerd Theissen, *Biblical Faith: An Evolutionary Approach* (London: SCM, 1984); and Philip Hefner, *The Human Factor: Evolution, Culture, and Religion* (Minneapolis: Fortress Press, 1993).

18. See the different approaches of Jerry D. Korsmeyer, *Evolution and Evil: Balancing Original Sin and Contemporary Science* (Mahweh, N.J.: Paulist, 1998); Marjorie Hewitt Suchocki, *The Fall to Violence: Original Sin in Relational Theology* (New York: Continuum, 1994); Sebastian Moore, *Jesus the Liberator of Desire* (New York: Crossroad, 1989); Gabriel Daly, *Creation and Redemption* (Dublin: Gill & McMillan, 1988); Charles Birch and John B. Cobb Jr., *The Liberation of Life: From the Cell to the Community* (New York: Cambridge University Press, 1981).

19. Denis Edwards, "Original Sin and Saving Grace in Evolutionary Context," in Russell et al., eds., *Evolutionary and Molecular Biology*, 377–92.

20. Karl Rahner, "The Theological Notion of Concupiscentia," in *Theological Investigations* (Baltimore: Helicon, 1961), 1:347–82.

21. Stephen J. Duffy, *The Dynamics of Grace: Perspectives in Theological Anthropology* (Collegeville, Minn.: Liturgical, 1993), 226.

22. Rahner's position can be found in, among many other places, his *Foundations of Christian Faith: An Introduction to the Idea of Christianity* (New York: Crossroad, 1993), 116–37. For a good discussion of the relationship between Rahner's theology of grace and the work of James Alison, see John P. Edwards, "The Self Prior to Mimetic Desire: Rahner and Alison on Original Sin and Conversion," *Horizons* 35 (Spring 2008): 7–31.

23. *Lumen Gentium*, 16; *Gaudium et Spes*, 22. This theme often appears in the encyclicals of John Paul II. See his *Redemptor Hominis*, translated as *Redeemer of Man* (Homebush, New South Wales: St. Paul, 1979), 20–21; *Dominum et Vivicantem*, 53, translated as *The Holy Spirit in the Life of the Church* (Boston: St. Paul, 1986), 91; *Redemptoris Missio*, 10, translated as *On the Permanent Validity of the Church's Missionary Mandate* (Homebush, New South Wales: St. Paul, 1991), 23.

24. Karl Rahner brilliantly establishes and explores the radical unity between these two loves in his "Reflections on the Unity of the Love of Neighbour and the Love of God," in *Theological Investigations* (New York: Seabury, 1974), 6:231–49.

25. Schwager, *Banished from Eden*, 53.

26. Marcus Borg, "Executed by Rome, Vindicated by God," in Jersak and Hardin, *Stricken by God?* 161.

27. Ibid.

28. Schwager, *Banished from Eden*, 59–60.

29. Girard, "Violence, Scapegoating and the Cross," 342.

30. Ibid., 342–46.

31. Moore, *The Contagion of Jesus*, 33.

32. Schwager, *Banished from Eden*, 136–37.

33. Ibid., 70–71.

34. Schwager, *Must There Be Scapegoats?* 214.

35. Alison, *Undergoing God*, 64.

36. Karl Rahner, "Dogmatic Questions on Easter," in *Theological Investigations* (New York, Seabury, 1974), 4:129.

Chapter 9: Final Fulfillment

1. Walter Kasper, "Hope in the Final Coming of Jesus Christ in Glory," *Communio: International Catholic Review* 12 (Winter 1986): 380.

2. Karl Rahner, "The Hermeneutics of Eschatological Assertions," in *Theological Investigations* (New York: Seabury, 1966), 4:323–46. See also his *Foundations of Christian Faith: An Introduction to the Idea of Christianity* (New York: Seabury, 1978), 431–47.

3. Rahner, "The Hermeneutics of Eschatological Assertions," 4:330.

4. "It may therefore be said that whenever we have a prediction which presents its contents as the anticipated report of the spectator of a future event—a report of an event in human history which of itself excludes the character of *absolute* mystery and hence deprives the eschatological event of its hiddenness—then a false apocalyptic is at work, or a genuine eschatological assertion has been misunderstood as a piece of apocalyptic because of its apocalyptic style and content." Ibid., 330.

5. William M. Thompson, "The Hope for Humanity: Rahner's Eschatology," in *A World of Grace: An Introduction to the Themes and Foundations of Karl Rahner's Theology*, ed. Leo J. O'Donovan (New York: Seabury, 1980), 158.

6. Karl Rahner, "Marxist Utopia and the Christian Future of Man," in *Theological Investigations* (London; Darton, Longman & Todd, 1969), 6:62.

7. Joseph A. Fitzmyer, *Romans: A New Translation with Introduction and Commentary*, Anchor Bible 33 (New York: Doubleday, 1993), 507.

8. Ibid., 509.

9. Ibid., 505.

10. Brendan Byrne, *Romans,* Sacra Pagina 6 (Collegeville, Minn.: Liturgical, 1996), 255.

11. Ibid., 255.

12. Ibid., 255–57.

13. Ibid., 257.

14. N. T. Wright, *Evil and the Justice of God* (London: SPCK, 2006), 75.

15. See also N. T. Wright, "Redemption from the New Perspective? Towards a Multi-Layered Pauline Theology of the Cross," in *The Redemption: An Interdisciplinary Symposium on Christ as Redeemer,* ed. Stephen T. Davis, Daniel Kendall, and Gerald O'Collins (Oxford: Oxford University Press, 2004), 69–100.

16. Wright, *Evil and the Justice of God,* 75.

17. Ibid.

18. Tom Wright, *Surprised by Hope* (London: SPCK, 2007), 104.

19. Christopher Southgate, *The Groaning of Creation: God, Evolution and the Problem of Evil* (Louisville: Westminster John Knox, 2008).

20. See Byrne, *Romans,* 256.

21. See Holmes Rolston III, *Genes, Genesis and God: Values and Their Origins in Natural and Human History* (Cambridge: Cambridge University Press, 1999), 303–7.

22. *First Letter to Serapion* 1.25 (Norman Russell, *The Doctrine of Deification in the Greek Patristic Tradition* [Oxford: Oxford University Press, 2004]).

23. Andrew Louth, *Maximus the Confessor* (London: Routledge, 1996), 73.

24. See Brian Daley, "'He Himself Is Our Peace' (Ephesians 2:14): Early Christian Views of Redemption in Christ," in Davis et al., *The Redemption,* 170.

25. *Ambigua* 41 (PG 91:1308D). Translation by Daley in "He Himself Is Our Peace" 171.

26. *Ambigua* 41 (PG 91:1312A). Translation by Louth in *Maximus the Confessor,* 160.

27. See Robert John Russell, *Cosmology: From Alpha to Omega* (Minneapolis: Fortress Press, 2008), 300–301. See also Russell's pioneering response to these issues (301–27).

28. Karl Rahner, "Dogmatic Questions on Easter," in *Theological Investigations* (London: Darton, Longman & Todd, 1974), 4:129. See also Rahner, "Resurrection," in *Encyclopedia of Theology: A Concise Sacramentum Mundi,* ed. Karl Rahner (London: Burns & Oats, 1975), 1438–42.

29. Karl Rahner, "Immanent and Transcendent Consummation of the World," in *Theological Investigations* (London: Darton, Longman & Todd, 1973), 10:289.

30. Karl Rahner, "The Festival of the Future of the World," in *Theological Investigations* (London: Darton, Longman & Todd, 1971), 7:183.

31. Ibid.

32. Ibid.

33. Rahner returns to this parallel between death and the final transformation of universal history in "The Theological Problems Entailed in the Idea of the 'New Earth,'" in *Theological Investigations* (London: Darton, Longman & Todd, 1973), 10:269.

34. Paul Evdokimov, *In the World, of the Church: A Paul Evdokimov Reader* (Crestwood, N.Y.: St. Vladimir's Seminary Press, 2001), 25.

35. Jürgen Moltmann, "Cosmos and Theosis: Eschatological Perspectives on the Future of the Universe," in *The Far Future Universe: Eschatology from a Cosmic Perspective*, ed. George F. R. Ellis (Philadelphia: Templeton Foundation Press, 2002), 261. See his *The Coming of God: Christian Eschatology* (London: SCM, 1996), 257–319.

36. Richard Bauckham, "The Future of Jesus Christ," in *The Cambridge Companion to Jesus*, ed. Markus Bockmuehl (Cambridge: Cambridge University Press, 2001), 271–73.

37. See Rahner's essays "The Theological Problems" and "Immanent and Transcendent Consummation of the World," in *Theological Investigations*, 10:273–89.

38. Russell, *Cosmology,* 308.

39. Rahner, "The Theological Problems," 270.

40. J. Massyngberde Ford, *Revelation: Introduction, Translation and Commentary* (Garden City, N.Y.: Doubleday, 1975), 95.

41. Thomas Aquinas *Summa theologiae* 1a.8.1.

42. Alexander Schmemann, *The Eucharist: Sacrament of the Kingdom* (Crestwood, N.Y.: St. Vladimir's Seminary Press, 1988), 125.

43. Ibid.

44. Ibid., 126. I am grateful to Theodore McCall, whose thesis "Ecology and Eschatology: Moving towards a Model of Ecological Eschatology" (Ph.D. diss., Flinders University, 2008) has led me to focus on Schmemann's work.

45. John F. Haught, *God after Darwin: A Theology of Evolution* (Boulder, Colo.: Westview, 2000), 43. Process philosopher Alfred North Whitehead proposed what he called "objective immortality," the idea that creatures make an impression on God and this impact remains in God beyond death. See his *Process and Reality: An Essay in Cosmology* (New York: Harper & Row, 1929, 1957), 526–33.

46. Elizabeth A. Johnson, *Friends of God and Prophets: A Feminist Theological Reading of the Communion of Saints* (London: SCM, 1998), 201.

Chapter 10: Prayers of Intercession

1. N. T. Wright and John Dominic Crossan, "The Resurrection: Historical Event or Theological Explanation? A Dialogue," in *The Resurrection of Jesus: John*

Dominic Crossan and N. T. Wright in Dialogue, ed. Robert B. Steward (Minneapolis: Fortress Press, 2006), 16–47. In chapter 2, I referred to the work of Marcus Borg, who also endorses participatory eschatology.

2. Ibid., 42–43.

3. William A. Barry, *A Friendship like No Other: Experiencing God's Amazing Grace* (Chicago: Loyola Press, 2008), 42.

4. Ibid., 61.

5. William A. Barry, *God and You: Prayer as a Personal Relationship* (Mahweh, N.J.: Paulist, 1987), 61–62.

6. Ibid., 62–63.

7. Brian Gallagher, *Taking God to Heart: A Living Spirituality* (Sydney: St. Paul's, 2008), 61.

8. Karl Rahner, *Christian at the Crossroads* (London: Burns & Oates, 1975), 57.

9. Karl Rahner, *Happiness through Prayer* (London: Burns & Oates, 1958, 1978), 65.

10. Karl Rahner, *Prayers for a Lifetime* (New York: Crossroad, 1985), 93. This prayer appeared earlier in *Encounters with Silence* (Westminster, Md.: Newman, 1960), 45–52.

11. Rahner, *Happiness through Prayer*, 67.

12. Herbert McCabe, *God Still Matters* (London: Continuum, 2002), 218.

13. Ibid., 61–62.

14. Augustine of Hippo, "Letter CXXX: To Proba," in "The Letters of St. Augustine," trans. J. G. Cunningham, in *The Confessions and Letters of St. Augustine with a Sketch of His Life and Work,* Nicene and Post-Nicene Fathers, ed. Philip Schaff, (Grand Rapids: Eerdmans, 1979), 1:462.

15. Ibid., 1:463.

16. Ibid., 1:467.

17. Ibid., 1:468.

Index

Alison, James, 130, 141, 196n2, 197n22
Anatolio, Khaled, 112, 116, 193n4
anthropic principle, 10, 11
Aquinas, Thomas, ix, 8, 28, 47, 48, 53, 54, 58, 61, 77, 80–84, 89, 90, 161, 165, 187n33
Athanasius, ix, 97, 107, 109–19, 122, 141, 150, 162, 170, 192n6, 194n25
Augustine, 23, 175, 176, 177, 201n14

baptism, 74
Barbour, Ian, 2, 61, 181n2
Barry, William A., 171, 172–73, 201n5
Bartholomew, D. J., 52, 53, 187n29
Bauckham, Richard, 156, 157, 200n36
Birch, Charles, 61, 197n18
Bobrinskoy, Boris, 122, 195n46
Bonaventure, 165
Borg, Marcus, 23, 24, 126, 138, 139, 184n22, 184n26
Byrne, Brendan, 148, 199n10

Carnley, Peter, 101, 192n17
cause
    created, 8, 24, 28, 42, 47, 48, 49, 58, 60, 61, 63, 68, 81, 91, 100, 168, 172, 178, 179
    creaturely, 46, 47, 49, 60, 61, 63, 69
    efficient, 41, 42
    hidden, 83
    natural, 77
    particular, 85
    primary, 46, 47, 48, 58, 79, 80, 81, 100
    sacramental, 95
secondary, 8, 46, 53, 54, 55, 60, 61, 62–64, 65, 68, 69, 70, 74, 78, 80–84, 87, 89, 90, 91, 92, 99–100, 102, 104, 105, 106, 168, 169, 172
Church, the, x, xi, xii, 71, 72, 74, 101
    early Church, the, 26, 80, 101, 109, 121
    liturgical life of, 72, 101, 102, 115, 141, 142, 162
    pastoral practice of, 77, 122, 135

CPSIA information can be obtained
at www.ICGtesting.com
Printed in the USA
FFOW01n2331040915
16614FF